First World War
and Army of Occupation
War Diary
France, Belgium and Germany

18 DIVISION
55 Infantry Brigade
Queen's Own (Royal West Kent Regiment)
7th Battalion
20 July 1915 - 31 January 1918

WO95/2049/2

The Naval & Military Press Ltd
www.nmarchive.com
Published in association with The National Archives

Published by

The Naval & Military Press Ltd

Unit 10 Ridgewood Industrial Park,

Uckfield, East Sussex,

TN22 5QE England

Tel: +44 (0) 1825 749494

www.naval-military-press.com

www.nmarchive.com

This diary has been reprinted in facsimile from the original. Any imperfections are inevitably reproduced and the quality may fall short of modern type and cartographic standards.

© **Crown Copyright**
Images reproduced by permission of The National Archives, London, England, 2015.

Contents

Document type	Place/Title	Date From	Date To
Heading	WO95/2049-2		
Heading	18th Division 55th Infy Bde 7th Bn West Kent Regt Jly 1915-Dec 1917 To 53 Bde 18 Div		
Heading	18th Division WO95/2049 121/6874 7th West Kent Vol. I Jly To August 15 Dec 17		
War Diary	Codford	20/07/1915	26/07/1915
War Diary	Havre	27/07/1915	28/07/1915
War Diary	Longeau	29/07/1915	29/07/1915
War Diary	Villers Bocage	31/07/1915	07/08/1915
War Diary	N' Bray	08/08/1915	15/08/1915
War Diary	Bray	16/08/1915	18/08/1915
War Diary	Bonnay	19/08/1915	22/08/1915
War Diary	Trenches	23/08/1915	30/08/1915
Map	D1 Sheet 2 Scale 1:2,000.		
Map	Appendix I Scale:- 1:2,000.		
Map	Scale: 1:2,000		
Heading	18th Division WO95/2049 121/7432 7th West Kent Vol 2 Sept & Oct 15		
War Diary	Meaulte	03/09/1915	06/10/1915
Miscellaneous	3rd Army Circular Memorandum. Leakage Of Information.	09/09/1915	09/09/1915
Heading	18th Division WO95/2049 121/7593 7th West Kent Vol 3 Oct 15		
War Diary		07/10/1915	25/10/1915
War Diary		18/10/1915	26/10/1915
War Diary		05/11/1915	05/11/1915
War Diary		27/10/1915	05/11/1915
Miscellaneous	Report On Sniping In Trench Warfare. App. II	20/10/1915	20/10/1915
Miscellaneous	18th Div. No. G. Report On Machine Gun Action In E.I. 6th-15th Octr. App III	06/10/1915	06/10/1915
Heading	18th Division WO95/2049 121/7678 7th W. Kent Vol 24 Nov 15		
War Diary	Dernancourt	06/11/1915	14/11/1915
War Diary	Trenches	15/11/1915	23/11/1915
War Diary	Dernancourt	23/11/1915	27/11/1915
War Diary	Trenches	30/11/1915	30/11/1915
Miscellaneous	3rd Army. Adjutant General's Branch Extracts From Routine Orders, Etc.	03/11/1915	03/11/1915
Heading	18th Div WO95/2049 121/7936 7th R.W. Kent Vol. 55 Bde Dec 15		
War Diary	Trenches	01/12/1915	31/12/1915
War Diary		28/12/1915	29/12/1915
Heading	181 WO95/2049 7 R.W. Kent Vol 6 Nov 16		
Heading	18 7th W. Kent Vol 7		
War Diary		03/01/1916	31/01/1916
War Diary	Dernancourt	01/02/1916	04/02/1916
War Diary	Pont Noyelles	05/02/1916	06/02/1916
War Diary	La Houssoye	16/02/1916	08/03/1916
Heading	18 7 R W Kent Vol 8		
War Diary		14/03/1916	16/03/1916

War Diary	Corbie	16/03/1916	17/03/1916
War Diary	Grovetown Camp	18/03/1916	31/03/1916
Miscellaneous	A.G. Base	01/05/1916	01/05/1916
War Diary	Y2	01/04/1916	30/04/1916
Miscellaneous	Ref. Albert Combined Sheet Apr/11 Amiens Sh 17		
Miscellaneous	Ref (1) Amiens Sheet 17 (2) Albert Combined Sheet	30/04/1916	30/04/1916
War Diary	Y.2.	02/05/1916	05/05/1916
War Diary	St Pierre	06/05/1916	31/05/1916
War Diary	St Pierre	15/05/1916	30/05/1916
War Diary	St Pierre	06/05/1916	25/05/1916
War Diary	Rail	26/06/1916	27/06/1916
War Diary	Avenue	27/06/1916	30/06/1916
Operation(al) Order(s)	Operation Order By Lt Col J.T.W. Fiennes Commanding 7th Royal West Kent Regt Appendix 6	24/05/1916	24/05/1916
Operation(al) Order(s)	Operation Order By Lt Col J.T.W. Fiennes Commanding 7th R.W Kent Regt Appendix 9	29/05/1916	29/05/1916
Operation(al) Order(s)	Operation Order By Lt Col J.T.W. Fiennes Commanding 7th Royal West Kent Regt Appendix 7		
Miscellaneous	A Form. Messages And Signals.		
Miscellaneous	Account of Attempted Paid on the Germain Trenches At The Salient near A. 9.9.05.60 Night 24th/27th June Appendix 8	27/05/1916	27/05/1916
Heading	55th Bde. 18th Div. War Diary WO95/2049 7th Battalion Royal West Kent Regiment. July 1916		
War Diary	Trenches	01/07/1916	12/07/1916
War Diary	La Motte	01/01/1917	08/01/1917
War Diary	Le Titre	09/01/1917	09/01/1917
War Diary	La Motte	10/01/1917	11/01/1917
War Diary	Domleger	12/01/1917	12/01/1917
War Diary	Le Meillard	13/01/1917	14/01/1917
War Diary	Raincheval	15/01/1917	16/01/1917
War Diary	Hedauville	17/01/1917	31/01/1917
Miscellaneous	Honours And Awards.		
War Diary	Hedauville	01/02/1917	11/02/1917
War Diary	St Pierre Divion	12/02/1917	19/02/1917
War Diary	Front Line	20/02/1917	27/02/1917
War Diary	Trenches	28/02/1917	28/02/1917
Miscellaneous	Narrative Of Operation February 14th 1917 App 19	17/02/1917	17/02/1917
Miscellaneous	Patrol Reports. App 20		
War Diary	Boom Ravine	01/03/1917	02/03/1917
War Diary	E. Miraumont Road	03/03/1917	03/03/1917
War Diary	Warwick Huts	04/03/1917	12/03/1917
War Diary	St Pierre Divion.	13/03/1917	15/03/1917
War Diary	Hessian Tr	16/03/1917	18/03/1917
War Diary	Loupart Line	19/03/1917	19/03/1917
War Diary	Bihucourt.	20/03/1917	20/03/1917
War Diary	Kitchener Huts.	21/03/1917	21/03/1917
War Diary	Senlis. Villiers	22/03/1917	22/03/1917
War Diary	Bocquage	23/03/1917	23/03/1917
War Diary	Ferriers.	24/03/1917	26/03/1917
War Diary	Wittes	27/03/1917	20/04/1917
War Diary	Ham-En-Artois	21/04/1917	21/04/1917
War Diary	Bethune	22/04/1917	27/04/1917
War Diary	Sains-Les-Pernes	28/04/1917	30/04/1917
War Diary	Trenches.	01/05/1917	04/05/1917
War Diary	Beurains	05/05/1917	14/05/1917

War Diary	Camp. S. 16	15/05/1917	21/05/1917
War Diary	Trenches	22/05/1917	31/05/1917
Miscellaneous	App 21		
Miscellaneous	The 7th Battalion Royal West Kent Regiment At Zero Hour Was Disposed As Follows App 22	07/05/1917	07/05/1917
Operation(al) Order(s)	7th Battalion Royal West Kent Regiment. Order No. 57.	21/05/1917	21/05/1917
Operation(al) Order(s)	7th Battalion Royal West Kent Regiment. Order No. 59	31/05/1917	31/05/1917
Operation(al) Order(s)	7th R.W. Kent Order No. 57	21/05/1917	21/05/1917
Operation(al) Order(s)	7th Royal West Kent Order No. 56		
Operation(al) Order(s)	7th R W Kent Order No. 60 App. 27		
Miscellaneous	Operation Against Enemy Posts In A.3.6	01/06/1917	01/06/1917
Operation(al) Order(s)	Annex To Operation Order No. 60		
War Diary	Trenches.	01/06/1917	02/06/1917
War Diary	Camp	03/06/1917	15/06/1917
War Diary	Camp Coigneux.	16/06/1917	30/06/1917
Miscellaneous	Operation Report For Night 2nd And 3rd June 1917 App 29	02/06/1917	02/06/1917
Operation(al) Order(s)	7th Royal West Kent Order No. 61	02/06/1917	02/06/1917
Miscellaneous	7th Battalion Royal West Kent Regiment. App 31		
Miscellaneous	7th Battalion Royal West Kent Regiment.		
Miscellaneous	7th Battalion Royal West Kent Regiment. App. 32		
Miscellaneous	7th Battalion Royal West Kent Regiment.		
War Diary	Coigneux	01/07/1917	02/07/1917
War Diary	Halloy	03/07/1917	04/07/1917
War Diary	Nr Abeele	05/07/1917	06/07/1917
War Diary	Palace Camp	06/07/1917	06/07/1917
War Diary	Trenches	07/07/1917	23/07/1917
War Diary	Canal Reserve Camp	24/07/1917	24/07/1917
War Diary	Ottawa Camp	25/07/1917	27/07/1917
Operation(al) Order(s)	7th Royal West Kent Regiment Order No. 58	01/07/1917	01/07/1917
Operation(al) Order(s)	7th Royal West Kent Regiment Order No. 59	03/07/1917	03/07/1917
Operation(al) Order(s)	7th Royal West Kent Regiment Order No. 59		
Miscellaneous	Supply Arrangements		
Miscellaneous	7th Royal West Kent Regiment Order No. 60	05/07/1917	05/07/1917
Operation(al) Order(s)	7th Royal West Kent Regiment Order No. 61	06/07/1917	06/07/1917
Operation(al) Order(s)	7th Royal West Kent Regiment Order No. 62	11/07/1917	11/07/1917
Operation(al) Order(s)	7th Royal West Kent Regiment Order No. 62	16/07/1917	16/07/1917
Miscellaneous	Table of Working Parties Issued With 7th Royal West Kent Regiment Order No. 61		
Operation(al) Order(s)	7th Royal West Kent Regt Order No. 63	23/07/1917	23/07/1917
Operation(al) Order(s)	Preliminary Order. 7th Battalion Royal West Kent Regiment Order No. 64		
Operation(al) Order(s)	7th Royal West Kent Regiment Order No. 64	30/07/1917	30/07/1917
Miscellaneous	O.G's Coys App 42		
War Diary	Ottawa Camp.	28/07/1917	30/07/1917
War Diary	New Dickebusch	31/07/1917	02/08/1917
War Diary	Trenches	03/08/1917	07/08/1917
War Diary	Chateau Segard	08/08/1917	10/08/1917
War Diary	New Dickebusch Camp.	11/08/1917	11/08/1917
War Diary	Nr. Abeele	12/08/1917	15/08/1917
War Diary	Nr. Zeggers Cappel.	16/08/1917	31/08/1917
Miscellaneous			
War Diary	Near Zeggers Cappel.	01/09/1917	23/09/1917
War Diary	Near St. Jan Ter Biezen	24/09/1917	30/09/1917
Miscellaneous			
Operation(al) Order(s)	7th Royal West Kent Regiment Order No. 65	14/08/1917	14/08/1917

Type	Description	Start	End
Miscellaneous	Training Programme-Week Ending 25th August 1917 "A" Company 7th Battalion Royal West Kent Regiment App 44		
Miscellaneous	Training Programme-Week Ending 25th August 1917 "B" Co 7th Battalion Royal West Kent Regiment App 4	25/08/1917	25/08/1917
Miscellaneous	Training Programme-Week Ending 25th August 1917 "C" Company 7th Battalion Royal West Kent Regiment		
Miscellaneous	Training Programme-Week Ending 25th August 1917 "D" Company 7th Battalion Royal West Kent Regiment	25/08/1917	25/08/1917
Miscellaneous	7th Battalion Royal West Kent Regiment. Week Ending 25th August 1917	25/08/1917	25/08/1917
Miscellaneous	7th Battalion Royal West Kent Regiment.	17/08/1917	17/08/1917
Miscellaneous	7th Battalion Royal West Kent Regiment App 45	01/09/1917	01/09/1917
Miscellaneous	Copy Of Letter From Brigadier General Commanding 55th Inf. Brigade. App 46		
Miscellaneous	Week Ending 8th September 1917 App 47 Allotment of Bombing Pits at (B. 20. a. 7. 3.)		
Miscellaneous	Training Programme-Week Ending 1st September 1917 "A" Company 7th Battalion Royal West Kent Regiment.		
Miscellaneous	Training Programme-Week Ending 1st September 1917 "B" Company 7th Battalion Royal West Kent Regiment.		
Miscellaneous	Training Programme-Week Ending 1st September 1917 "C" Company 7th Battalion Royal West Kent Regiment	01/09/1917	01/09/1917
Miscellaneous	Training Programme-Week Ending 1st September 1917 "D" Company 7th Battalion Royal West Kent Regiment	01/09/1917	01/09/1917
Miscellaneous	Training Programme-Week Ending 6th September 1917 "A" Company 7th Battalion Royal West Kent Regiment.	06/09/1917	06/09/1917
Miscellaneous	Training Programme-Week Ending 6th September 1917 "B" Company 7th Battalion Royal West Kent Regiment.	06/09/1917	06/09/1917
Miscellaneous	Training Programme-Week Ending 6th September 1917 "C" Company 7th Battalion Royal West Kent Regiment.	06/09/1917	06/09/1917
Miscellaneous	Training Programme-Week Ending 6th September 1917 "D" Company 7th Battalion Royal West Kent Regiment.	06/09/1917	06/09/1917
Miscellaneous	7th Battalion Royal West Kent Regiment. App 48	15/09/1917	15/09/1917
Miscellaneous	Training Programme-Week Ending 22nd Sept. 1917 App 49 "A" Company 7th Battalion Royal West Kent Regiment.	02/09/1917	02/09/1917
Miscellaneous	Training Programme-Week Ending 22nd Sept. 1917	22/09/1917	22/09/1917
Miscellaneous	7th Battalion Royal West Kent Regiment. App 50	20/09/1917	20/09/1917
Miscellaneous	7th Battalion Royal West Kent Regiment. App 51	29/09/1917	29/09/1917
Operation(al) Order(s)	7th Buffs Order No. 81	22/09/1917	22/09/1917
Operation(al) Order(s)	Administrative Instructions To Accompany 7th Buffs Order No. 81	22/09/1917	22/09/1917
War Diary	School Camp Near St. Jan-Ter-Biezen.	01/10/1917	09/10/1917
War Diary	Dirty Bucket Camp Line	10/10/1917	13/10/1917
War Diary	Gournier Farm	14/10/1917	14/10/1917
War Diary	Dirty Bucket Camp.	15/10/1917	24/10/1917
War Diary	Poperinghe	25/10/1917	26/10/1917
War Diary	Parroy Camp	27/10/1917	31/10/1917
War Diary	School Camp Near St. Jan-Ter-Biezen.	01/10/1917	09/10/1917

War Diary	Dirty Bucket	10/10/1917	10/10/1917
War Diary	Camp	10/10/1917	10/10/1917
War Diary	Line	11/10/1917	13/10/1917
War Diary	Gournier Farm	13/10/1917	14/10/1917
War Diary	Dirty Bucket Camp.	15/10/1917	24/10/1917
War Diary	Poperinghe	25/10/1917	26/10/1917
War Diary	Parroy Camp	27/10/1917	31/10/1917
Operation(al) Order(s)	7th Battalion Royal West Kent Regiment. Order No. 67	09/11/1917	09/11/1917
Operation(al) Order(s)	7th Battalion Royal West Kent Regiment. Order No. 69	23/10/1917	23/10/1917
Miscellaneous	55th Infantry Brigade. Account Of Operations From 9th To 14th Oct. 1917	14/10/1917	14/10/1917
Map	Poelcappelle		
Operation(al) Order(s)	7th Battalion Royal West Kent Regiment Order No. 68	11/10/1917	11/10/1917
Miscellaneous	Appendix.	30/10/1917	30/10/1917
Miscellaneous	55th Infantry Brigade. Account Of Operation From 9th To 14th Oct. 1917	14/10/1917	14/10/1917
Miscellaneous	Appendix 54. 7th Battalion Royal West Kent Regiment Report On Operations Near Poelcappelle.	13/10/1917	13/10/1917
Miscellaneous	7th Battalion Royal West Kent Regiment. Report On Operation Near Poelcappelle. App 54	13/10/1917	13/10/1917
Miscellaneous	7th Battalion Royal West Kent Regiment. Report On Operation Near Poelcappelle. App 45	10/10/1917	10/10/1917
Miscellaneous	7th Battalion The Royal West Kent Regiment		
Miscellaneous	55th Infantry Brigade. Account Of Operation From 9th To 14th Oct. 1917		
Miscellaneous	Appendix 54. 7th Battalion Royal West Kent Regiment Report On Operation Near Poelcappelle.	13/10/1917	13/10/1917
Miscellaneous	7th Bn. RW Kent Regt October & November 1917		
Miscellaneous	7th Battalion The Royal West Kent Regiment		
Miscellaneous	55th Infantry Brigade. Account Of Operation From 9th To 14th Oct. 1917	14/10/1917	14/10/1917
Miscellaneous	Appendix 54. 7th Battalion Royal West Kent Regiment. Report On Operation Near Poelcapelle.	13/10/1917	13/10/1917
Operation(al) Order(s)	7th Battalion Royal West Kent Regiment Order No. 70 App 56	26/10/1917	26/10/1917
Operation(al) Order(s)	7th Battalion Royal West Kent Regiment Order No. 71	02/11/1917	02/11/1917
War Diary	Parroy Camp	01/11/1917	01/11/1917
War Diary	Privet Camp	02/11/1917	03/11/1917
War Diary	Larry Camp	04/11/1917	30/11/1917
Miscellaneous			
War Diary	Parroy Camp	01/11/1917	01/11/1917
War Diary	Privet Camp	02/11/1917	02/11/1917
War Diary	Parry Camp	04/11/1917	30/11/1917
Miscellaneous			
Miscellaneous	7th Battalion The Royal West Kent Regiment.		
War Diary	Larry Camp.	01/12/1917	07/12/1917
War Diary	Baboon Camp	08/12/1917	10/12/1917
War Diary	Line	11/12/1917	14/12/1917
War Diary	Baboon Camp	15/12/1917	16/12/1917
War Diary	Nortleulinghem	17/12/1917	28/12/1917
War Diary	Portsmouth Camp.	29/12/1917	31/12/1917
Operation(al) Order(s)	7th Battalion Royal West Kent Regiment Order No. 72	07/12/1917	07/12/1917
Operation(al) Order(s)	7th Battalion Royal West Kent Regiment Order No. 73	09/12/1917	09/12/1917
Operation(al) Order(s)	7th Battalion Royal West Kent Regiment Order No. 74	15/12/1917	15/12/1917
Operation(al) Order(s)	7th Battalion Royal West Kent Regiment Order No. 74	27/12/1917	27/12/1917
Operation(al) Order(s)	7th Battalion Royal West Kent Regiment Order No. 76	30/12/1917	30/12/1917

Type	Description	From	To
War Diary	J Camp.	01/01/1918	02/01/1918
War Diary	Baboon Camp.	03/01/1918	06/01/1918
War Diary	In The Line	07/01/1918	10/01/1918
War Diary	J Camp.	11/01/1918	18/01/1918
War Diary	Baboon Camp.	19/01/1918	21/01/1918
War Diary	In The Line	22/01/1918	24/01/1918
War Diary	J Camp.	25/01/1918	31/01/1918
Operation(al) Order(s)	7th Battalion Royal West Kent Regiment Order No. 77	01/01/1918	01/01/1918
Miscellaneous	Artillery Arrangements Before And During The Attack Appendix "B"		
Operation(al) Order(s)	7th Battalion Royal West Kent Regiment Order No. 77a	05/01/1918	05/01/1918
Operation(al) Order(s)	Instructions To Be Read In Conjunction With Preliminary Order No. 64		
Operation(al) Order(s)	7th Battalion Royal West Kent Regiment Order No. 78	07/01/1918	07/01/1918
Operation(al) Order(s)	7th Battalion Royal West Kent Regiment Order No. 80	17/01/1918	17/01/1918
Miscellaneous	Copies No. 1		
Operation(al) Order(s)	7th Battalion Royal West Kent Regiment	20/01/1918	20/01/1918
Miscellaneous	Amendments To Battalion Order No. 81	21/01/1918	21/01/1918
Operation(al) Order(s)	7th Battalion Royal West Kent Regiment Order No. X	23/01/1918	23/01/1918
Operation(al) Order(s)	7th Battalion Royal West Kent Regiment Order No. 82	24/01/1918	24/01/1918
Operation(al) Order(s)	7th Battalion Royal West Kent Regiment Order No. 83	30/01/1918	30/01/1918
Heading	1915 July 1917 Dec Royal West Kent (Queen's Own)		
Miscellaneous	A/740/82 Casualties Of 7th R.W. Kent Rgt		
Miscellaneous			

WO95/2049(2)

WO95/2049(2)

18TH DIVISION
55TH INFY BDE

7TH BN WEST KENT REGT

JLY 1915 - DEC 1917

18th Division   WO95/2049

121/6874

7th West Kent
Vol. I
July 3 August 15   Dec 17

Army Form C. 2118

WAR DIARY
INTELLIGENCE SUMMARY
(Erase heading not required.)

Place	Date	Hour	Summary of Events and Information	Remarks and references to Appendices
~~Critical~~ CODFORD	20/7/15		Reduced to War Scale	
"	22/7/15		Received orders to proceed abroad	
"	23/7/15	3 p.m.	Battalion assembled 950 strong for address by Brig. Gen. A. Martyn Comndg 55th I.B., Lieut. O.C. 1st Bn. R.W. Kent Regt.	
"	25/7/15	12 noon	Received and issued detailed orders re entrainment	
"	26/7/15	3 am	Entrained in three parties between 3am and 6am; proceeded to Southampton, embarked on board S.S. MONAS QUEEN 6.45 pm, cast off at 7 pm.	
HAVRE	27/7/15	3 am	Arrived HAVRE; fine crossing, speed 15 Knots	
		7 am	Battalion disembarked, and marched to Rest Camp, No 2, at SANVIC distance, 5 miles.	
	28/7/15	8.45 am	Marched out of camp, proceeded to GARE DES MARCHANDISES; Entrained at once in one train, moved off at 2.30 p.m., via ROUEN — AMIENS. one man kicked out of the train by a savage mule, train stopped; 2 officers and six men went back, but before they could bring him up, the train had to go on; informed R.T.O. at ROUEN who was unable to arrange for them to come on by next train.	

Army Form C. 2118

2

WAR DIARY
INTELLIGENCE SUMMARY
(Erase heading not required.)

Instructions regarding War Diaries and Intelligence Summaries are contained in F.S. Regs., Part II. and the Staff Manual respectively. Title Pages will be prepared in manuscript.

Place	Date	Hour	Summary of Events and Information	Remarks and references to Appendices
LONGEAU	29/7/15	2.30 am	Arrived here at 2.30 am, detrained, and marched via AMIENS to VILLERS BOCAGE, distance 10½ miles, arriving at 7.40 am. Battalion went into billets. Accoutrements placed out of bounds by Brigadier.	
VILLERS BOCAGE	31/7/15		Battalion Route march.	
	1/8/15		MAJ. GEN. MAXSE met Captain and upwards of the Brigade, and complimented the Brigade on the way they have had been carried out, and that the 1st Division had a good name already. Informed in that we were in the 10th Corps of the 3rd Army.	
	2/8/15	2.20 pm	Brigade paraded for inspection by GEN MORLAND Comdg. 10th Corps. Owing to bad weather the inspection was cancelled.	
	4/8/15	3 pm	Brigade inspected by GEN. MORLAND who expressed himself well satisfied with the appearance of the Battalion.	
	5/8/15	6 pm	Battalion paraded to march with SS & I.B. to BONNAY. A Company formed the Advance guard; marched via COISY – QUERTRIEUX – PONT NOYELLE arriving BONNAY at 12.30 am. Battalion went into billets; billets very poor & dirty.	
	7/8/15	6.45 pm	Lost a man drowned whilst bathing in the River ANCRE. BUFFS and ourselves paraded to march towards BRAY. Bivouacked night of 7th/8th in a wood some two miles West of BRAY. 6th Cheshires & 1st Cornwalls passed us on the road, going to the Trenches beyond BRAY.	

Army Form C. 2118

WAR DIARY
INTELLIGENCE SUMMARY
(Erase heading not required.)

3

Place	Date	Hour	Summary of Events and Information	Remarks and references to Appendices
Nr BRAY	8/8/15 and 9/8/15		Received intimation that Battalion was to be attached to Units of 13th Brigade for instruction, as follows:- 1 Coy to 1/R.W.Kent Regt, Hd. Qrs. and 1 Coy to 2nd West Ridings (Duke's) each dividing officers, N.C.O. and men to be attached to similar 'opposite number' for 48 hours.	
	9/8/15	9.3 p	A Coy went to 1/R.W.Kent Regt, in CARNOY, B Sector. B Coy - - 2/West Ridings in C Sector	
"	10th + 11th	9.30 p	A Coy relieved by C. Coy. - B Coy relieved by D Coy	
"	12th 13th	9.30 p	A & D Coys again went into the trenches for 48 hours. This time each Platoon was attached to a Company and took over entirely from a Platoon of the Battn. holding the trenches for 24 hours, and the whole Company took over as a complete Unit from a Company in the firing line. This scheme worked very well. B Coy had one man slightly wounded in the face by stone, etc from a "sausage".	
"	14/8/15 15/8/15		C & D Coy relieved A & B Coys and carried out same scheme. C Coy had two men slightly wounded. The O.S.C. Battn to whom we were attached report that all ranks behaved very well, and shewed great keenness to learn.	
BRAY	16/8/15 17/8/15		Whole Battalion billeted at BRAY	
"	18/8/15	7 pm	55 I.B. H.Q. , 7th BUFFS & 7th R.W.K. paraded and marched to BONNAY.	

Army Form C. 2118

WAR DIARY

INTELLIGENCE SUMMARY

(Erase heading not required.)

Instructions regarding War Diaries and Intelligence Summaries are contained in F.S. Regs., Part II. and the Staff Manual respectively. Title Pages will be prepared in manuscript.

Place	Date	Hour	Summary of Events and Information	Remarks and references to Appendices
BONNAY	19/8/15 to 22/8/15		Battalion billeted at BONNAY. Battalion marched to SERNANCOURT and billeted there, night 22nd/23rd	
TRENCHES	23/8/15	7 pm	Marched from SERNANCOURT to Trenches; distance – 6 miles; took over Sector A1 (76 – 83) from 1/CHESHIRES; relief was carried out and completed at 10.45 pm.	App. I.
			NOTES ON TRENCHES: (see Appendix I). A lot of work required on trenches required especially left Sector (80-83), where banquette required rebuilding, parapets must bullet proof, paradoes built up, communication trenches deepened. There were no sniping posts worthy of the name, either in front line or further back. Dug outs were insufficient in number, and very few were bomb-proof. In the case of a heavy enemy bombardment, hardly a man could have escaped. Cooking carried out in French boilers in Dug Outs (named the CITADEL) 800x back from Battn. H.Q. Water brought up to B CITADEL in rail way trucks drawn by H.A. horses from BRAY. Carts can come up to Battn. H.Q. by night. Battalion disposed of in trenches as follows:— A Coy — Right Sector — 76 to 79 A Coy — Left Sector — 80 – 83 A Coy in Support at R2 (Battn. H.Q.) C Coy in Reserve at R3	

WAR DIARY / INTELLIGENCE SUMMARY

Army Form C. 2118

Place	Date	Hour	Summary of Events and Information	Remarks and references to Appendices
Trenches	24/8/15		Work on parapets begun at once, C & A Coys sending up large working parties to front line. Situation quite quiet. Two men of B Coy accidentally wounded themselves.	5-
"	24th/25th	Night	Quiet: 8th E. Surrey on our left did a good deal of firing. Zone 81 B — 82 A danger zone with mines underneath. This portion was not held but patrolled every 10 minutes by one bomber and one rifleman. One man killed in a listening post, shot in the head.	
"	25/8/15	10.45 a.m.	Quiet in the morning. 1 German dropped from shells beyond the CITADEL 82 C Batt, I R.F.A. registering. Two men killed; shot in the head by bullet, coming through the parapet.	
		10 p.m.	Mine exploded by Germans opposite TT; no damage; near edge of crater about 25x from our parapet. Germans bombed the crate all night long trying to prevent our occupying it; we prevented them occupying it by M.G. fire. Estimated dimensions of crater, given by 2nd Lieut I. HEATON who reconnoitred it shortly after explosion :— 50x by 30x by 30'.	
	26/8/15		Germans appeared to have got to their edge of crater, where the debris is piled higher than on our side; enemy trenches immediately opposite were rendered invisible from the front for about 50 yards.	
	27/8/15		Shallow mining, at a depth of six to ten feet below the ground commenced from three different points opposite the new crater (77), to	

WAR DIARY
INTELLIGENCE SUMMARY
(Erase heading not required.)

Army Form C. 2118

Instructions regarding War Diaries and Intelligence Summaries are contained in F.S. Regs., Part II. and the Staff Manual respectively. Title Pages will be prepared in manuscript.

Place	Date	Hour	Summary of Events and Information	Remarks and references to Appendices
	27th	5.30pm	make bombing posts to prevent Germans occupying crater, under superintendance of Lt CHRISTIE, R.E. (It should be mentioned here that a Battn. bombing section had previously been formed, consisting of 4 O.N.C.O.'s & men, under 2nd Lt. PYMM, 7th R.W.K.) Six men wounded during the day. German mine under 81.B blown by one of our comrades; 30 yards of our parapet knocked down; sides and rear edge of crater occupied and consolidated during the night without loss. Mentioned well. It is considered by the 178th Tunnelling Coy that the Germans were in the act of laying their charge, so the blow was well timed.	
	28/8/15		Enemy snipers rather too active, but nevertheless our posts not yet completed.	
		6pm to 6.30	6 Inch Howitzer Battery C/65, bombarded one particular post opposite 81 with considerable success. One man slightly wounded by short burst. Enemy replied with about 60 "whiz-bang" (common shell) on Battn. H.Q. with no result except one man very slightly scratched.	
		9.30pm	178th Tunnelling Coy blew a German mine opposite 80 by Cannon. Effect : result — successful ; no crater formed.	
	29/8/15	3.30pm	Shallow mines opposite 60 at 77 fused out about 20 yards. C 62 Batty R.F.A. registered on German lines.	

WAR DIARY or INTELLIGENCE SUMMARY

Army Form C. 2118

Place	Date	Hour	Summary of Events and Information	Remarks and references to Appendices
		6 pm	Battn. relieved by 7th Buffs. Relief completed without casualties at 1.15 a.m. Total casualties during tour in Trenches = O.R. 3 killed and 13 wounded. Behaviour and bearing of all ranks was excellent; men were cheery throughout.	
	30/8/15	4.30 am	Battn. less A & B Coys arrived in billets at MEAULTE. A Coy to BECORDEL-BÉCOURT; B Coy in reserve to A.1 at POINT 107.	

Captain & Adjutant
7th R.W. Kent Regt.

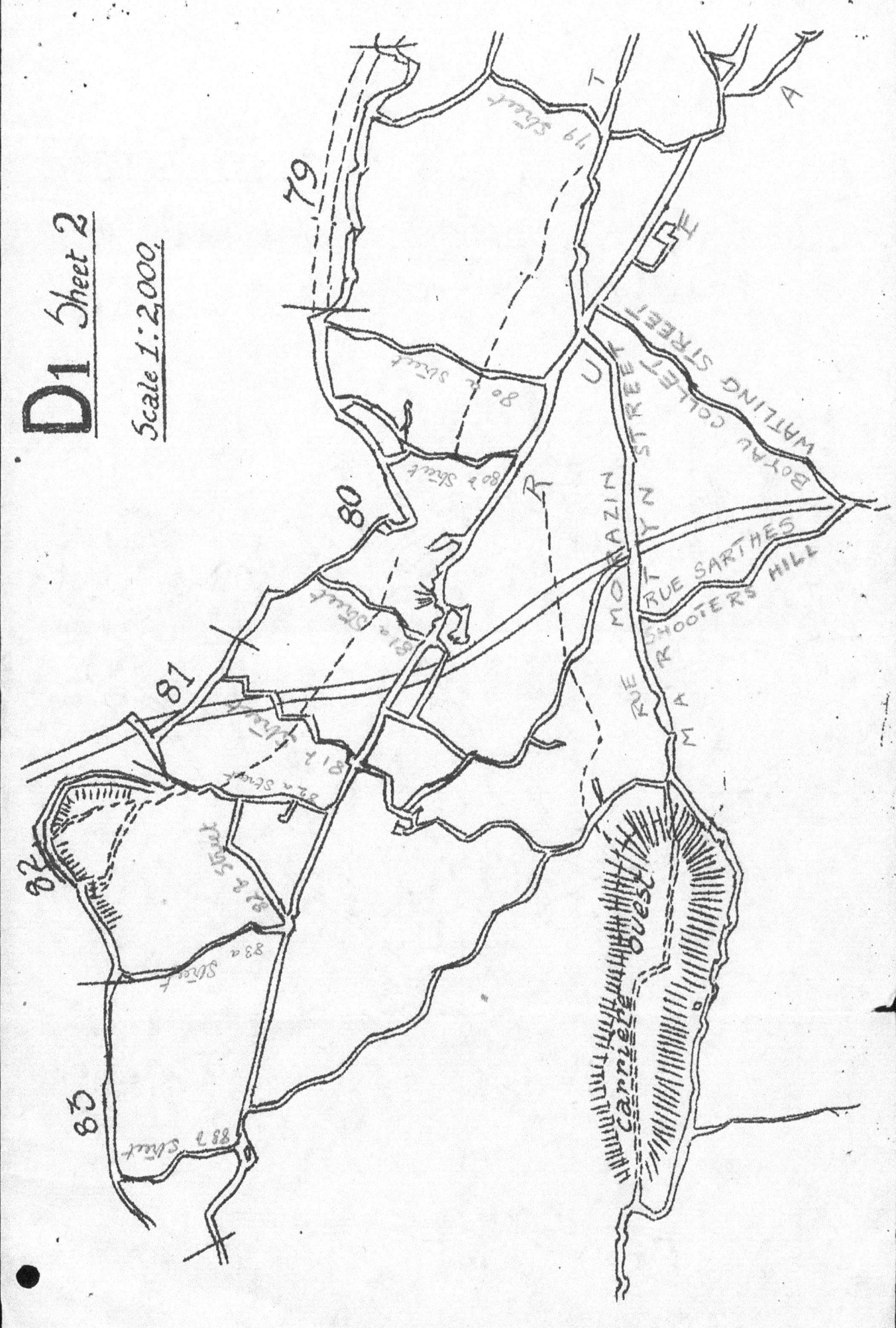

APPENDIX I.

N.

Scale:-
1:2,000.

78

R 78 Street
H 77b Street
O 77a Street
R 76b Street
76a Street
76 Street

MANCHESTER
OVER
ALBERT
ROAD

77

CARRIER

KENT
Portland Avenue

Scale:- 1:2000.

PARK LANE — Bn Hd Qrs
R. OLD

To R 3, about 300x
To CITADEL

18th Hussein

WO95/2049

121/7432

4th without
vol 2
Sept & Oct 15

Army Form C. 2118

WAR DIARY
INTELLIGENCE SUMMARY
(Erase heading not required.)

Instructions regarding War Diaries and Intelligence Summaries are contained in F.S. Regs., Part II and the Staff Manual respectively. Title Pages will be prepared in manuscript.

Place	Date	Hour	Summary of Events and Information	Remarks and references to Appendices
MEAULTE	3/ix/15		55th I.B. relieved by 54th I.B. Battalion relieved by 6th NORTHANTS. Marched to billets at RIBEMONT and MERICOURT arriving at 1.30 a.m.	
	4th 15 16th		Billets	
	17th	11 a.m.	Paraded to march to the trenches; on the distance was considerable (8 to 9 miles) a long halt was made (1 p.m to 6 p.m.) for dinner and tea. Relieved 6th SEAFORTHS in sector E1, which had not been previously occupied by the battalion; relief completed at 10.30 p.m. Disposition of 18th Division had been changed as follows :- 54th I.B. on the right, A.1 and A.2; 55th I.B. in the centre, A.3 and E.1; 53rd I.B. on the left, E.2 and E.3, each Brigade having two battalions up. Battalion distributed as follows :- Firing Line, A Company on the right, B in the centre and C on the left: A Company in Local Support being N. and N.E. edge of redoubt found Becourt wood: Battalion H.Q. at CHATEAU BECOURT; this Chateau being the only building in BECOURT which had not been knocked about, it appeared to be an admirable position for Battn H.Q. but it also had very good and made bomb proof and cabin above after a few days work.	
	17th to 26th		In the trenches; German trenches varying from 350 to 500 yards away. Fairly quiet sector; supported by B/84 Battery, Capt NORRIS. Work completed included entire relieving of fire parapet, deepening and digging communication trenches, and making Dug Outs.	
	22nd/23rd	6 p.m 3.30 a.m	A Company with some R.E. and B Company & 4 R. SUSSEX PIONEERS dug new trenches by night: men dug well, no casualties	
	23rd/24th	Mdnght	Same trenches completed	

WAR DIARY
INTELLIGENCE SUMMARY

(Erase heading not required.)

Army Form C. 2118

Place	Date	Hour	Summary of Events and Information	Remarks and references to Appendices
	23rd		Slow bombardment of German trenches from 12.30 pm to 8 pm.	
	24th		Same programme. This weather was unfortunately broken and rain and thunder storm in progress. One rifle field-gun/c was wounded on the patrol. Capt HOLLAND and Lt WARREN brought the wounded man and Lt McKENZIE found and brought in the dead man under heavy rifle & M.G. fire, which was plucky but foolish.	
	25th		Bombardment of German trenches from 2 pm to 4.30 pm. All these three days enemy scarcely replied except by a few rifle-grenades which did no damage.	
	26th/27th		Relieved by 7th BUFFS; relief completed by 12.30 am. Relief somewhat delayed owing to muddy state of trenches. Marched to billets at DERNANCOURT leaving D Company up to carry out mining & tunnelling fatigues.	
			NOTE: During tour in the trenches casualties were:—	
			Killed – O.R. 2	
			Wounded – O.R. 10 (including 3 accidentally)	
			(Of the one was S.M. TAPP who had an accident while testing a rifle grenade)	
	27th/5th		Battalion in billets at DERNANCOURT: exercises carried out consisted chiefly of attack practice assaulting from the trenches, route marching, bayonet fighting, physical drill and handling of arms. A draft of 23 men arrived.	
	6th		Relieved 7th BUFFS in E1: relief completed at 10.30 pm.	C. R. Anhahn Lt Col
				7th R.W.K.

3rd Army Circular Memorandum.

LEAKAGE OF INFORMATION.

1. On occasions, movements of troops, which some individuals consider may be likely to take place, have formed the subject of open discussion by Officers and other ranks.

2. The injury to our Military cause which may be done by this is incalculable. It is to be impressed on all ranks that they are absolutely forbidden to discuss in public any Military movements or operations, whether on a large or small scale. It is their duty as good soldiers to "know nothing" about such matters, and, if questioned, to adopt an attitude of "complete ignorance". Any infringement of this rule is to be severely dealt with.

3. Spies, both male and female, and the enemy's intelligence agents are undoubtedly among us, therefore every officer and man should be on his guard. It is only by the loyalty and discretion of all ranks that anything approaching secrecy can be maintained. It is the essential duty of every soldier to at once check any indiscreet conversation on the part of others at all times and in all places.

4. Unguarded talk at railheads, railhead towns or estaminets is extremely harmful, and therefore the particular attention of all personnel of rear-work services, such as railheads, supply-columns, ammunition sub-parks, casualty clearing stations, etc., should be drawn to these instructions.

5. All ranks should be similarly be warned that, should they unfortunately fall into the hands of the enemy, they must decline to give any information beyond their rank, true name and regimental number.

6. These instructions should be read out on parade to all units.

9th September, 1915.

WLATER CAMPBELL, Major-General.
D.A. & Q.M.G., 3rd Army.

18th Hussars

7th Hussars
Vol 3
Oct 15

VOL 3

Army Form C. 2118

WAR DIARY
INTELLIGENCE SUMMARY
(Erase heading not required.)

Instructions regarding War Diaries and Intelligence Summaries are contained in F.S. Regs., Part II. and the Staff Manual respectively. Title Pages will be prepared in manuscript.

Place	Date	Hour	Summary of Events and Information	Remarks and references to Appendices
	7th Oct		Germans all doing more firing than when Battalion was last in this sector (i.e. 10 days ago). Their snipers seemed to have got the upper hand. As this Battalion makes rather a point of sniping, this situation was taken in hand at once. Twenty (20) picked men under an officer (2/LT C.G. TINDALL) were struck off all duties and were kept for sniping purposes only. Battn H.Q still at the CHATEAU, which became daily more dangerous owing to stray bullets. Germans were seen daily doing a lot of work in their trenches, relying on their snipers to cover them and give them immunity from our rifle fire. Artillery quiet, except in retaliation; importance owing to shortage of ammunition.	Vide Appendix II
	9th		We have got three sniping posts in we now, and they have already begun to make themselves felt. Enemy put up a dummy horse and rider carrying a flag in front of this line, from a s.p. during the night, significance unknown; it was soon shot down.	
	10th		Very quiet all day; nothing worth note occurred	
	11th		The coming of day revealed a German flag on the ground about 100 yards in front of enemy trenches. It is thought this was a trap in order to induce one of our patrols to come and capture it.	
	11th/12th Night		Some went out in the direction of this flag, but found no	

WAR DIARY
INTELLIGENCE SUMMARY

(Erase heading not required.)

Army Form C. 2118

Instructions regarding War Diaries and Intelligence Summaries are contained in F.S. Regs., Part II. and the Staff Manual respectively. Title Pages will be prepared in manuscript.

Place	Date	Hour	Summary of Events and Information	Remarks and references to Appendices
	12th		saw nothing, except the sounds of digging and various kinds of work going on in German lines. Col. PRIOR received orders to proceed to England, on account of his departure deeply regretted by all ranks. Maj. J.T. WYKEHAM-TIENNES took over the Command. During the day a point (x20 D61) in the German lines, from which we had been worried at nights by M.Gs and rifle grenades, was shelled by our 4.5" trenches. Before nightfall our M.Gs were laid on this point, and during the night fire was opened at intervals. Also at dawn a German working party was caught there. A full account of this incident is given in Appendix III. — As far as could be ascertained, Germans were doing a lot of work on their 1st & 2nd line trenches, "constructing" new entanglements in front of their 2nd line trenches, this work being screened by the rows of their 1st line trenches. The fact that their own German trenches are nearly everywhere on higher ground than our own makes this work able to go on without being seen by us.	Vide Appendix III.
	12/13th	Night	A patrol went out about 200x in front to listen; one man was heard from the German line, followed shortly afterwards by a Very light, & M.G. fire	

Army Form C. 2118

WAR DIARY
INTELLIGENCE SUMMARY
(Erase heading not required.)

Place	Date	Hour	Summary of Events and Information	Remarks and references to Appendices
	13th		Owing to our patrols being in a shell crater, they were not hit. Enemy whizz-bang battery evidently received their weekly allowance of ammunition, as they were lined with it. No damage. Our reserve company (A Coy) spent this and the next two days making fire steps, parapet and traverses in the new trenches mentioned at the bottom of Page 8, which runs between the 2nd line of this Sector. Enemy spotted this work on the 14th, & being warned to periodically on that day, 1st & 16th, only two were slightly wounded as a result of this.	
	14th			
	15th			
	16th		Battn. relieved by 7th Buffs. During our tour in the trenches the situation was at all times normal. Our snipers and machine guns were particularly successful. The infiltre of LEWIS GUN in the trenches is now firmly established. Battn. arrived in billets at DERNANCOURT at 11.30 p.m. Total Casualties from 6th Oct – 16th Oct. Other ranks:- Killed 4, Wounded 8.	
	17th /23rd		Battalion in Rest billets: bombing, trenched mortar & vis (on &a on the numerous fatigues would allow) to make every officer & N.C.O. a competent instructor & deny	

1875 Wt. W593/826 1,000,000 4/15 J.B.C. & A. A.D.S.S./Forms/C. 2118.

WAR DIARY
INTELLIGENCE SUMMARY

Army Form C. 2118

Instructions regarding War Diaries and Intelligence Summaries are contained in F.S. Regs., Part II. and the Staff Manual respectively. Title Pages will be prepared in manuscript.

(Erase heading not required.)

Place	Date	Hour	Summary of Events and Information	Remarks and references to Appendices
	18th		Men on efficient bombers. The following changes in Company command took place:- Capt A.E. Peidgin, Batt. Command A Coy vice Lt Col R.C. Ryall. " R.B. Holland (2nd Capt B Coy) to command B Coy vice Capt A.E. Phillips " T.T. Waddington (2nd Capt C Coy) " C " - Capt W.G. Summers transferred to A Coy as 2nd Captain	
	17th	1030 am	Batt. inspected by Brig. Gen. A. Martyn; he was accompanied by Lt. Gen. Sir T. Morland Commdg 10th Corps.	
	22nd		The Brigade appointed to command 67th Bde and take them out to Salonika; his authority greatly regretted by all Temp. Lt Col. Elmslie Commdg 7th Buffs temporarily assumed command of SS I.B. Maj Osborne, Brigade Major appointed to command 12th Middlesex, SS. I.B. Capt 247ER, 2nd Capt C Coy to be acting Staff Captain SS, I.B	
	25th		Relieved 7th Buffs in E.I. Relief complete at 9pm.	
	26th		Distribution:- Right Sector ..... D Coy Centre " ..... A " Left " ..... C " Reserve ..... B "	
	26th Oct to 5th Nov		Battalion in the trenches for 9 days; then tour being very much	

Army Form C. 2118

WAR DIARY
INTELLIGENCE SUMMARY
(Erase heading not required.)

Instructions regarding War Diaries and Intelligence Summaries are contained in F. S. Regs, Part II. and the Staff Manual respectively. Title Pages will be prepared in manuscript.

14

Place	Date	Hour	Summary of Events and Information	Remarks and references to Appendices
	27/28th	night	The same as the preceding ones, 7th QUEENS on our right at Sect A3; 6th BERKSHIRES on our left in B2.	
	28th/29th	night	We put up 125 x wire entanglement in front of our trenches; no casualties.	
	29/30th	night	A patrol went out at midnight and stayed out for two hours, encountering no hostile patrols; they reported wire going on in German trenches.	
	30th/31st /1st Nov	night	We put up another 125 x rG entanglement; no casualties. Our wiring party counted 5 officers & 1 o.r.; only 4 men worked on a trench.	
	1st/2nd	night	A patrol crawled out and reported Germans working in front of their trenches; on their return Very lights were sent up, but Germans working parties were not altogether located.	
	2nd		During the night 2nd/3rd a good deal of rain fell; ten of the parapet fell in in several places; also communication trenches & traverses were affected to an only very slight length of trench have so far been bombed by R.E.	
	3rd and 4th		These days were spent in repairing damage to trenches. The Germans also appeared to have difficulty with their trenches, as several working parties were seen and fired on by our Artillery, with, in several cases, considerable success.	

Army Form C. 2118

WAR DIARY

INTELLIGENCE SUMMARY

(Erase heading not required.)

Instructions regarding War Diaries and Intelligence Summaries are contained in F.S. Regs., Part II. and the Staff Manual respectively. Title Pages will be prepared in manuscript.

Place	Date	Hour	Summary of Events and Information	Remarks and references to Appendices
	4th/5th	night	We put up 50 x more wire, with no casualties.	
	5th	11 p.m.	Relieved by 7th Buffs. During the tour the only change in the Enemy's moral behaviour was the rather larger number of "whiz bangs" (77mm shells) fired by them into this Sector; the reason was not apparent, but our total Casualties of 3 killed and 9 wounded (all other Ranks) are the 3 men killed and how of the wounded were caused by these shells, on every occasion that they abtely fired, every immediately retaliated on previously registered targets. Battalion marched to rest billets at DERNANCOURT.	

R.A. Humphries Capt
adjutant
7th R.W. Kent Regt

REPORT ON SNIPING IN TRENCH WARFARE.   App. II

During the period of training immediately preceeding departure for France an order was received by the Divisional Commander requiring battalions to train a certain number of selected men as snipers. This order had already been anticipated in so far that the general lines of organisation and training had already been discussed and decided upon, as far as was possible in theory. On receipt of the above mentioned order, the formation and training of the battalion snipers was immediately proceeded with on the previously determined lines, namely:-

Twenty four specially selected men under a subaltern officer were drawn from the companies and struck off all other duties during their course of special training; as far as possible the men selected fulfilled the following conditions.
  (a) Country bred.
  (b) Preferably game keepers and poachers.
  (c) Intelligent and fairly well educated.
  (d) At least first class shots.
  (e) Sober and of good physique.

EARLY TRAINING.

The course of training comprised the following subjects, and was carried out as far and as thoroughly as equipment and local conditions permitted.
1. Practice in quick shooting and vanishing and moving targets from behind all kinds of cover up to 600 yards with all types of sights.
2. Use of Aperture, Lens and Telescopic Sights, (The necessary equipment for this was bought out of private funds) both in theory and practice, and the care and adjustment of the same.
3. Eyesight training and use of Rangefinder, Telescope and Binoculars.
4. Use of natural cover and assimilation to background. Construction, siting and concealment of artificial cover, value of silence and of immobility as a help to concealment (taught mainly by demonstration).
5. Map reading, judging distance, by eye and by observation.

This training was continued after arrival in France whenever opportunity offered and is still continued when in rest billets.

The first Sector of trenches occupied by the Battalion afforded all the practice necessary to test and adapt the training and organisation. The trenches were close together, at no point more than 100 yards apart, the German snipers were in complete ascendancy, and it was impossible to show even a periscope over the parapet without it being smashed. On the right of the Sector, the ground sloped away behind the fire trench affording no position from which the German line could be seen. On the left flank matters were reversed, and good positions were found about 100 yards in rear of the fire trenches; these positions commanded, and at points enfiladed the hostile trenches.

The first step was to make a prolonged reconnaissance with a telescope, locating by flash and movement the enemy's sniping posts. This reconnaisance was carried out from disused communication trenches covered with weeds, and proved successful in locating the enemy posts. Positions were then selected and work commenced on them.

On the left where the ground was high, disused trenches were utilised, protected positions being made in them by tunnelling into the parapet and boring a hole on the enemy's side under a thorough large bunch of long weeds. The hole made was no larger than was absolutely necessary, infinite pains being taken to leave the ground on the enemy's side absolutely undisturbed. When the necessary excavation was completed, loophole plates were inserted, the whole forming a completely covered in bullet proof "conning tower", in which the man could shoot and observe undisturbed, and which having been constructed from the trench outwards was absolutely invisible from the front.

On the right of the sector a different state of affairs was found to exist, as the ground sloped back from the fire trench and no commanding positions were to be had. It was finally decided to utilise the parados of the fire trench, access to which was obtained from a supervision trench a few yards to the rear; in this parados two posts were built similar to those constructed on the left. In this sector one other post was made in the parapet of a disused trench about 15 yards in front of the fire trench.

After two days a considerable diminution in volume and accuracy of the enemy's fire was observed, but the third day the enemy's snipers were found to be shooting from different positions, thus proving they had been forced to evacuate their

P.T.O.

old ones.

The battalion was then relieved and did not return to that sector.
During this tour of duty the following lessons were learnt.
1. That two men were necessary to each post, one to shoot, the other to observe; therefore two loopholes fairly close to each other were necessary.
2. If disturbance of the natural contour of the ground was to be avoided, the loopholes had to be shoved up with timber as work proceeded.
3. The Officer i/c Snipers and the Snipers would have to be attached to Battalion Headquarters, and struck off all duties while in trenches, if delay and confusion was to be avoided.
4. Regular reliefs for each post were necessary if a constant watchfulness from dawn to dark was to be obtained.

The battalion's next tour of duty was in a different sector of the trench line. The Officer i/c of Snipers and his twenty four men were attached to Battalion Headquarters and struck off all duties. The men were divided up into pairs and told off in two reliefs to each post.

The ground was again very similar to that of the sector first occupied, high ground on the left and falling away in the centre and on the right. In this sector the distance of the German trenches varied between 300 yards and 600 yards.

A reconnaisance was made and two posts were built on the rising ground on the left and an existing French post on the right was occupied for the time being.

On this sector being taken over by the battalion, it was found that the Germans again had superiority of fire, and further experience of this sector disclosed the following facts.
1. German sniper was top dog.
2. Further measures were necessary in order to counteract his superiority. To meet the situation three more posts were constructed and in three days such complete control of the situation was obtained that difficulty was experienced in preventing the men in the fire trenches sitting on the parapet. If additional evidence of superiority were required it was furnished by the crop of periscopes which grew like asparagus from a bed along the German line.

Experiments were now made with different types of posts, one type especially proving very effective. It was constructed by tunnelling out from a disused communication trench into a large patch of rank weeds on the forward slope of a hill, reliance for protection to sniper's head and shoulders being placed upon cover afforded by rank herbage, and assimilation of colour to background, in which great assistance was found in the use of veils and snipers coats provided by the Brigade.

ORGANISATION OF DUTIES AND EQUIPMENT OF POSTS.

Posts were numbered in the order in which they were constructed and four men in two reliefs allotted to each; reliefs were organised in periods of three hours each, commencing a quarter of an hour before dawn and ceasing at nightfall. The following equipment is allotted to each post and handed over clean to each relief.
1. To those posts furthest from enemy's lines, telescope-sighted rifles and a telescope for use by observer.
2. To intermediate posts rifles fitted with Lens sights, observers being provided with binoculars.
3. To posts nearest enemy's line, rifles fitted with aperture sights, observers with binoculars.

This distribution was necessitated by the inadequate number of telescopic and Lens sighted rifles available. As previously stated the men worked in pairs, one observing and the other in readiness to shoot.

The posts were so arranged that each has a definite portion of the enemy's line to observe, an unceasing watch being kept on the whole front of the sector from dawn to dark.

On vacation of the posts at dusk all rifles and optical equipment are cleaned and brought to Officer i/c of Snipers for his inspection, these implements remaining in his charge during the night and being drawn from him again at "STAND TO" on the following morning.

As evidence of material results obtained, the following incidents are described being substantiated by evidence of independent witnesses.
1. Two men seen patrolling German front line trench; they stopped and got up on firing step, one man took aim at our trenches while the other stood behind him, fired on by our snipers the man watching was seen to collapse and fall backwards into the trench.

2. Early on a foggy morning the mist suddenly lifted and a German was seen sitting on the parapet smoking a pipe. He was fired on and was seen to fall backwards on to the parapet and roll into the trench.
3. A German was seen to get out of the trench and run along the parapet; he was hit and fell face foremost on to the parapet rolling into the trench.
4. A German was seen placing sandbags on the parados, he was hit and collapsed sliding down the parados yelling.

In addition to these material results, evidence of successful neutralizing effect is available in the fact that excepting the first occasion on which the Battalion was in the trenches, only one casualty has been suffered from German snipers by day.

This neutralizing effect has been obtained by careful location and registration of snipers' posts and loopholes, and instant fire being turned on them as soon as occupied. On one occasion a hostile machine gun was silenced by the accurate fire of the snipers against its emplacement.

A recent elaboration of the system in force has been made in combining sniping with collection of information. To each post is given a tracing of that portion of the trench map, scale 1/10,000, with which it is directly concerned; on this map ranges to marked points are shown thus serving the double purpose of a range sheet and a map by which positions of enemy activity can be accurately described. Each post is required to furnish to the Officer i/c Snipers a report at the end of the day on the following headings.
(a) New work done by enemy during the night.
(b) Machine guns, trench mortars, snipers, observation posts, new loopholes, etc. located during day.
(c) Germans seen, place, colour of uniform, apparent age, physique and equipment.
(d) Action taken; if hit, evidence in support.
(e) General.

This addition to the system has been found of great value as the Officer i/c Snipers combines intelligence duties with Command of Battalion Snipers.

The men display the greatest keenness and rivalry in collection of information and in their work in general.

S U M M A R Y.

OBJECTS.

(a) Neutralisation of enemy snipers.
  Minimising casualties and admitting of free movement behind fire trenches of Officers and working parties.
(b) Infliction on enemy of casualties whenever opportunity offers.

ORGANISATION AND TRAINING. ESSENTIALS.

Snipers must be regarded and trained as specialists and struck off all other work, attached to Headquarters Co. and must be under the command of a specially selected officer, the best qualified available, who should be similarly struck off all other work.

A definite system providing that all portions of the enemy's front within the Battalion Sector shall be ceaselessly watched from dawn to dark must be instituted.

Adequate equipment in telescopic and lens sights and in telescopes must be provided.

Men must be specially trained in use of sniping equipment and must be selected for skill with the rifle, intelligence and trustworthiness. Everything must be done to foster the feeling that the man is a specialist, and holds his position by virtue of his skill and woodcraft.

ORGANISATION.

Snipers should be organised in pairs and never separated, each man taking his turn in shooting and observing. A regular system of reliefs must be in force, reports should be required from each post at a definite time each day under headings which should be given to the men. Careful steps should be taken to ensure that all equipment is kept in good condition. All posts where circumstances permit should be roofed in and made as comfortable as possible as the posts have to be occupied in all conditions of weather.

P.T.O.

TRAINING.

- Musketry.
- Judging Distance.
- Range Taking.
- Observation of Bullet Strike.
- Use and care of Optical Sights.
- Use and care of telescopes and binoculars.
- Use of natural and construction of artificial cover.
- Assimilation of colour to surroundings.
- Construction of all types of bullet proof cover.
- Value of immobility and silence.
- Map reading.
- Writing of simple reports.
- Eyesight training.
- Location by means of flash and sound of hostile riflemen.

It cannot be too strongly insisted upon that success can only be obtained by infinite pains in the selection of men, organisation, training, reconnaissance of ground and by constant and unremitting effort to devise new expedients to meet ever varying conditions.

All efforts will, however, be negative if the relieving Battalion is not equally well organised for sniping purposes, and gives away by careless use positions selected.

Oct. 20th. 1915.

(signed) Charles C. Tindall.
2nd. Lt. 7th Batt. Royal West Kent Regt.

App. III

18th Div.No.G. 826

REPORT ON MACHINE GUN ACTION IN D.I. 6th - 15th OCTR.

The system of Machine gun action in the trenches in force in the Battalion depends for its success upon careful and continuous reconnaissance of the enemys line both by day and night. All traces of work done during the night is carefully registered and ranged on during the day, particularly in cases where it seems probable that the work is incomplete and will be continued the following night. Temporary emplacements are constructed wherever necessary to facilitate the cross fire of two or more guns upon the determined spot, and fire is opened at uncertain intervals during the night. The same system is employed to deal with hostile machine guns the positions of which have been located, ground in the sectors right and left being sometimes borrowed for use temporarily when increased effect can thereby be gained. Guns however are never moved more than 50x outside their own sector for this purpose and then only for a few minutes.

The Machine Gun Officer and Sniping Officer are in close touch make use of their combined local knowledge and thus each reaps the advantage of the others knowledge which frequently necessitates combined work

The following instances are given to illustrate action of guns:-

During Oct.12 Point X20 D 61 was shelled by our 4.5" Howitzers which did considerable damage to enemy works at this point. The machine guns were laid on damaged portion of work - range 430x and during night 12/13th Octr. opened fire at intervals. A listening post opposite to and 250x from point 61 reported cries of pain following first burst of fire from Machine Guns. The morning of the 13th was foggy the German lines being invisible up to 6.30.a.m. At this time the mist lifted very suddenly disclosing a hostile working party of about 30 men repairing wire outside their trenches between points X20 d61 and X 26 B87. Two guns immediately opened cross fire on party at range of 600x. Loud yells were heard by our sentries along the whole of our line but the effect could not be definitely seen owing to the fog descending again and blotting out target. On the morning of the 14th a similar incident occurred: A German working party of about 10 men at point X 26 b 82 was discovered owing to fog suddenly lifting. Fire was opened and before the mist fell again 3 or 4 bodies could be distinctly seen lying on the ground. On many other occasions cries have been heard from the German lines following a burst of fire from guns laid by day on points where work is known to be in progress.

I am strongly of opinion that action by Machine guns should be on the lines I have described rather than by wild and indiscriminate shooting on the off chance that someone will be hit.

This system and the undoubted deterrent effect it has had upon the German Working Parties is due to the energy in reconnaissance and initiative displayed by my M.G.Officer Lieut.B.McKenzie.

Oct.20th.1915.

(sd)J.T.W.FIENNES. Lt.Colonel,
Commanding 7th R.W.Kent Regt.

WO95/2049

7th W. Kent.
Vol 4

18th Division

D/
768

Nov. 15?

Army Form C. 2118

WAR DIARY
or
INTELLIGENCE SUMMARY

(Erase heading not required.)

Vol. IV

Instructions regarding War Diaries and Intelligence Summaries are contained in F.S. Regs., Part II. and the Staff Manual respectively. Title Pages will be prepared in manuscript.

Place	Date	Hour	Summary of Events and Information	Remarks and references to Appendices
DERNAN-COURT	6th to 14th		Rest billets: Average of 430 men on fatigue daily, a good deal of work done in improving billets, watering, flooring and making beds. Battalion practised in bombing.	
Tunnelle	15th	6.20 pm	Relieved 7th BUFFS in E.1.	
"			Distribution: Right Sector ... D Coy Centre " ... A Coy Left " ... B Coy Reserve ... C Coy	
"	15th/16th	night	Foggy and snowed during the night. Lt C.S. STEVENSON wounded by Rifle Grenade.	
"	16th		Very quiet — weather cold	
"	17th		"	
"	18th	6am to 2pm	Very foggy; afternoon quite fine but occasional bursts of M.G. fire. 2/Lt PROUD and one man patrolled to within 100x of enemy's trenches at this point nearly 50x distant, and saw Germans repairing their line; on being detected M.G. fire was opened in their direction.	

Army Form C. 2118

WAR DIARY
INTELLIGENCE SUMMARY
(Erase heading not required.)

Instructions regarding War Diaries and Intelligence Summaries are contained in F.S. Regs., Part II. and the Staff Manual respectively. Title Pages will be prepared in manuscript.

Place	Date	Hour	Summary of Events and Information	Remarks and references to Appendices
Trenches	18th	7pm	A large Trench M.G. explosive plate, which could not be taken down a trench, was taken across country, its emplacement it was required for.	17
"		7pm	Enemy shelled our transport coming up, doing no damage.	
"	19th		Weather still very severe.	
"	"	11.45 pm	Enemy shelled vicinity of CHATEAU BECOURT with 77mm guns; no reply was made as it was thought that then we were caught mid before to locate our batteries by flashes; we were caught once before in this way.	
"	20th	11am to 12 noon	Enemy distributed over 100 4.2 Howitzer & 77mm Field gunshells over our sector; our 18 pdrs and 6 inch howitzers replied.	
"	21st	11am	Our artillery successfully shelled enemy working parties.	
"	"	2pm	Altered distribution of Companies to 2 Companies in front line, one in support (Countesatoca Company), and one in reserve (redoubt), by order of G.O.C. 18th Division.	

Right Sector ...... A Coy
Left " ...... B Coy
Support " ...... C Coy
Reserve " ...... D Coy

Army Form C. 2118

WAR DIARY
INTELLIGENCE SUMMARY
(Erase heading not required.)

Instructions regarding War Diaries and Intelligence Summaries are contained in F.S. Regs., Part II. and the Staff Manual respectively. Title Pages will be prepared in manuscript.

Place	Date	Hour	Summary of Events and Information	Remarks and references to Appendices
Trenches	23rd	Morning	Note. The support Company is so organised, as to have two complete working parties always ready for immediate action.	
BERTRAN- COURT	"		Relieved by 7th Buffs. Arrived Billets 1.30 p.m.	
"	24th		Col. TIENNES proceeded to England on leave; Capt A.B. PHILLIPS temporarily in command.	
"	24/29		Rest Billets. — About 250 men on fatigue daily; Comparatively small numbers enabled a day to be struck off all fatigues in order to carry on training in bombing, musketry and other subjects.	
"	29th	10.10 p.m.	Test alarm given from Bde. H.Q. — Night class but cold. All Coys and M.G. Section ready to move off in 20 minutes; Transport in 55 minutes.	
TRENCHES	30th		Relieved 7th Buffs = E.1. Relief completed 11.45 a.m.	

O.H.Andrietta Capt
adjt
7th R. W. Kent Regt

3rd ARMY.

A.C./1266.

ADJUTANT GENERAL'S BRANCH

EXTRACTS FROM ROUTINE ORDERS, ETC.

The following extracts of orders are published as it is thought they may be of use, especially to New Divisions joining the 3rd Army.

1. **CORRESPONDENCE.**

   Instructions regarding the rendering of Correspondence and Returns are contained in 3rd Army Circular Memorandum dated 8th September, 1915.

2. **CASUALTY REPORTS.**

   The method of reporting Casualties to Army Headquarters is also contained in the Circular Memorandum quoted above.
   The cause of any accidental casualty should be stated very briefly in the telegraphic daily casualty returns; the casualty return is not to be delayed, however, for the insertion of the information.
   A brief telegraphic report should also be made separately, stating the circumstances attending any injuries to officers or men caused by the accidental explosion of grenades.

3. **FIGHTING STRENGTH RETURNS.**

   The weekly Fighting Strength Return will be rendered to Army Headquarters by 8-30 a.m. on Sunday. Instructions for the compilation are contained in 3rd Army Circular Memo.
   No Officer is to be struck off the strength of a unit unless he is either:-

   (i) A casualty in action (Killed, wounded or missing).
   (ii) Transferred or attached to another unit, or to the Staff.
   (iii) Invalided home by the order of the medical authorities in this country.

   As regards (ii)

   Officers may be struck off the strength if they are permanently transferred or posted to another unit, by order of General Headquarters, or appointed to the Staff. The unit must have a recognised establishment.
   Officers temporarily transferred to equalize numbers of officers in units, or to command units, under authority given to Divisional or Corps Commanders, and officers appointed to command of composite companies or as Divisional Claims Officers cannot be struck off the strength.

N.C.O's and men who are attached to Trench Mortar Batteries will be borne on the strength of their units, but should be shewn on A.F. B.213 as detached from their units on special duty, and reinforcements demanded to replace them.
(Authority:- A.G., G.H.Q., D.133 dated 2/8/15).

Men attached to Tunnelling Companies are not to be struck off the strength of their units till their transfer is completed, i.e. not until a notification has been received from R.E. Records that a regimental number has been allotted.

All men assisting in tunnelling operations, other than men belonging to Tunnelling Companies, must not be struck off the strength of their units, but drafts may be demanded from the Base by entering the number so employed on the back of the perforated sheet attached to A.F.B.213 as "Employed assisting Tunnelling Companies"

No "other ranks" are to be struck off the strength unless they are either:-

(i) Casualties in action (Killed, wounded or missing)
(ii) Evacuated sick out of the Divisional area.
(iii) Permanently away on extra-regimental employment.

As regards (iii) a man cannot be struck off the strength of his unit unless he is taken on the strength of another unit which has a recognised establishment.

For instance, batmen to officers and interpreters, cooks, etc., on Headquarters of formations may be struck off strength, but men in charge of bath houses, men employed in Brigade Mining Sections, Grenade Companies etc., may not be struck off the strength.

N.C.O's and men undergoing training in clerical duties should be borne on the strength of their units, but should be shown on Army Form B.213 as "Permanently employed at Headquarters....... as a Clerk" and reinforcements demanded in their place.

ARMY FORM.B.213.

Attention is directed to General Routine Order 1175 regarding the compilation and rendering of Army Form B.213.

4. COURTS-MARTIAL.

Courts-Martial procedure and other disciplinary matters are contained in 3rd Army Circular Memorandum on Courts-Martial dated 14th July, 1915.

5. TRENCH MORTAR BATTERIES.
1. Establishment.

The numbers to be maintained with each Trench Mortar Battery are as follows:-

3rd Army Memo AG/76/12 d/ 18/8/15.

Royal Artillery. 1 Officer, 1 Sergeant, 2 Corporals or Bombardiers and 8 Gunners.

Infantry. 1 Officer, 2 Corporals or Lance-Corporals, and 10 Privates.

Any reinforcements required will be trained at the Trench Mortar School, and on Battery Commanders notifying their requirements, the necessary arrangements will be made.

2 Command.

These Batteries for tactical employment and all administrative purposes are placed directly under the Brigadier commanding the Infantry Brigade to whose section they are allotted, and are under no circumstances to be commanded or administered by the Brigadier-General, Royal Artillery, of the Division concerned.

3. Royal Artillery Personnel.

The Battery as a unit is too small for promotion to be made in it. It is therefore necessary to promote throughout the Artillery Trench Mortar personnel of the Third Army.

For this purpose, nominal rolls of Trench Mortar Batteries are kept, with notes as to the individual capacity of all ranks. In order that these rolls may be kept up to date, Battery Commanders will notify the Commandant, Trench Mortar School, from time to time, of the names of any N.C.O's or men recommended for promotion.

When a vacancy for an N.C.O. occurs in a battery, the Battery Commander will notify the Commandant, Trench Mortar School and the Commandant will forward his recommendation to the M.G.R.A. 3rd Army for approval.

4 Infantry Personnel.

The Infantry personnel of Trench Mortar Batteries is found from among the Infantry Brigades to which those Batteries belong.

No Infantry Officer will be struck off the strength of his unit for service with Trench Mortar Batteries, without the previous sanction of General Headquarters.

N.C.O's and men who are attached to Trench Mortar Batteries will be borne on the strength of their units, but should be shown on A.F.B.213 as detached from their units on special duty, and reinforcements demanded to replace them.
(Authority:-A.G., G.H.Q., D.133 dated 2/8/15).

On a vacancy occurring for a N.C.O. in a Battery, its Battery Commander will notify the Infantry Brigadier. The Infantry Brigadier will then make the necessary promotion, either from those in the Battery, or from his Brigade. The Battery Commander will notify the Trench Mortar School.

If the man so selected for promotion, has not been trained in Trench Mortar work, the Infantry Brigadier will arrange to send him first to the Trench Mortar School.

6. TUNNELLING COMPANIES, R.E.

The Tunnelling Companies are Army Troops, and are, as far as personnel is concerned, administered by the Chief Engineer, 3rd Army.

A.R.O's 76 & 111.   Officers Commanding Tunnelling Companies will render a weekly state direct to Chief Engineer, 3rd Army, showing the strength on Saturday of their respective Companies, and the numbers required to complete to War Establishment.

A.F.B.213 will be rendered as usual to D.A.G., Base, through the ordinary channel, in accordance with G.R.O.1175 (ii) dated 27th September, 1915.

Names of Officers and other ranks who are considered suitable, and volunteer, for transfer to Tunnelling Companies, will be called for as circumstances require. The Chief Engineer, 3rd Army, will make arrangements direct with Divisions for their inspection, and from those chosen, vacancies in existing Companies will be filled, or new Companies formed.

The selected men will at first be attached to the Company to which they are posted, and the O.C. Company is to take steps to have their transfer documents completed as soon as possible.

All Officers and men attached to Tunnelling Companies can be replaced by drafts (if available) from the Base, but they are not to be struck off the strength of their units till their transfer is completed, i.e. not until a notification has been received from R.E. Records that a regimental number has been allotted.

All men employed assisting in tunnelling operations, other than men belonging to Tunnelling Companies, must not be struck off the strength of units, but drafts (if available) may be demanded from the Base by entering the number so employed on the back of the perforated sheet attached to A.F.B.213 as "Employed assisting Tunnelling Companies"

Only regular soldiers of the Old and New Armies can be transferred. Men of the Special Reserve and Territorial Force require to be discharged and re-enlisted.

The selection of Officers for these Companies will continue to be made at General Headquarters.

7. DISCHARGES.

A.R.O. 93.

Soldiers due for discharge on termination of engagement, under the first para of General Routine Order 507, dated 3rd January, 1915, will be sent to the Base Depot of their unit or formation, for passage to England, and should arrive at the Base 14 days before the date due for their discharge. No previous authority from G.H.Q. will be required.

The date of discharge should be verified with the Officer in charge of Records before the soldier is sent to the Base.

When men under Suspension of Sentence become due for discharge, and they are not willing to re-engage for the duration of the war, applications for instructions as to their disposal will be forwarded to Corps Headquarters 30 days before the date of their discharge.

8 TRANSFERS.

D.A.G. 3rd Echelon No.9404 dated 17/9/15.

1. Transfers of N.C.O's and men from one unit to another can only be permitted when the transfer would be for the benefit of the Public Service.

2. N.C.O's and men of the Territorial Force cannot be transferred to a unit of the Regular Army. They must be discharged and re-enlisted.

9. PROCEDURE IN REGARD TO MEN UNDER AGE.

A.G. G.H.Q. A/2702 dated 14/9/15.

In all cases regarding the retention, or otherwise, in this country of men who are reported to be under age, Corps Commander will refer the case to D.A.G., 3rd Echelon.

Lads who are under 17 years of age, according to their birth certificate, which should be produced, will be sent to England, unless they are passed fit for service and wish to remain at the front.

Those over 17 will be retained with their unit, unless they are certified by a Medical Officer as unfit for service at the front.

When applications are received for men to be discharged or sent to England on the grounds of being under age, a report should be rendered to 3rd Army "A" stating how the case has been disposed of.

10. PERSONNEL SENT TO THE BASE.

A.R.O. 93.

1. Officers, N.C.O's and men sent down to the Base will invariably be provided with written orders showing their destination, the place at which they are to report, and the reason for which they are being sent down. The A.G., G.H.Q., or D.A.G., 3rd Echelon authority should be quoted on the orders. If this is not possible a copy of the authority should accompany the man.

Commanding Officers of units will be held responsible that those instructions are carried out.

2. Men transferred to the Base on Medical grounds.

A.R.O. 13.

No men are to be transferred to the Base on Medical grounds other than through the ordinary channels of the Medical Units in the Field, unless they have been personally inspected and reported upon by the A.D.M.S. of the Division. Each man, on transfer, should be accompanied by a statement drawn up by the A.D.M.S. of a Division stating exactly in what particulars, and for what reason, the man is unfit for service at the front.

11. N.C.O'S and MEN PROCEEDING HOME TO TAKE UP TEMPORARY COMMISSIONS.

A.G. G.H.Q. A/7870.

N.C.O's and men selected by the War Office for appointments to commissions to units at home are to be sent to England via BOULOGNE. When accommodation is available they will travel by the packet steamer, otherwise they will proceed by the leave boat.

Candidates should be in possession of proper authority to travel, to be produced to the M.L.O. at Boulogne, and should also have explicit instructions as to where to report on arrival in England.

It is not necessary for candidates to be sent to their Base Depots for despatch.

Candidates should be in possession of Form M.T. 393, or failing that, written authority from their Commanding Officer.

12. DIVISIONAL INSTRUCTORS AT THE BASE.

G.H.Q. O.B./ 645.

One Officer and two N.C.O's detailed from each Division for training reinforcements, selected primarily on account of their fitness for that duty, will be sent to the Base where their Divisional Base Depots are situated, and will be employed to train the reinforcements of their own respective Divisions. They will be relieved every 2 months by others similarily selected.

Whenever practicable N.C.O's who have a good knowledge of the types of grenades in use, and who are good musketry instructors, should be selected.

13. PURCHASE OF SPIRITS.

A.R.O. 61.

The purchase of spirits of any kind at estaminets or other houses is forbidden. Beer, cider and wine are the only alcoholic drinks that may be purchased by the troops.

Disobedience of this order is to be severely dealt with.

14. ESTAMINETS.

A.R.O. 25.

All cafes and estaminets in towns or villages where troops are billeted will be closed to the troops, except between the following hours:-

11 a.m. to 1 p.m.
6 p.m. to 8 p.m.

15. MOTOR CARS.

A.R.O. 60.

The hiring of civilian motor cars for private purposes is forbidden.

16. LETTERS.

A.R.O. 20.

It is forbidden to post letters or other communications in civil post boxes.

Any letters so posted will, on collection, be destroyed.

17. LEAKAGE OF INFORMATION.

Attention is directed to the pamphlet issued with Army Routine Order 86 dated 9th September, 1915, a copy of which is attached.

18. SELF-INFLICTED INJURIES.

The procedure to be adopted in cases of self-inflicted injuries is laid down in 3rd Army Circular Memorandum No. 7.

19. POSTING OF OFFICERS.

Applications for the services of Officers serving at home cannot be entertained.

20. LEAVE.

1. Leave may be granted at the discretion of Corps Commanders. The period of leave is for eight days, and will date from day of departure from this country to day of departure from England, viz:- a man leaving his unit on a Monday must return by the leave boat on the following Monday.
2. Except under very exceptional circumstances leave will not be granted to Officers or men who have been less than 3 months in the country.
3. The grant of leave to Brigade Commanders, Divisional Commanders, and Senior Officers of Corps Staffs will be reported to 3rd Army Headquarters.
4. The numbers of all ranks who may be allowed to proceed daily by the leave boat will be notified to Corps from time to time. This allotment is not to be exceeded under any circumstances.

5. Only Staff Officers and regimental officers of the rank of Lieut-Colonel are entitled to travel by the packet steamer, and authority to travel by packet steamer will not be given to officers other than these.

6. Arrangements should be made for men proceeding on leave to be formed into parties, either regimental, brigade or Divisional, under the charge of a suitable number of officers, who will remain in charg until the troops are entrained on the other side. The same procedure will be adopted for the return journey, and men should assist by joining their parties at Waterloo Station as quickly as possible.

The officer to command the troops on board will be detailed by the embarkation staff at the Port. Officers in charge of parties must report as soon as they arrive on board to the Officer in command of troops, both on the outward and return journies.

7. All Officers, non-commissioned officers and men proceeding on leave from the 3rd Army, other than Staff Officers and regimental Officers of the rank of Lieut-Colonel, will proceed and return via HAVRE and SOUTHAMPTON, and their leave tickets should be endorsed accordingly.

8. A separate leave ticket must be issued to each man.

9. N.C.O's and men whose final destination is Scotland or Ireland should be granted leave, as far as possible, on days other than Saturdays.

10. Rifles will be taken, but all ammunition must be collected from N.C.O's and men proceeding on leave before they leave their units.

11. Reports have been received that some soldiers, when proceeding on leave, arrive at Boulogne under the influence of drink.

In future, any soldier found in this condition, or found in possession of wine or spirits, either on arrival at the port, or on the way to the port, will be returned to his unit under escort and forfeit leave for six months.

This order is to be brought to the notice of all men before proceeding on leave.

Headquarters, 3rd Army.
November, 1915.

H.A.L. TAGART, Major-General.
Deputy Adjutant and Quartermaster General,
3rd Army.

WO95/2048

7th R.W. Kent
Vol. 5

121/7936

18th KW

SSB2

Dec 15

Army Form C. 2118

Vol. V — 19

WAR DIARY
or
INTELLIGENCE SUMMARY
(Erase heading not required.)

Place	Date	Hour	Summary of Events and Information	Remarks and references to Appendices
TRENCHES	1/1/15		E Surrey on our right. BERKSHIRES on our left. Trenches in a very bad condition, especially communication trenches, which fall in quicker than they can be cleared. One platoon of the Reserve Company employed daily in cutting stakes and brushwood for revetting. Distribution of Companies :- D. Company right sector C. " left " B. " Counter attack A. " Reserve	
	1/2nd			
	2nd		50 yards of wire put up during the night. Enemy shelled our front trenches and CHATEAU, with 77 m field gun during the morning. B/84 Batty replied with effect.	
	3rd		Quiet day, spent in repairing trenches. NORFOLKS relieved BERKS on our left.	
	3/4th		Half the Officers and N.C.O's of 15th LANCASHIRE FUSILIERS 96 I.B. came up for instruction for 24 hours.	
	4th	2.30 to 3pm	More rifle fire than usual during the night. 2nd half of Officers and N.C.O's of 15th LANCASHIRE FUSILIERS.- Enemy shelled our trenches with 77 m field guns, doing no damage. B/84 Batty retaliated.	
	5th	3/30pm	A Coy. relieved D Coy. - B Coy. relieved C.Coy. Reciprocal artillery fire throughout the day. Enemy tried to snipe some of our working parties in ABERDEEN AVENUE and SHUTTLE LANE who were somewhat exposed, but were unsuccessful.	

Army Form C. 2118

WAR DIARY
INTELLIGENCE SUMMARY
(Erase heading not required.)

Instructions regarding War Diaries and Intelligence Summaries are contained in F. S. Regs., Part II. and the Staff Manual respectively. Title Pages will be prepared in manuscript.

Place	Date	Hour	Summary of Events and Information	Remarks and references to Appendices
TRENCHES	5th		8 Platoon 15th LANCASHIRE FUSILIERS came up for instruction, each platoon took over a short frontage. In order to make room, two platoons of A. Company were withdrawn to billets in ALBERT, and two platoons of B. Company to CHATEAU building.	
	6th		Quiet day, weather foggy.	
	7th		Relieved by 4th BUFFS. — marched to billets in DERNANCOURT — less D. Coy to BECORDEL on TAMBOUR mining fatigue. Casualties — 4 wounded.	
	8th to 17th		Rest billets DERNANCOURT. Lieut & Q.M. J.R. Moloney the U/M officers joined 2 Lt & Chops = 10-12-15 to A. Coy Returned from England 2 Lt & Bromley = 11-12-15 to B. Coy 2 Lt B.H. Glover — 11-12-15 to D. Coy	
	18th		Relieved 8th E. SURREY Regt in D.3. Subsector 12 noon. Distribution of Companies:— C. Coy. Right Sector D. " Left " A. " Counter Attack B. " Reserve. A few rifle grenades and trench mortar bombs went fired into the sector during the afternoon causing no casualties. night Quiet. Germans heard working opposite the TAMBOUR,	

WAR DIARY or INTELLIGENCE SUMMARY

Army Form C. 2118

2/

Place	Date	Hour	Summary of Events and Information	Remarks and references to Appendices
TRENCHES	18th (continued)		which is a salient in our line, about 50 yards from the German front line, the intervening space being covered with mine craters.	
	19th		Our supporting Battery, A/84, shelled enemy trenches during the morning. There was no retaliation.	
	19/20th		An Officer's patrol under 2/Lt DENNIS. reconnoitred the crater and encountered no hostile patrol. 2nd Lt. D. CATHCART joined 19-12-15 to C. Coy.	
	20th		We bombed enemy's trenches with West Gun Catapult during the morning making good practice. Enemy replied with a few rifle grenades.	
	21st	5/6pm	Lewis guns fired on German Transport on FRICOURT Road	
		8/15am	Enemy blew a mine in front of the TAMBOUR, followed by two more explosions at 8/15am and 8/35am, which knocked down several yards of our parapet and buried several men. The enemy displayed no activity of any description during the rest of the day. Circumstances tend to point to the fact that the Germans had some mishap themselves. The undermentioned Officers and 15 N.C.O's and men were gassed while carrying out rescue work:-	

2/Lt. D.S. FREEMAN.
2/Lt. J. CROSS.
CAPT. T/LT. WADDINGTON
LIEUT. D. RUSSELL   } AT DUTY
2/Lt. F.H. LEWIN

WAR DIARY / INTELLIGENCE SUMMARY

Army Form C. 2118

Place	Date	Hour	Summary of Events and Information	Remarks and references to Appendices
TRENCHES	21st	3pm	A. Coy relieved C. Coy. B. Coy " D. Coy.	
	21/22nd		Enemy fired a number of rifle grenades and trench mortars into the TAMBOUR but caused no casualties. Our supporting Batty fired on German Tambour at 11.30 pm and Lewis Guns heard enemy transport on FRICOURT Road and fired on it range 2000 yards.	
	22nd		6" Howitzers and Field Guns shelled the German trenches during the morning with considerable effect.	
		11am	Our trench mortars fired eight rounds, all of which exploded and fell into the enemy's trenches.	
		3pm	A. thirteen pounder was brought up into a wood 200 yards 3 of our Battn. Headquarters, and fired some 40 rounds into the rear of D 1 Subsector. 9 Germans were shot by our snipers. A German working party digging a trench on the skyline, were scattered by our Lewis Guns — range 1500 yards.	
	22/23rd		German transport was again heard and fired on by our Lewis Guns (1 gun fired 3000 rounds in 40 minutes without a stoppage). It would appear that this proceedure causes considerable annoyance to the enemy as this transport now comes up at varying hours with vehicles at greater intervals.	

WAR DIARY
or
INTELLIGENCE SUMMARY
(Erase heading not required.)

Army Form C. 2118

23

Place	Date	Hour	Summary of Events and Information	Remarks and references to Appendices
	22/23rd		and efforts appear to have been made to deaden the sound of the wheels. 178th Tunnelling Company fired two camouflets at 5-12 pm and 9-30 pm; these were followed by artillery fire on German TAMBOUR. The mining officers consider that two German galleries were destroyed, and that the enemy were working in them at the time	
	23rd	10.30am 11.30am	Enemy fired a few shells near Batt: Headquarters, apparently searching for the 13 pounder which fired yesterday.	
	24th		24th Hey: Batty fired several rounds during the day.	
		12noon	Relieved by 8th E. SURREY Regt. Batt: marched to VILLE.	
	26th		Batt: returned to DERNANCOURT.	
	26th/31st		Billets and fatigues. A. Coy. in BECORDEL — TAMBOUR mining	
	28th		LIEUT. D. RUSSELL wounded in TAMBOUR	
	29th		CAPT. W.G. SUMMERS killed " "	
			LIEUT. E.J. INNOCENT wounded " "	
		7pm	C. Coy relieved A. Coy. on TAMBOUR mining fatigue.	

J W Frennie Lt Col

W09/2049
7 N.W. News
Vol 6

18

7th W. Kent
vol: 7

WAR DIARY or INTELLIGENCE SUMMARY

Army Form C. 2118

Volume VI

Place	Date	Hour	Summary of Events and Information	Remarks and references to Appendices
	Jan 3rd	4 Morning	Relieved 7th BUFFS in F.I. Reliefs complete 2.30 pm. Relayed in two states of numbers. Distribution of Battalion "A" Right, "B" left, "C" Double attack, "D" Reserve	
	" 4th	Morning	119 Heavy Battery fired short barrate at Point 7025. Enemy retaliates.	
	" 5th	9.45 am	Whizz bangs on front line.	
		10.30 am	Enemy sheltable attempted to enter our line but was prevented by A.P.G. fire	
	5/6th		Wires of patrols on patrols out	
	6th		Very noisy night, except for occasional bursts of machine gun fire.	
	7th		During the morning the enemy shelled the Battalion down the drainage	
	8th		Enemy artillery shelled BECOURT WOOD systematically, doing the day doing no damage.	
	9th		Very quiet. Considerable aerial activity.	
	9/10th		Enemy fired 40 shells at Right Company at 12 midnight for no apparent reason. Wire parties were out on the Right.	
	10th		2nd Lieut J.R.S. PROUD wounded by premature bursting of one of own mills grenades.	
	10/11th		Patrols & wiring parties out all night.	
	11th		Battalion relieved by 7th BUFFS, returned to DERNAN COURT.	
	12/13		Rest & XIIIG	
	13		Relieved 7th BUFFS in F.I.	
	14/15		Distribution of Companies "B" Co. Right Section "A" " Left " "D" " Rentre attack "C" " Reserve

QUEENS on our Right, ESSEX on our Left

WAR DIARY

INTELLIGENCE SUMMARY

Army Form C. 2118

Place	Date	Hour	Summary of Events and Information	Remarks and references to Appendices
	19/20		One patrol out.	25
	20.		Quiet day except for shelling. Mines dug out under [construction].	
	20/21st		Two wiring parties out, but were [disturbed] by bright moonlight.	
	21st		Quiet. Wind, WEST.	
	21/22nd		Raining. Wind, N.W. Wiring parties out all night. 2nd Lieut HEATON & one man examined German front line in front of Pt. 7025 & brought specimens of enemy wire at that point. Examined German field cables about 50 yards towards enemy T[G's?] outside during the night.	
	22nd		Our artillery fired 7H rounds on German trenches round X26 D9, & appeared to do considerable damage. Our Lewis guns were laid on the spot & swept it at intervals during the night.	
	22/23rd		Wiring parties out all night. (It appears that German Snipers are at another point in front of this sector)	
	24th	3 pm	Enemy's 9 & 2 Howitzer rather more active than usual. We fired 12 rifle grenades into the enemy front line trenches, they all burst. Enemy retreated a rifle grenade.	
		4 pm	Saw blue and red rifle grenade shining over their parapet, for his battery into action & wound - burst 2nd Lt. (H.E.) No more German rifle grenades were fired.	
	24/25th		Patrol & wiring parties out all night. German machine gun playing very [particularly] round Mr Heaton, several bullets falling inside the boundary. They have never attained the exact elevation so accurately before.	
	25th		Quiet.	
	25/26		Wiring & Patrols	

Army Form C. 2118

WAR DIARY
or
INTELLIGENCE SUMMARY
(Erase heading not required.)

Instructions regarding War Diaries and Intelligence Summaries are contained in F. S. Regs., Part II. and the Staff Manual respectively. Title Pages will be prepared in manuscript.

Place	Date	Hour	Summary of Events and Information	Remarks and references to Appendices
	26th	10am	French aeroplane slightly damaged, came over here flying low & going west. It came down 1000 x W of BECOURT WOOD. Enemy machine guns fired heavily at it. Passed over. Personally enough, nothing for minute of its passing, many heavy artillery did get on to it although it appeared could not be observed from any but these kinds, but it was dropped away no trace, to ALBERT & followed from 20,4,2 shells fell within 50x radius of Bn HQrs. First shell came from casualties. Shrunnes no damage. Battalion had permission went to ground.	
		12.30pm	2nd Ries. Battery retaliated on FRICOURT farm. When the enemy M.G. opened fire, B.H. Battery fired 2 salvos at a presumably registered emplacement, on which the gilles had been registered ready. Enemy M.G. fire was silenced during the night in consequence. Returned by 7th BUFFS. Platoon returned to billets in BERNANCOURT.	
		6pm	LT. WOODHOUSE slightly wounded 2h. O.R. 4 killed 9 wounded	
	27th		Owing to on duty, a great deal of clearing of communication trenches was done, was obtained for 30' from 3rd line towards the front. Round strongpoints were constructed for day sentries. Work on the KEEP was carried on by a Platoon R. SUSSEX PIONEERS & running of the same by us. Bombing material was carried out daily in BECOURT WOOD. Two more huts were erected by 2nd Rubents.	
	29th			
	30th		Owing to enemy gas attack S. of the SOMME, all works were ordered to carry respirators at all times. No gas was smelt here. Individual gunfire heard all day in the direction of SUZANNE.	

WAR DIARY
or
INTELLIGENCE SUMMARY
(Erase heading not required.)

Army Form C. 2118

Instructions regarding War Diaries and Intelligence Summaries are contained in F.S. Regs., Part II. and the Staff Manual respectively. Title Pages will be prepared in manuscript.

Place	Date	Hour	Summary of Events and Information	Remarks and references to Appendices
	31st		Owing to enemy bombardment of E.11, battalion were ordered to be ready to stand to at any moment.	
		5.35	Batt'n ordered to 'stand to'.	
		5.45	Am. Allot'd to an advance posts in light fighting order, with	
		6.10pm	Received orders to proceed as far as MOULIN du VIVIER.	
		6.15	Pm. 1st Echelon formed up in return & emergency rations.	
		6.20pm	Pm. moved off.	
		6.30pm	Pm. arrived at MOULIN du VIVIER. Ordered to return to billets	
		6.50	Pm. returned to billets	
			The undermentioned officers have gone to hospital during January.	
			LT. PYMM. 5th
			Capt FULLER. (R.A.M.C) 8th
			2nd Cross. 12th
			Capt WADDINGTON 19th
			The undermentioned officer joined on 23rd
			2nd Lt WRIGHT
			" FILE.

R. Armstrong Capt. adjt

for O.C.
7th R.W.K.

Army Form C. 2118

WO95/2049

WAR DIARY
or
INTELLIGENCE SUMMARY
(Erase heading not required.)

Place	Date	Hour	Summary of Events and Information	Remarks and references to Appendices
DERNANCOURT	Feb 1st		Received instructions that a Divisional school was to be formed and that Lt. Fuenes was to be commandant. The battalion was to be used for demonstration & instructional purposes.	
	2nd		Ordered to move to PONT-NOYELLES on the 5th March.	
	4th		Advance party proceeded to PONT NOYELLES.	
PONT-NOYELLES	5th		Battalion paraded at 9 A.M. to proceed to PONT-NOYELLES. Distance of 10½ miles, halted at 11 A.M. for ¾ hour to eat rations and arrived at PONT-NOYELLES at 1:30 P.M. Difficult to obtain billets as were very close on.	
	7th		Elementary training began, chiefly handling of arms & squad drill in extended order. Buttons were cleaned & every effort made to recover any smartness which had been lost during trench warfare.	
LA HOUSSOYE	10th		Moved to LA HOUSSOYE & Ostome a distance of about 3½ miles. 10th on billets of 6th NORTHAMPTONS, close to proposed position for Divisional School.	

Army Form C. 2118

WAR DIARY
or
INTELLIGENCE SUMMARY
(Erase heading not required.)

Instructions regarding War Diaries and Intelligence Summaries are contained in F. S. Regs., Part II. and the Staff Manual respectively. Title Pages will be prepared in manuscript.

Place	Date	Hour	Summary of Events and Information	Remarks and references to Appendices
	16th		B & C Coys were moved to QUERRIEUX to assist the R.E. in the construction of a railway line. Hours of work 7 A.M. to 4 P.M. The Battalion sends 3 90 boys carried on with Platoon & Company trainings for the rest of the month.	
	17th		During the month Capt. C.G. WEBBER proceeded to England to transfer to the Home Service Battalion, on the 19th Lieut. I.H. SKINNER rejoined the Battalion on the 14th 2nd Lieut. D.C. PHIPPS } joined the Battalion on the 14th " H.M. COCKLE } 2nd Lieut. B.H. GLOVER joined the 103rd T.M.B on the 6th "	

1 MAR 1916

Arthur J. Phipps Major
Comm 7th Service Battn R. W. Kent Regt

Army Form C. 2118.

WAR DIARY
or
INTELLIGENCE SUMMARY
(Erase heading not required.)

Place	Date	Hour	Summary of Events and Information	Remarks and references to Appendices
LAHOUSSOYE	1918 March 1st		A Divisional school was formed and Colonel Fiennes having been appointed Commandant left the Battalion to take command of the School. Major Phillips took command in his place. The Adjutant (Captain Armsthwaite also proceeded to the School to act as instructor. Distribution of the Battⁿ Battⁿ: less B & C Coys and details at LA HOUSSOYE B & C Coys under Captain HOLLAND formed a Wing at QUERRIEUX 3 miles away and were employed on — Railway construction. Details (40 men O.R.) were attached to the 18 Div School ¼ mile away.	
	7th		Brigadier General Jackson came over from St GRATIEN to see the School & the Battⁿ	
	8th		D Coy were used as demonstration coy fr the school both in	

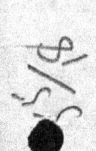

18.

7 R W Kent
Vol 8

Army Form C. 2118.

WAR DIARY
or
INTELLIGENCE SUMMARY
(Erase heading not required.)

Place	Date	Hour	Summary of Events and Information	Remarks and references to Appendices
	1916 May			
	14th		Close order drill & the attack in the open. A Coy employed entirely on fatigue for school.	
	15th		Ordered to move together with rest of the Brigade to Y Sector. D Coy to remain as Demonstration Coy for School. Wing formed under Lieut C.S. EMDEN consisting of D Coy complete with Pack mules & corbies & 2 HD Horses 1 Limbered G.S. Wagon and Two mules. Quartermasters stores & Heavy baggage sent by two lorries direct to SUZANNE with small advance party to take over QM stores a/17th MANCHESTER. Three guides were sent with this party to report to 2nd R.S.F. & learn the trenches before the Bn arrived.	
	16th		Bn less Wing concentrated at CORBIE. Left LAHOUSSOYE & QUERRIEUX at 12 NOON. B & C Coy joined Bn at LA NEUVILLE &	

WAR DIARY
or
INTELLIGENCE SUMMARY

(Erase heading not required.)

Army Form C. 2118.

Place	Date	Hour	Summary of Events and Information	Remarks and references to Appendices
CORBIE	16-17		Marched into CORBIE at 1 P.M. The Instruments of the Drums were returned to D Coy. B⁺ Billeted in CORBIE	
	17th		Moved out of CORBIE at 5.A.M & marched to GROVETOWN CAMP a distance of 10 miles. Last quarter of a mile was in zone of Artillery fire. B⁺ moves across country by Platoons at 100 yds distance. Comfortable camp under canvas. Relieved the 1st & 2nd Battns of Kings Liverpool Regiment.	
GROVETOWN CAMP	18		No Baggage wagons accompanied unit - but 4 lorries were provided for transport. Start Moved to SUZANNE at 6.15 P.M. marching via BRAY. Companies moved at 100 yd distance until clear of BRAY and then B⁺ moved by platoons at 50 yds distance. Arrived SUZANNE at 9.30 & billeted without trouble. Transport in	

WAR DIARY
or
INTELLIGENCE SUMMARY

Army Form C. 2118.

(Erase heading not required.)

Place	Date	Hour	Summary of Events and Information	Remarks and references to Appendices
	March 1916			
	19		lorries	
			Moved out to relieve 2nd R.S.F. in Y11 subsector at 6.30 P.M.	
			C. Cy moved to reserve Coy billets in SUZANNE	
			A Cy relieved FARGNY MILL	
			B Cy " Q WORKS and 13 TRENCH (2 platoons in each)	
			HQ took over BATTLE DUGOUTS	
			Transport 7 P.M. Storm remained in SUZANNE	
			Relief complete by 9.15 P.M. no casualties.	
			9th EAST SURREYS on Right – Y(i)	
			7th BUFFS – Left Y(iii)	
Y11	20th		Patrol from MILL under 2nd Lieut WOOD HOUSE located	
			GERMAN post in marshes opposite our island, foot & found	
			200 yds track running on road between the two. 62nd R.E. B.H.Q	
Y11	21st		Heavy shelling on Y11 KNOWLES front pushed by Germans, equip.	

Place	Date	Hour	Summary of Events and Information	Remarks and references to Appendices
Y(ii)	27th		Attack unsuccessful. No effect on our sector except for fair shells round 13 Trench. Hostile MG registered on Bridge near M1+1 but soon silenced by our Field guns.	
V(ii)	2.3		Rifle grenades registering on M11.6 on 18 pounder notches. Ordered to move Bn HQ to ravine where only one dugout was ready. HQ Self. back to SUZANNE with exception of C.O, Adjutant & 6 Runners. Officers reconte. Reserve the L.G's, Bombers reconnoitres in the o.l.s.	
	2.		Transport came up to MARICOURT RD by night to a dump about ½ mile from RAVINE. (Companies more) withdrawn rations & R.E. material from the DUMP to HQ.	

WAR DIARY
or
INTELLIGENCE SUMMARY

(Erase heading not required.)

Army Form C. 2118.

Place	Date	Hour	Summary of Events and Information	Remarks and references to Appendices
Y11	25th		Work on New H.Q. dug-outs progressing speedily	
	26th		Capt Anstruther returned and took over adjutancy	
	27th		Our 4.5 Howitzers scored 8 hits on the CHAPEAU de GENDARME.	
	28th		Communication set up between ISLAND + HOUSE POSTS and COY H Qs in the MILL. Very considerable air activity.	
	29th		Germans sent over 8 Liddo into SUZANNE at night near Ru. Erys billets	
	30th		C.O. went home on leave. Capt Anstruther took over command of the Batt. Batt Conference held at 10.30 am.	
	31st		French artillery fired on Y Wood during the afternoon. Intra-Coy relief took place in evening B Coy took over the right sector and A Coy the left. C Coy went into Rug Regt billets in SUZANNE. Capt Waddington went sick on leave and was evacuated to 13th Duc School. Trench s/O strength on March 9th.	
			2/Lt WRIGHT } attended first course at 14th Duc School	
			2/Lt BROWNLEE }	

2/Lt HOGG
2/Lt WOODHOUSE } attended 2nd course at 4th Div School.

Capt R.B. HOLLAND went to the 4th ARMY SCHOOL on 26th inst
Lieut B. McKENZIE rejoined 13th inst
Lieut. E.T. INNOCENT   —   11th inst
2/Lt R. BARTHOLOMEW 9th Bn was attached from 13th inst.

R Ambrother Capt
Commdg
7 th R.W. Kent Regt

R.W.K 393
1/5/16

A.G.
Base
———

Herewith copy of War
Diary for the month of April
1916. Please acknowledge
receipt.

R. Ambrother Capt
ADJUTANT.
7th SERVICE BATTn R. W. KENT REGt

WAR DIARY
or
INTELLIGENCE SUMMARY

Army Form C. 2118.

XVIII / VIII

17 Volyn West Rdiv

Vol 9

Place	Date	Hour	Summary of Events and Information	Remarks and references to Appendices
Y2	1st 1/7/16	8.15pm	An intercepted message by the French learned in that an attack from N. and S. of the SOMME might be expected during next few days.	
"	2nd	3h	Trench mortars near TARGNY MILL	
"		10pm	A patrol went out to obtain enemy positions N of TRENCH (A/29/d), and it reports that they had a Lewis group at the N. and S. End of it about 50 yds apart, which were visited once during [night].	
"	3rd	10am	Enemy shelled Bn H.Q. with 10.5 cm Howitzers, about ten (10) rounds of damage Y3.	
"		?	Buff relieved Queens - Y3.	
"	5th 2/7 to 4h		Deliberate fire of an enemy 77mm battery apparently directed out on Second line (P2) in SPUR WOOD, about 40 shell burst over in the area; work on trenches progressed normally.	
"	7th		Up to this time it had not been definitely ascertained whether enemy posts were actually laced in the earthworks of (Streets LODGE WOOD (G.S.B.) or whether them from was only PStreets war on substantial front, ISLAND POST (A.29/d/33), was occupied up on the (runaway) fly wire and uncertainty. During the last few days patrols from 8th & SUPPER REGT. in Y1 had tried to reach LODGE WOOD from VAUX Causeway/B.	

2449 Wt. W14957/M90 750,000 1/16 J.B.C.&A. Forms/C.2118/12/

Army Form C. 2118.

WAR DIARY
or
INTELLIGENCE SUMMARY
(Erase heading not required.)

Instructions regarding War Diaries and Intelligence Summaries are contained in F. S. Regs., Part II. and the Staff Manual respectively. Title Pages will be prepared in manuscript.

Place	Date	Hour	Summary of Events and Information	Remarks and references to Appendices
			and on this day, about 4 pm one of their patrols, accompanied by 2nd Lt NEWBOLD headed FARGNY MILL Coming from the South without encountering any signs of the enemy himself, but a great deal of material such as sandbags, shovels, wire-cutters etc were found lying about. Therefore during the night 7/8th we pushed up a few posts. 12 men strong to LODGE WOOD and established a strong point at the S.E. corner from there by day and the advanced place was called NEW CROSS, being 700x S.E. of FARGNY MILL & 700x N.W. of FOUR TREE POST (G.6.b.c) held by the enemy.	
Y 2	9th	4 am	At Stand to' in the morning two loaded Mills bombs were found close to one How. Sap; they were expert in, the lowest mines were found to contain 22 lbs each of Gun-Cotton	
	10th/11th	night	These rifle & M.G. activity during the night; one SB was distinguished by a dog which came out of the German lines & barked at them, whereupon enemy sent up lights & opened fire.	
	11th/12th 7/pm		Heavy bombardment in the direction of CARNOY lasting half an hour 7th QUEENS relieved 7th BUFFS in Y3	
	12th		Exceptionally quiet all day	
	12th/13th	11.45am	Heavy bombardment lasting one hour in the direction of CARNOY.	

WAR DIARY
or
INTELLIGENCE SUMMARY
(Erase heading not required.)

Army Form C. 2118.

Place	Date	Hour	Summary of Events and Information	Remarks and references to Appendices
V2	13th	1 p.m.	Enemy shelled Bn. H.Q. with eight 15 cm shells; no damage.	3
	13th/14th		Wire put up inside the edge of LODGE wood about 100 yards South of NEW CROSS. A patrol under Lt HACKETT which went out towards FOUR TREE POST heard a party in the wood.	
	14th	5 to 7	Two sections of the day patrol on NEW CROSS went out & cut the enemy wire again in the afternoon and reached the wire to the North	
		21.45	of FOUR TREE POST. This post appears to be a semi-circular work strengthened round the West end of such traversing; it was occupied by day; our patrol returned safely without being discovered.	
			Corps Commander had tea at Bn. H.Q.	
	15th		Scaled to kill TARGNY MILL with one Platoon only; obtained at 5.30/... with Coy Commanders at 5.30/-.	
	"	8.30	German M.G. silenced by howitzers of 9 Sqd. Shooting of A/84 Battery.	
	16th	10.15	One of our aeroplanes brought down in action behind the CHATEAU de GENDARMES, apparently in square A/30 Lord SEDCARI.	
		2 p.m	A patrol from E.SURREY REGT with this trench guard to see and went out led by 2/Lt SWINDEN of D Coy to reconnoitre FOUR TREE POST more closely; 2/Lt SWINDEN showed himself and was killed by Gemma H.G. 2/Lt SWINDEN's Lce/Corp also killed by them. They were unable to afterwards brought in his body but were unable to get. his body away also 5 killed during the attempt his body because in positions and disabled fire. They were emptied this porter received a...	

Army Form C. 2118.

WAR DIARY
or
INTELLIGENCE SUMMARY
(Erase heading not required.)

Place	Date	Hour	Summary of Events and Information	Remarks and references to Appendices
Y 2	17th		Identification, & brought back safely there. Lt. INNOCENT went to M.G. section at CAMBRES (or a machine gun course. Camb gun. Reduced the garrison 58 on front line, which in this sector consists only of a number of Saps & these I saps covered to a minimum, the strip being consisted to a recent cutting out precaution against the enemy attempting TIRGNY hill used for various unit gun-posts. And one platoon to collect attack garrisons, & has new cross roads to distribute them. Sergt. Morph's Ammunition party are now cross from hr. Sergt Morph stated that it indeed be almost impossible (so we hope) for the Boche use if he did into our trenches at any point to take any prisoners and come tr. at unce) to organised that even the lightest post get out without - having several from ours on round again. Further, unless each man in the Eriacle hr. been killed with the officers. Sposts and singled that he is a German first, & till I gun first, and the rest of afterwards, not use luck in other words.	
17/18th Night		A great deal of work put up at the west end of this sector of wire wheel with tangle wire hits to hold our sector safe, been doing the covers position just in rear of	

Army Form C. 2118.

WAR DIARY
or
INTELLIGENCE SUMMARY
(Erase heading not required.)

Instructions regarding War Diaries and Intelligence Summaries are contained in F. S. Regs., Part II. and the Staff Manual respectively. Title Pages will be prepared in manuscript.

Place	Date	Hour	Summary of Events and Information	Remarks and references to Appendices
	18th 19th		In Mill Quiet	
Y.2	20th	4pm 7pm	Artillery active in Y3. Enemy shelled Bn. Hd-Qrs.	
"	21st		Enemy opened rapid artillery fire on right of Y3 and on left twice during the day. Rain all day.	
"	22nd	3pm	Enemy fired about 100 shells (15 cm, 10.5 cm and 77 mm) into to M.1. Some damage was caused to the trenches, but no sustained in Counatta.	
"	23rd		(Easter day) Very quiet. One of our batteries reported always hostile infantry sending patrol from 9th Bn, 9th Int. to "C" Coy.	
"	24th		2nd Lt J. Forsyth joined A/9/4 for 5 minutes; two slight Counatta.	
"		4pm	Enemy bombarded	
"	25th	12 noon	Our artillery bombarded "Y Wood" (A.23.a) intensely for 5 minutes. Considerable aerial activity during the day. Very lot.	

2449 Wt. W14957/M90 750,000 1/16 J.B.C. & A. Forms/C.2118/12.

WAR DIARY or INTELLIGENCE SUMMARY

Army Form C. 2118.

(Erase heading not required.)

Place	Date	Hour	Summary of Events and Information	Remarks and references to Appendices
Y2	25th/8th	2.45AM	Enemy fired some heavy shells into open ground to rear of TARGNY MILL.	
"	26th	12 noon	A German M.G. was located by our snipers. A/84 Battery was informed, who fired on it and obtained two direct hits dispersing the enemy.	
"	"	1.30 pm	A working party repairing trench damage was dispersed by shrapnel.	
"	"	9 pm	Mill bombarded with howitzers & trench mortars. One man of a working party slightly wounded.	
"	27th		Considerable aerial activity, mostly our own.	
"	"	10 pm	Trench mortar bombs in the M.I.L., no damage.	
"	28th		Very quiet – Wind S.W. Received operation orders re relief and move.	
"	29th		Quiet in front line. Considerable enemy battery activity on both sides. Wind shifted to N.E. German used up balloon for testing wind in the evening.	
"	30th		During the afternoon the enemy registered on some	

Place	Date	Hour	Summary of Events and Information	Remarks and references to Appendices

Coy on communication trenches. Wind shifted to S.W. again. Issued Operation orders.

General

Companies have been changed round every 6 days — making 12 days in the trenches and 6 days at SUZANNE.

CAPT HOLLAND returned from and CAPT LATTER proceeded to 4th Army School on 23rd.

CAPT SNELGROVE to hospital 20th.

Total Casualties:—
3 O.R. Wounded.

App V

(signature) Capt
for O.C.
7th R.W.K.

Rg. ALBERT combined sheet APR/11
AMIENS " sh. 17
Preliminary Operation Orders by
Major A. E. PHILLIPS.
Comdg. 7th R.W. Kent Regt.
28 April, 1916

1. The Bn will be relieved on the night 2/3rd May and will march to PICQUIGNY (8½ miles N.W. of AMIENS)

2. The march will be performed in four stages, as under:—
   (a) Night 2/3rd R. BOIS CELESTINS
                         (1 mile N. of CHIPILLY)
   (b) 3rd   LA HOUSSOYE
   (c) 4th   ARGOEUVRES
                         (5 miles N.W. of AMIENS)
   (d) 5th   PICQUIGNY

3. SUPPLIES.   On 1st May no supplies will be drawn
   On 2nd May, ration for 3rd May taken from refilling point R. BOIS CELESTINS

On 2nd May, supply wagons will refill at MERICOURT LOCK at 7.30 a.m. and proceed under orders of O.C. Batt'n to LA HOUSSOYE.

On 4th May supply wagons will refill at LA NEUVILLE at a time to be notified later and proceed to ARGOEUVRES.

On 5th May refilling point ST. SAUVEUR; détrainement PICQUIGNY

4. Transport. Two baggage wagons will report to Q.M. Stores at 10 a.m. on 2nd May. Four motor lorries will arrive in SUZANNE at 8.20 a.m., 8.40 a.m., 9 a.m. and 9.20 a.m. respectively.

The Transport Officer will arrange for guides to meet each of these lorries and guide them to Q.M. Stores. These lorries are not to remain in SUZANNE more than HALF AN HOUR.

The above transport will be loaded as under:-

(a) Motor lorries :-
   Q.M. stores
   Orderly Room (less actual requirement)
   Officers Kits in excess of 30 lbs.
   Signalling gear
   350 blankets rolled in tens
   Pioneers tools
   Snipers rifles
   Spare transport gear
   Waterproof sheets rolled in twenties
   10 Camp Kettles

   The whole of the Reserve Coy will be at the disposal of the Q.M. for loading these lorries, which will proceed direct to PIQUIGNY.
   Sgt. SPENDLOWE, Orderly Sgt WEST and 3 men per Coy & H.Q. will proceed with these lorries and will be provided with four days rations.

(b) Baggage wagons :-
   One wagon will be allotted to 'A' & 'B' Coys and one to 'C' Coy & H.Q.
   Remainder blankets in tens

Officers Kits
Spare rations (limited to above
 per Coy.)
Orders on loading of these
will be issued later.

5. From 1st May rations for the
H.Q. Coy will be divided into
three equal parts (roughly 50
rations in each part) and
issued one part to each Coy.
Units of H.Q. will be divided
up and attached as under:-
  Signallers
  O. Room   } Leading Coy
  H.Q. Officers Staff

  Q.M. Stores
  Police
  Pioneers   } Centre Coy
  D Coy L. gunners
  Transport   } Rear Coy.

NOTE Sewers Gunners & Officers
grooms, Stretcher bearers to move
with their Coys.

The Chaplain will be attached
to "D" Coy & the Interpreter to "A" Coy
from 2nd May.

6. O.C. Coys will arrange to have
Officers kits & baggage divided
into two parts:—
   (a) Packs, necessities (to accompany
       the Battn).
   (b) Surplus (to go ahead in lorries)

7. Further details will be issued
   in due course.

         [signature] Capt
                      & Adjt
         7th R.W. Kent Regt

SECRET   COPY No 6   APP. 12

Reinforcements - Bn H.Q.
2 Platoons ordered at 3.5

Operation orders by Major A.E. Phillips
Commanding 7th N. Staffs Regt.

30-ix-16

1. The Battalion will be relieved by
the 2nd Royal Scots Fusiliers
on the 2nd prox. the relief will
commence about 6pm
a/c duty it [illegible] will
be to S. PIERRE B. GIRK (1½
miles N.W. of Dieuvam), via
BOIS CELESTINE & MOUISSUE
and ST. SAUVEUR [illegible]
[illegible]   E. Pinckner ATR/11
push 2

2. The order of relief will be as —
    a) "R" works
    b) A/24/4
    c) "O" works
    d) FARM ...
Lists of trench stores will be
carefully completed and signed

by an officer of both incoming & outgoing companies. Time and place for guides to meet incoming units will be notified later.

3. The battalion will march to BOIS CELESTINS in order:—
   (Refs PP)
   A Coy — leaving SUZANNE by platoon starting at 2 p.m.
   Route — CAPPY DOUBLE — BRAY — ETINEHEM (use the track running through E C of L. 10) — Bois CELESTINS (F. 34. c).
   C Coy will follow this route.
   The Headquarters Coy will march after HQ Company.
   Other Companies by platoon after that. Route — SUZANNE — BRAY (use road running through L.17, L.16) — MAY DOUBLE — Chipilly cross roads (F. 21. G. 78) — Chipilly — Bois CELESTINS
   Transport in small parties via CAPPY DOUBLE — BRAY —

3 men and to Camp Orderly
Officer for nights of 2/3rd and
3rd [inst?]

8. An advance party under 2/Lt
O C Johnson consisting of
C.Q.M. S[?], and Sanitary per-
-sonnel will proceed in
advance to take over the
camp.

9. Reveille on the 3rd will be
at 7.15 a.m.
Breakfast at 8.30 a.m.
Dinners at 12.30 p.m.

[list:]
No 1. Files
No 2. A Coy
No 3. B
No 4. C
No 5. [?] Police
No 6. Q.M.
No 7. T.O.
No 8. H T [?]
No 9. Sgt Maj [?]
No 10. Adjutant

[signature] Capt
[signature] O.R.E.K.

Army Form C. 2118.

1 West Kent
Volume 9 Vol 90
XVIII

WAR DIARY
or
INTELLIGENCE SUMMARY
(Erase heading not required.)

Instructions regarding War Diaries and Intelligence Summaries are contained in F.S. Regs., Part II. and the Staff Manual respectively. Title Pages will be prepared in manuscript.

Place	Date	Hour	Summary of Events and Information	Remarks and references to Appendices
Y.2.	2/5/16	11.15 p	Relieved by 2nd Royal Scots Fusiliers. Officers nightly marched by platoons to BOIS DES CELESTINS. Distance 10 miles.	
	3/5/16		Battn. marched to LA HOUSSOYE, distance 11 miles. Moved off 2 p.m. Arrived 7 p.m.	
	4th "		Marched to ST. SAUVEUR via AMIENS, distance 18 miles. Moved off 6.30 a.m. arrived 10 p.m.	
	5th "		Marched from ST SAUVEUR to ST PIERRE & GOUY, distance 7 miles. Moved off 4.30 p.m. arrived 6 p.m. During the march 40 men proceeded by barge and 3 men fell out on the line of march.	
ST. PIERRE	6/31m		Rifles. Battalion - Brigade training	
	"15"		Lieut A.H.S. STAGG Suffolk Regt attached for duty as Transport Officer.	
	19"		Colonel FIENNES rejoined the Battn from 18th Gds School	
	29"		Capt. T.T. WADDINGTON rejoined the Battn from England.	
	25"		Lieut J.B. MATTHEWS accidentally wounded at Trench Mortar Demonstration	
	30"		"D" Co. rejoined the Battn.	
	12"		Bombers and s.m. & half visited the Battn. during training.	

Anstruther Capt
for Colonel

WAR DIARY
or
INTELLIGENCE SUMMARY
(Erase heading not required.)

Army Form C. 2118.

7. W. Kent
Vol X

Place	Date	Hour	Summary of Events and Information	Remarks and references to Appendices
ST PIERRE	1st		Capt Leather took over command of 'A' Coy vice Capt Snelgrove to England	
	2nd		2nd Lt Johnson proceeded to be attached to 53rd Bde. for Staff Duties	
	7th		Undermentioned Officers joined from 9th Bn, and posted to Companies as under:—	
			2nd Lt G. Scurrell — A Coy	
			" F.A. Ottini — B Coy	
			" H.T. Bishop — A Coy	
	8th		8th Bn R.W Kent Regt attached to 55th Bde M.G Coy. Received orders to move up to the line	
	3rd		Military Honours:— Capt T.D Anstruther (Adjutant) — mentioned from C.S.M C. Pearson (C Coy) — D.C.M	
			(D Coy) Capt. Woolpart — Mentioned in dispatches	
	6th	12 noon	Regimental Transport proceeded by road to CORBIE	
	10th	11.30am	Battalion entrained at PICQUIGNY & railed to MER COURT	
		1.50pm	Arrived MER COURT detrained, had dinners, met 7 new pt	
		2.45pm	Moved off and marched to BOIS des TAILLES, where Battalion had tea	
		5.1?	Marched by Platoons to BRAY arrived BRAY 9.30pm, went into billets	

WAR DIARY
or
INTELLIGENCE SUMMARY

(Erase heading not required.)

Army Form C. 2118.

Place	Date	Hour	Summary of Events and Information	Remarks and references to Appendices
	10th		2nd Lt. A.C. Dennis attached to 12th Middlesex on Conducting Reinforcements.	
	11th		"A" & "D" Coy proceeded to CARNOY for fatigue. "B" & "C" Coys received Lecture - BRAY and marches to the Trenches daily for fatigues.	
	12th			
	13th		2nd Lt. H.T. Gregory joined Brigade & posted to "D" Coy. "C" Coy moved up to CARNOY. Major Releap took command of the three Companies. Disposition was of attack one Company to LARGE WOOD " " " CARNOY defences.	
	14th		Received orders to relieve 8th & Surrey L.A. Issued orders 2nd Lt. H.G. Bushell joined & posted to "B" Coy.	
	15th	12 noon	Relieved 8th R. Surreys 4 1/2 R. Sussex. R.Sept Fusiliers (30th Div.) on our right. Disposition - Three Companies in the front line. C Coy on the right. A " " " Centre. D " " " Left. B Coy in reserve. No extra neces~	

WAR DIARY or INTELLIGENCE SUMMARY

Army Form C. 2118.

(Erase heading not required.)

Instructions regarding War Diaries and Intelligence Summaries are contained in F. S. Regs., Part II. and the Staff Manual respectively. Title Pages will be prepared in manuscript.

Place	Date	Hour	Summary of Events and Information	Remarks and references to Appendices
	15th/16th		in this Subsector for a counter attack Company, which seems strange.	
	16th		German active with rifle & M.G. fire	
			Enemy very active in this subsector. German aeroplane flew low over our lines. Fired at by Lewis gun. But unmolested by A.A. guns.	
		1.30 PM		
		3 PM	2/Lt LUCAS wounded	
	17th		Germans active with Trench Mortars	
	18th		Enemy shelled CARNOY VALLEY slightly.	
	19th		Ditto	
	20th	4.45 PM	Relieved by 7th BUFFS. Relieved 30th E Surreys in RAI-AVENUE Carnoy Valley for batgm. Capt WARRE took on duties as Camp Commandant GROVETOWN CAMP, whilst 1st Lieu Transport is to be.	
	21st		Rae Avenue, 2nd Lt. Savage, Bond and Officer proceeded to 1st Div. School of Instruction.	
	22nd		Raid Avenue. It is almost inexplicable why the enemy	

2449 Wt. W14957/Mgo 750,000 1/16 J.B.C. & A. Forms/C.2118/12.

Army Form C. 2118.

WAR DIARY
or
INTELLIGENCE SUMMARY
(Erase heading not required.)

Instructions regarding War Diaries and Intelligence Summaries are contained in F. S. Regs., Part II. and the Staff Manual respectively. Title Pages will be prepared in manuscript.

Place	Date	Hour	Summary of Events and Information	Remarks and references to Appendices
	22nd/23rd		do not shell this valley. It is packed with men all wearing about with open fires & dumps, and a centre of considerable activity in every respect. Battery emplacements are being dug to shield themselves from fire from the forward slopes. It is night.	
	23rd/24th		A large fatigue party carried up gas cylinders to CC front line. There were rumours of a "Special Gas Coy". D.T.S.	"V" day
	24th	At Al Freun 4 Major Phillip mentioned in despatches. Received Brigade Operation Order No 27. K attack & open trench. 2nd Captains H.H L/S HACKETT and SKINNER proceeded to 1st line transport in GROVETOWN, also 2nd Lts HOGG & FORSYTH. 2nd Lt NEWBOLD continues adjutant. School, a temp. Instructor starting running up to Div. School & this Bombardment began behind front line.	"V" day APP XVI
	25th		Bombardment continued. Issued Operation orders JU/3 Sec APP VI	APP XII
		12 noon	Ordered to carry out a raid on German Trenches; 2nd Lt BROWNLEE Selected. Issued OT. order, A JU/2, See A/14 VII	APP VIII

Army Form C. 2118.

WAR DIARY
or
INTELLIGENCE SUMMARY
(Erase heading not required.)

Instructions regarding War Diaries and Intelligence Summaries are contained in F.S. Regs., Part II. and the Staff Manual respectively. Title Pages will be prepared in manuscript.

Place	Date	Hour	Summary of Events and Information	Remarks and references to Appendices
			The Raid failed & 5 men are missing, see Report App. VIII	App VIII
R...	26th		2nd Lts C. da Silva formed parties & O. Coy and sent to Div. School.	"W" day
			Heavy fatigues. Relieved & new wire by day & by night.	
	27th		2 Lts. P. Stevens, H. Buffie, J.S.C. Carter joined 1st line Transport & sent to Div. School	"X" day
AVENUE		10.30 PM	Sgt G Sumpsey attempted a raid, but were not very successful.	
			Attempted to remove more wire but prevented by enemy shelling.	
	27th/28th		Gen. fatigues.	"Y" day
	28th	1 PM	Informed by Brigade that "Z" day was postponed indefinitely 8th E. Surreys relieved 8th E. Surreys charge this of Queen.	
		5.30 PM	5 Coy went to Billets in BRAY to make room for R.E. Avenue for E. Coy R.E.	
		6.30 PM	C. Coy proceeded to BRAY to make room for mi company 7th Queen.	
		6 PM to 7 PM	Canon Valley shelled with 15cm H.E.	

2449 Wt. W14957/M90 750,000 1/16 J.B.C. & A. Forms/C.2118/12.

Army Form C. 2118.

WAR DIARY
or
INTELLIGENCE SUMMARY
(Erase heading not required.)

Instructions regarding War Diaries and Intelligence Summaries are contained in F.S. Regs., Part II. and the Staff Manual respectively. Title Pages will be prepared in manuscript.

Place	Date	Hour	Summary of Events and Information	Remarks and references to Appendices
	28/29th	2 AM	Larnor valley & Rail Avenue trenches heavily shelled. "A" Company particular had some casualties to report from heavy casualties.	"Y/1" day
		5.30 AM		
	29th		Bombardment continued	App IX
		2 P	Ordered to raid German trenches. 2/L/5 Hearn & Woodhams selected. Op. Order N° Ty/4. See App IX.	
		10.30P	Raid had to be cancelled owing to proposed time & special reasons at that time; only warned at the last for the movement. The "Special Ration" were issued but the Raid would not with any organisation, but the Raid would not take place on account	
	30th		(This will appear Vol. X). Casualties :— Killed O.R. 5 Wounded, 2nd Lt Evens, O.R. 28 Missing, O.R. 5	("Y/2" day)
			NOTE: The undermentioned have received parchment certificates from the Div'l Gen'l Commander in recognition of gallant conduct and devotion to duty :—	

Army Form C. 2118.

WAR DIARY
or
INTELLIGENCE SUMMARY
(Erase heading not required.)

Place	Date	Hour	Summary of Events and Information	Remarks and references to Appendices
			1086 C.S.M. Pearson E. "C" Co.	
			595 Sgt. Spradlow W. "A" "	
			1952 Pte. Harper G. "D" "	
			1515 R/W.M.Sgt. Bowman W.R. "C" "	
			2239 Pte. Hammond T. "D" "	
			2363 " Bagwell A. "D" "	
			5217 " Hull A.E. "D" "	
			3256 S/M Swindell T.P.	

C.W. Armstrong Capt.
a/adjt
for O.C.
7th R.W. Kent Regt.
30 – vi – 16

APPENDIX b. Copy No 1

Tg. MARICOURT and
LONGUEVAL 1:10,000   JU/3.

Operation Orders by Lt-Col J.T.W. Fiennes
Commanding 7th Royal West Kent Regt
24-VI-16

1. Information.   The 55th Inf. Bde will attack the
                  German trenches on the right
                  of the 18th Division, with the
                  53rd Inf. Bde on it's left and
   the 21st Inf. Bde of the 30th Division on
   it's right.   The final objective of the
   55th Inf. Bde is from the triangle formed
   by the trenches in the S.E corner of S.27.a
   (western end of MONTAUBAN) inclusive
   along MONTAUBAN ALLEY as far
   as the trench running North at S.26 d 67
   exclusive. The 55th Inf. Bde will attack
   on a frontage of two battalions (about
   900 yards); 8th E. Surrey Regt on the
   right, 7th Queens on the left. 7th Buffs
   in Support.

2. Intention.   The 7th R.W.Kent Regt will be
                  in Brigade Reserve in RAIL
                  AVENUE, and will move up
   in rear of the 7th Buffs as far as
   our front line system between BATTY
   ROAD and NE end of COKE AVENUE.

2/

Battalion report centre will move to the E Surrey report centre at N. end of COKE AVENUE on it's vacation by that battalion.

3. Frontages and objectives.

Companies will move up in four lines of sections in file at   interval and   distance.

'C' Company on the right will move to

'D' Company on the left will move to

'A' Company

'B' Company less two platoons

Company Commanders, whenever halted, will at once set to work repairing trenches in their vicinity, particularly communication trenches.

4. Carrying Parties.

O.C. 'B' Company will detail two platoons to carry from the Brigade Dump to 'A' and 'B' Dumps. These platoons will work backwards and forwards, and will be kept together in sections. They will wear green shoulder straps. Platoon Commanders to report to LT KNIGHT 92nd R.E. at 6pm on Y/Z night for instructions.

5. Dumps

(a) In our lines:—
Brigade Dump at junction of MERCHISTON and COKE AVENUES under CAPT MITCHELL
DUMP 'A' at Mine Craters under LT CARROLL (8th E Surrey)
DUMP 'B' at N end of COKE AVENUE under Lt WILLIAMS (8th E Surrey)

(b) In enemy lines:—
DUMP 'C' – A2.d.75
DUMP 'D' – A2.d.95

A dump will be established in MONTAUBAN as soon as possible.

6. Strong Points.

Strong points are to be constructed by the leading battalions as follows:—
No 1.– Junction of BACK LANE and BACK TRENCH (A3.c.15.15)

4

No 2. — Junction of MINE ALLEY and POMMIERS TRENCH (A.2.d.76.80)

No 3. — Junction of BRESLAU ALLEY and POMMIERS TRENCH (A.3.c.15.70)

No 4. — North of DUG OUT TRENCH on the POMMIERS TRENCH (A.3.c.47.00)

No 5. — Junction of TRAIN ALLEY and MONTAUBAN–TALUS BOISÉ road (A.3.C.75.55)

No 6. — (by 53rd Inf Bde) — Junction of MONTAUBAN ALLEY and trench leading North to Battery emplacement 4640 (S.2b.d.63.66.)

No 7. — Junction of MONTAUBAN ALLEY and trench leading to western end of MONTAUBAN (S.27.c.03.78.)

No 8. — The triangle (S.27.a.7.)

No 9. — The two most westerly houses of MONTAUBAN.

No 10. — THE TWINS.

No 11. — Junction of MILL TRENCH and MINE ALLEY (A.3.a.35.55)

7. Artillery. The right group Artillery is affiliated to the 55th Inf Bde. An artillery liaison officer will be told off for duty with each battalion

8. Machine guns.   No. 4 Section 55th Coy M.G. Corps (4 guns) will be in Bde reserve with the 7th R.W. Kent Regt CARNOY VALLEY.

9. Wire.   The 7th R.W. Kent Regt will be responsible for removing all wire behind our front line between U/V night and Y/Z night. Tasks will be allotted to Companies in due course.

10. Forward Saps.   Three saps will be available for communication across "No man's land" immediately after the assault. 'UP' saps will be marked at each end by RED flag, & 'DOWN' by BLUE flag.

11. S.A.A.   170 rounds will be carried on each man, with the exception of Grenadiers, Company Runners and Lewis gunners, who will carry 50 rounds each. Extra ammunition required will be issued to Companies on Y day at a time to be notified later. Indents to be submitted to the Sergeant Major by 6 p.m. on X day.

6.

12. Grenades — The battalion will carry it's complement of 1280 Mills grenades only. They will be distributed as follows:—

16 Platoon parties of 6 men each carrying 10 = 960
Battalion bombing party of ten men each carrying 20 = 200
Reserve carried by Hd Qr Guard, 6 men each carrying 20 = 120

The Battalion bombing party, vide Appendix I, will report at Battn Hd Qrs at 6pm on 'Y' day. When the Battalion moves forward as ordered in paras 2 and 3, O's C Companies will arrange to collect all grenades left in our front line trenches, and send them to either 'A' or 'B' dump.

13. Lewis Guns — Each Lewis Gun team will be strengthened by four additional men to carry S.A.A. Lewis Gun teams will wear light blue shoulder straps. S.A.A. will be carried in the special buckets prepared for this purpose; 5 magazines to be carried in

each bucket.

14. Traffic.   On and after 'U' day, all UP traffic will proceed by BEDFORD, COKE, FUSILIER and PRINCES only, and all DOWN traffic by BATTY, QUEENS, MERCHISTON and SHEFFIELD.

15. Distinguishing Marks.

(a) Yellow patches will be worn on the back of the haversack in such a way that they may be easily seen from the rear.

(b) One red and yellow flag will be carried by each platoon. These are to be waved by platoons only when they are the furthest advanced troops, and in Touch with the enemy. They are never to be stuck in the ground.

NOTE. The 30th Division will use a blue and yellow flag instead of a red and yellow one.
The 7th Division (on the left) will wear a pink patch, 1 foot square, on the haversack which will be worn on the back

16. Communication   If the Commdg. Officer
                    moves from his Report
                    Centre, the Sig. Off. will
arrange to send out a telephone
party with him.

The 55th Inf. Bde. Sig. Sec. will be
responsible for the working of all
lines between report centres and
Brigade Hd. Qrs.

The 55th Inf. Bde. Hd. Qrs will
remain at A.25.d.65 (S. of BILLON
WOOD) till MONTAUBAN ALLEY
is made good, when they will move
to the Brigade Dump.

A Divisional Visual Station
has been established at A.13.d.21

XIIIth Corps Contact Patrol
Aeroplane will be distinguished by
a broad black band under both
lower planes, and by streamers
from the end of both planes. The
firing of a white Very light by
the aeroplane means :- "I am
ready to receive a message".

Attacking Infantry will signal
to aeroplanes (and Observation
balloons) by means of :-
(1) Flares (in batches of three)
(2) Mirrors (if available)

(3) Ground Shutters

Flares and mirrors mean :— "I am here, and, so far as I know, within 50 yds of the actual firing line."
The supply of flares is very limited, and they will only be used when the leading infantry have either

   (1) Reached the 1st, 2nd or 3rd objective
   (2) Been prevented from reaching any of their objectives.

and then only if the aeroplane fires a white light.

7. Equipment   Packs will be stored in CARNOY VALLEY. Time and exact place to be notified later. The haversack will be carried on the back, with waterproof sheet and mess tin. Smoke helmets will be carried ~~if the youth stood close at~~ all waterbottles will be full at the hour of assault. All ranks will be warned to economise water as there will be none available for some considerable time after the final objective is reached. Each man will carry two

sandbags folded over the entrenching tool carrier. By the morning of 'Z' day every man will be in possession of a full oil-bottle, pull-through and flannelette.

18. Rations and Water	Preserved meat will be substituted for fresh meat during operations. On the night before the assault men will be issued with their rations for the next day, which must be intact at the hour of assault, unless the assault takes place late in the day. Rations will not be consumed without orders from an officer. Water has been stored in tanks in QUEEN St, PRINCES St, GEORGES and MARY St; 125 filled petrol tins are now stored at Batt. Hd Qrs.
19. Medical arrangements	The 55th Fd Amb will be responsible for collecting all wounded in the 18th Division, and will establish Adv. Dressing Stations for the 55th Inf Bde at :-

11

(a) The dug-outs off MERCHISTON (A14 a95)
(b) For walking cases in dug-outs at BRONFAY FARM.

Cases of wounded men in advance of our present front line will be collected into suitable dug-outs, which will be marked by Regim'tl M.O's and their position notified to 55th Fd. Amb.

20. Veterinary.   Veterinary arrangements have been notified to T.O.

21. Prisoners.   Prisoners will be marched back across the open to BILLON FARM. Prisoners, when captured, must at once be disarmed and searched for concealed weapons. Officers must be kept apart from other ranks. Documents will be collected and handed over to the man with the red, white and blue sack (vide para 21), or to the Intelligence Police at BILLON FARM. Escorts must watch that no papers are destroyed during the march. After handing over prisoners, escorts will rejoin at once and report at Batln Hd Qrs on their arrival. Strength of

escorts should be approx. 10%. All prisoners should, when practicable, be sent to Battn H.Q. before proceeding to BILLON FARM.

21. Reinforcements.   Reinforcements will be sent direct to 1st Line Transport in GROVE-TOWN CAMP. Reserve rations will be kept there in case drafts arrive without rations. When notification of their arrival is sent, the Q.M. will send a cyclist to railhead (HEILLY) to meet them. The Q.M. will send drafts up with a guide as far as Bde H.Q; from there a Bde runner will guide them to Battn H.Q. They should invariably be sent up with a days rations.

22. Casualties.   O.C. Coys will take care to see that casualties are reported promptly and accurately, and in accordance with S.R. 580 recently circulated.

24. Police. Sgt Spudlowe will be in charge of the Brigade Police. Posts will be established at at the ends of communication trenches to collect stragglers.

25. Removal of S.A.A etc from casualties. All ammunition and bombs will be collected from casualties. All ranks will be warned that if they are wounded, they must hand over S.A.A and bombs before being carried or proceeding to the rear.

26. Intelligence. No 4216 PTE BARWELL, 'D' Coy. has been detailed to collect documents etc from dug-outs and from the enemy's dead. He will carry a sack with a red, white and blue disc on it. All ranks will be warned what his duties are, and if he becomes a casualty his sack must be collected by the nearest man, and the work continued

27. Miscellaneous.

(a) No papers or orders are to be taken forward of our line. No maps other than MARICOURT and LONGUEVAL 1:10,000 and tracings of enemy trenches, which will not be marked with strong points

(b) No men will fall out to take wounded back

(c) The personal effects of Officers killed will be sent to the QM and forwarded under registered package direct to :—

    Deputy Adjutant General
      G.H.Q.
        3rd Echelon
          Base.

(d) Ration indents may be amended at Refilling point but notice of any alteration should be given to S.O. 55th Inf. Bde as early as possible.

(e) A Sergeant and 4 Loaders will be detailed to report to 55th Supply Coy A.S.C.

(f) Company Gas N.C.O's will be responsible that Vermorel Myato Sprayers. ~~and Ayton gas fans~~ are taken forward.

15.

(g) 2/Lt BARTHOLOMEW and four runners have been detailed to act as guides for the 9th Division.

(h) 2/Lt BUSHELL will hold himself in readiness to superintend the loading of trucks at BRONFAY and pushing them to CARNOY. Ten men will be detailed for this purpose.

(i) All ranks will be reminded that secrecy regarding forthcoming operations is one of the main factors of success. Therefore the utmost care & discretion must be used when corresponding with friends at home.

(k) The word 'RETIRE' will never be used, and if heard never attended to, as it can only come from a German.

(l) No private letters, or papers that might be of value to the enemy as information, or for purposes of identification will be carried on any person during the attack.

(m) All ranks are reminded that the Iron Ration is not to be broken into except by the order of an officer. Disobedience of this order is a Court Martial Offence.

(n) All ranks will be warned that if taken prisoner, they can only be required to give their name and Regiment, and that the German will use every means to extract information, such as dressing up a German who speaks English perfectly in the uniform of a British soldier, and mixing him up with prisoners.

Copy No 1 — DIARY.
" 2 — C.O.
" 3 — 2nd in Command.
" 4 — A. Coy
" 5 — B. "
" 6 — C. "
" 7 — D. "
" 8 — QM + T.O.
" 9 — S.O. & I.O.
" 10 — M.O.

P. Anstruther Capt
Adjutant
7th R.W. Kent Regt

Copy No. 1

APPENDIX 9

JV/4

Operation Orders by Lt.-Col. J.T.W. Fiennes
Commanding 7th R.W. Kent Regt.
29-VI-16

Intention

1. A raid will be carried out against the German trenches tonight. The object of the raid is to ascertain if the enemy is holding his line, and whether he occupies the 1st or 2nd line trench, to engage him and destroy his morale, and to bring back prisoners.

   Point of Starting — Head of PRINCES STREET

   Approximate point of entry — A.8.b.56

   Hour of entering enemy's trench 11.15 PM (ZERO)

2. Composition and Organisation — 2nd Lt J. HEATON will command the party and he will be assisted by 2nd Lt WOODHOUSE. The party will consist of these two officers, three N.C.Os and 23 other ranks,

2.

and will be divided up as under:-

'A' – Right blocking party – 1 N.C.O. and 6 men
'B' – Left blocking party – 1 N.C.O. and 6 men
'C' – Main body, (for clearing dug-outs & killing Germans) – One officer, 1 N.C.O. and 8 men.
'D' – Covering party, (to remain outside the German trench at point of entry) – one officer & 3 men

3. **Equipment** Details of equipment have been given verbally to the officers concerned.

4. **Artillery** The artillery will barrage the whole of the German front line opposite this sub-sector, beginning at — 0/10. At ZERO the barrage will lift between the points A.8.b.80.71 and A.8.b.23.63 on to BRESLAU SUPPORT. The raiding party will enter the German trenches im-

-mediately the barrage lifts.
At 0/20 the barrage will lift from BRESLAU SUPPORT between A.8.b.87.88 and A.8.b.21.90, but will remain concentrated on these points. Artillery support will not cease until the whole raiding party has returned to our lines.

The F.O.O. will install a telephone at the head of PRINCES STREET, at the starting point.

5. <u>Password</u>   The password will be 'WHISKEY'

6. <u>Signal</u>   The signal to leave the German trenches will be given by LT HEATON or LT WOODHOUSE and will be a blast on a siren whistle.

7. <u>Direction and Touch</u>   The ground will be reconnoitred by officers and N.C.Os. by day, and a compass ~~bearing~~ and back

4.

bearing taken to the objective from the starting point. The men before they go out will have the direction of prominent objects such as the craters pointed out to them. Touch will be kept by means of a tape reeled out by the leading man of the party, and cords will be used for lateral touch.

8. **Medical** — The M.O. will arrange to be at the starting point at ZERO with the necessary bearers and appliances.

9. **Synchronisation of Watches** — Watches of all concerned will be synchronised with that of the O.C. 7th R.W. Kent Regiment at 8 p.m.

Copy No 1 — Diary
"   No 2 — O.C. 7th R.W. Kent
"   No 3 — O.C. 7th Queens
"   No 4 — Lt Heaton
"   No 5 — F.O.O.

R. Ashton the Capt.
Adjt
7th R.W. Kent Regt

Statement of N° 1452 Pte MARTIN,
in continuation of 'Account
of attempted raid on night
of 25th/26th, para 3, forwarded
under my No. A28 of 26-VI-16.

Pte Martin was the second man
to go after the cut party. He
thought he saw them & pro-
-ceeded some distance in that
direction and encountered wire
which he started cutting.
When through he lay down &
listened, but heard nothing of
them; about five minutes after-
-wards he heard a conversation
on his right, & shortly after that
a party of men passed along the
[line?] & he found he had [traced?]
within about 12 yards of
them, making a good deal of
noise, talking, shouting etc.,
From his description his
position would probably have
been on or about A 9 a 25.65. After
things had quietened down he

started to try & get back again, but in doing so he made a noise, at which lights were put up, and a German appeared head & shoulders above the parapet, saw him & shouted "Come in here!" Instead then made off, & a German came out of the trench and followed him. He ran on some distance and then turned round and fired two shots at the German, whereat the pursuit ceased. He then wandered about trying to find his way back and at last came upon a trench, which, hearing no movement inside, he got into. This may have been the Salient at A.9.a.05.60. but he had no idea where he was. He knows it was a German trench because he heard voices to his right talking in an unfamiliar tongue, but no one came near him the whole night. Just before dawn

Copy No 6   APPENDIX 4   July

Operation orders by Lt-Col. J.T.W. Fiennes, Commanding 7th Royal West Kent Regt.

25-VI-16

1. The battalion will carry out a raid upon the German front line trenches at the "Salient", A.9.a.10.5.6 at 12.30 AM night 25th/26th June.

2. Raiding party under 2/Lt BROWNLEE will consist of 1 officer & 25 O.R. organised as follows:—
   "A" Party, 1 N.C.O. & 5 men } Trench
   "B" Party, 1 N.C.O. & 5 men } blocking
   "C" Party, 2 N.C.O. & 6 men, clearing Dug Out
   "D" Party, 1 N.C.O. & 5 men, Take over Prisoners

3. Right Group R.A. and Trench mortar battery will co-operate.

4. Raiding party will leave the trenches at A/9.a.20.45 at 12.30 a.m. night 25th/26th. The signal to

2.

move will be the bursting on the Salient (A.9.a.05.10.) of 3 heavy Trench Mortar bombs, at the same time the artillery will place a barrage on the German lines at the following points:

(1) Salient at A.9.a.56.70.

(2) Junction of communication trench E. of Salient with BRESLAU SUPPORT (A.9.a.17)

(3) Along BRESLAU SUPPORT to and including junction of communication trench W. of Salient with BRESLAU SUPPORT (A.8.b.99), thence along communication trench to its junction with BRESLAU TRENCH at A.8.b.87.

(4) WEST along BRESLAU TRENCH from point A.8.b.87.

This barrage will continue until return of Raiding Party to point of departure.

(5) Details of equipment have been issued to officers concerned.

(6) Identification is required. If no live prisoner is captured, every effort must be made to collect papers, identity discs, shoulder straps, pay books, etc, from

the killed or wounded.

7. CAPTAIN HOLLAND will be in command of the operation, but will remain in our trenches at the point of departure. He will be in touch with the F.O.O. of the Batteries concerned, & with the T.M. Officer, both of whom will report to him at 12 midnight at the point of departure from our trenches.

8. The M.O. will arrange to be in attendance with such stretcher bearers etc as he considers necessary in a dug out which will be placed at his disposal by the O.C. 8th E. Surrey Regt.

9. The raiding party will be in position ready to start at 12.15 A.M. night 25th/26th.

Copy No. 1 to Diary
 "   2 — O.C. 7th R.W.R.
 "   3 — Capt Holland
 "   4 — O.C. 8th E. Surrey
 "   5 — Capt Butler, D.T.M.O.
 "   6 — 84th Bde. R.F.A.

R. Amtruther Capt
adjt
7th R.W. Kent
Regt

"A" Form.
MESSAGES AND SIGNALS.

Army Form C. 2121.

TO: 4th Army A   13th Corps.

Sender's Number: A 703
Day of Month: 14
AAA

Fighting strength return 7th Bat.
The Buffs now 13 ... aaa
... ... 32 Off. 979
O.R. ... two ... ...
30 O.K. Col. three 34
Off 979 O.R. Col. ...
1 O.K. Col. A 34
... 993 O.R. Col. B.
13 ... 115 O.R. aaa
Col. two reinforcements Off.
2/L N.W. LODER and 2/Lt.
H. OWEN 20 O.R. aaa
Addressed 4th Army repeated 13th
Corps.

From: 3rd Division
Place:
Time: 3-55 pm

Ralph Berry Captain

"A" Form.
MESSAGES AND SIGNALS.
Army Form C. 2121.

| TO | 30th DIVISION. | | |

Sender's Number.	Day of Month.	In reply to Number.	
* S.402	14	R.B.2	A A A

Herewith copy of strength return as requested and This was forwarded on Friday evening. to 55° IB aaa

From 7 Buffs
Time 11.50 pm

J Phillips Capt. a/s
for L Col

APPENDIX 8   1

Account of attempted raid on the
German trenches at the salient
near A.9.a.05.60., night 24th/25th June

1. The party was composed of one officer
and 28 other ranks, and was
split up as follows:—

   'A' — Trench blocking party — 1 N.C.O. & 5 men
   'B' —   "   "   — 1 N.C.O. & 5 men
   'C' — Clearing dug-outs   — 1 N.C.O. & 4 men
   'D' — Taking the prisoners   — 1 N.C.O. & 5 men
   'E' — Clearing dug-outs   — 1 N.C.O. & 4 men

   2nd Lieut. T. Briggs was in charge
   of the party.

2. The party was due to leave our
   trench at 9 p.m., but owing to
   delay in laying the communication trench, did not actually
   leave our front line at A.9.a.15.45.
   until 11.45 p.m. The artillery barrage
   started punctually at 12.30 a.m.

3. The party proceeded to the German
   wire in the following formation:—
   Two columns in single file at

2

at pass intervals 'A' & 'C' on the left and 'B' & 'D' on the right. 'D' party was provided with a white tape which was paid out as they proceeded.

On arrival at the German a gap in the German wire at 1.9.a.05.55, Lt Brownlee was informed that 'D' party were not present; a man who thought he had seen them go off to the right, went some distance to try and find them, but returned without having succeeded. [crossed out] went off to try and find them, and he did not return. Then Lt Brownlee noticed that the Artillery barrage had ceased, this and the fact that the whole of 'D' party was missing decided him to return to our lines, with a view to organising a search for the missing men and to obtain instructions from CAPT HOLLAND who was in charge of the operations from our own trenches. He reached our trenches about 1.5 AM, and Capt Holland passed out to bring his party inside; Lt Brooker then went out with a Corporal and one man and scoured the ground but without success. They went out again a third time in another direction, but was unable to find any trace of the missing men.

4. The artillery F.O.O. was taken up by Capt Holland to the front line about 6 pm where he was shewn where to install his telephone instrument and instructed to have his line laid and to report to Capt Holland at this spot at 12.05 AM. Owing to a misunderstanding the line was not laid to the place indicated, and the artillery officer lost his way and did not report to Captain Holland at all.

He subsequently returned to the signal office of A 1 Sub-sector, and stopped their bar

Page about 1 A.M.

5. As regards 'D' party, some light has been thrown on their movements by the return of one of the party Pte Lea who was wounded by shrapnel.
He states that he was at the rear of the party, and cannot explain how the Corporal, who was leading, lost touch with the remainder. They however reached a gap in the German wire about A.9.a.30.65, passed through it, and lay down just in front of the German parapet to consider the situation. Then a german came out of the trench a little way to the right and started walking towards our lines. The corporal shot him. This gave the alarm, lights were sent up, german heads appeared over the parapet and bombs were thrown at our party, badly wounding

the Corporal, and he thinks, killing or wounding several others. He then dragged the Corporal some distance back into a shell crater, and returned for help. He himself being wounded he was unable to go out again to guide the search party. He firmly avers that the German parapet was thickly manned after the alarm had been given, and this evidence is corroborated by that of several officers in our trenches, who heard a lot of shouting, and could distinctly see faces in the German lines when lights went up.

6. The failure of the raid is attributed to the following causes:—
   (a) Latrines unstated
   (b) 'D' party losing itself, and subsequently giving the alarm by firing a

shot. (It should be stated that after the whole party had left our parapet, it was halted and Lt Bonnalie himself ascertained that all were present, and in touch).

(c) Absence of the F.O.O. and of his telephone.

(d) As 'D' party were in possession of three ladders their absence ~~the stopping of the barrage~~ made it inadvisable for the rest of the party to get ~~~~ into the German trenches.

7. Reference the red ~~~~ in para 3, this man has rejoined this morning, but is too badly shaken to give a coherent account of what happened to him. Any information that may be got out of him will be forwarded later.

8. Attached are copy of operation orders, and instructions # 2/2 from O.C. Right Group, B.T.A.

R.V. Lewis Lt-Col.
26-II-16 Commdg 7th R.W. Kent Regt.

he got out of the trench, and lay down in a shell crater about 20 yards from it, where he apparently had several narrow escapes from being hit by our own shrapnel and trench mortar bombs which, he says, were falling all around him. Then about 10.30 AM a cloud of smoke came over from our lines, which he took advantage of, and regained our lines near A.9.a.78.47 in safety. He was very much shaken on his return.

R. A. Matthews Capt
for Lt Col
Comm'g 7th R.W. Kent Regt

27-V-16

55th Bde.
18th Div.

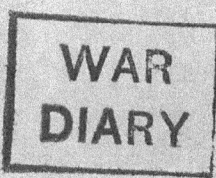

WO95/2047

7th BATTALION

ROYAL WEST KETN REGIMENT.

JULY 1916.

Appendices attached :- Operation Order.
Situation Report.
Map.

WAR DIARY of 7th Royal West Kent Regt Army Form C. 2118.

INTELLIGENCE SUMMARY
(Erase heading not required.)

Vol XI JULY

Place	Date	Hour	Summary of Events and Information	Remarks and references to Appendices
Trenches	July 1st	7.30 am	(2nd) The attack by 55th Bde commenced. 8th E Surreys were leading Batt on the right and 7th Queens on the left. The 7th Buffs were third Battalion, in support covering all what Brigade frontage, & 7th R.W. Kent Regt. the two platoons detached for carrying material from Brigade Dump to our front line, in Brigade reserve Lyn 8th Suffolk Regt. & 53rd Brigade were in Divisional Reserve in rear of 55th Brigade	
		8.10 am	A message was received from 8th E Surreys Report Centre that all was going well, but they had not heard whether the POMMIER LINE was taken.	
		8.12 am	The Brigade informed us by telephone that all appeared to be going well, but that the leading Battalions had met with much opposition when was anticipated, and had suffered considerable casualties	
		8.35 am	Ordered C. and B. Companies to move up to the forming up trenches as they became vacated by 7th Buffs. Each Company had 2 platoons to keep in touch with the Buffs. 2nd Lieut Tindall had been sent as Liaison Officer to H.Q. 7th Buffs. The other two became divisional Res.	
		8.47 am	The leading Platoon "D", "C" & then "A" in the centre, and "D" on the left started moving forward	
		9.30 am	Bn H.Q. started moving forward up COXE AVENUE. An eight Report Centre, leaving the Signalling Officer and Battalion Report Centre in its initial position.	
		9.42 am	The whole Battalion was clear of TRAIL AVENUE. Captain Washington intercepted a message from the Buffs to me, asking for help for the E. Surreys which were held up at TRAIN ALLEY, and stating that the whole Battalion (Buffs) had been thrown into his platoon. This message actually reached Bn H.Q. at 10.40 a.m, but at 9.45 am a message was sent to the 8th Suffolks informing them that Tindall Washington at 10.8 am being thrown into the fight they would have to move up to our original half line	

Army Form C. 2118.

WAR DIARY or INTELLIGENCE SUMMARY
(Erase heading not required.)

Instructions regarding War Diaries and Intelligence Summaries are contained in F.S. Regs., Part II and the Staff Manual respectively. Title Pages will be prepared in manuscript.

Place	Date	Hour	Summary of Events and Information	Remarks and references to Appendices
	1st		Sent 2nd Lieut Tindall to the Artillery as Liaison Officer. Platoon I.O. saw and	
		10.30 am	an officer [?] of "A", "C" and "D" Companies reported personally to me	App 10
			raised to them verbally orders to move forward with my O.O. 417 (App 10) and at	
		10.25 am	I received their orders arriving by runner of the above mentioned.	
			Officers, 2nd Lieut [?] Station of "A" Co was wounded, and 2nd Lieut Phillips "D" Coy	
			was temporarily knocked out by shell shock, and owing to the runner going to	
			"D" Coy becoming a casualty, that Company never got the orders	
			"C" Coy and "A" Coy were ready to move by 11.10 am and actually moved at 11.20 am	
			very shortly after this Captain Lester and 2nd Lieut Woodward were wounded	
			the advance of "A" Company soon became slower than that of "C" Company, the	
			Platoons lost touch and became somewhat advanced, but these Platoons were checked and	
			re-organized by R.S.M. Klein in the TONNIER LINE between 12 noon and	
			12.20 pm; and the 4th Platoon was at No.5. Strong Point about this time,	
			under the Lieut Tate, who was not anywhere near what he was at the line the	
			only Officer left in the Company. By this time (actually 11.45 am) three Platoons	
			of "B" Coy with Capt. Waddington had reached the final objective, passing	
			through elements of B. Surrey and Buffs, and two Platoons were at in the	
			TONNIER LINE	
		10.30 am	Battalion Report Centre moved to Right Rear Report Centre.	
		11.25 am	One Platoon of "D" Coy was sent to carry up S.A.A. and bombs to the final objective	
		11.45 am	a message from the Brigade informed us that the 20th R.F. had taken MONTAUBAN	
		12 noon	the Adjutant was sent out to find out where "D" Coy was, as they did not	
			appear to have moved. He found Capt Lender and his Coy still in our	
			trenches ventral, and it was only then discovered that the orders to move	
			(App. 10) had not been received by him. They were delivered to him	
			personally by the Adjutant at 12.15 pm.	

2449 Wt. W14957/M90 750,000 1/16 J.B.C. & A. Forms/C.2118/12.

WAR DIARY or INTELLIGENCE SUMMARY

Army Form C. 2118.

Remarks and references to Appendices: 3

Place	Date	Hour	Summary of Events and Information
	1st	12.25 pm	A message was received from Capt. Waddington that he had reached MONTAUBAN alley at 11.45 a.m. with two platoons & his own Coy, but that 3" L. Trench Mortar Battery and 1st Buffs and one platoon "C" Coy were not consolidating the line. After known g. m. time (11.20 am) to meet ninth as opposition at all, but one platoon under 2nd Lieut. Innocent got left behind & never came. (The officer having been killed in that has not been captured.) In HONTAUBAN alley until 3 p.m. one more action) and they did not arrive. The leading platoon of the meantime the 3 platoons from three more of "A" Coy under B.S.M. Kleen moved forward to the junction of MINE alley and W. end of HONTAUBAN, where they stopped at 12.45 pm to consolidate and engaged a German machine gun firing from HONTAUBAN alley about S. 26. & 13.
		3 pm	B.S.M. Kleen reported to Capt. Waddington in HONTAUBAN alley. About 5 p.m. Capt. Waddington moved down to bring his 3 platoons up into HONTAUBAN alley, which he did, arriving about 6 pm. The platoon of "A" Coy under 2nd Lieut. ?, passed over the POMMIER Shrine at 11.50 a.m. and pressed over the open down to MINE alley, and got in touch with Capt. Kleen and 2nd Lieut. Shelley of B. L. Company of the HILL and on the MAMETZ-HONTAUBAN road at 12.15 pm. They moved up into HONTAUBAN alley, on the left of a platoon of 1st Buffs, who were now on the left. There was not much 6 p.m. that C.S.M. Sellars when they started consolidating. It was not until 6 pm. that C.S.M. Sellars and 2nd Lieut. ?, with mentally? m.d., and 18th and 2nd Lieut. ?, both came command D "A" Coy. Montauban "D" Coy had moved up to the POMMIER Shrine which many machine between 12.30 pm and 1 pm. Number 15 platoon under 2nd Lieut. Wills appear to have received orders to storm POMMIER Shrine which they did, and did not seem to return.

Army Form C. 2118.

WAR DIARY
or
INTELLIGENCE SUMMARY
(Erase heading not required.)

Instructions regarding War Diaries and Intelligence Summaries are contained in F.S. Regs., Part II. and the Staff Manual respectively. Title Pages will be prepared in manuscript.

Place	Date	Hour	Summary of Events and Information	Remarks and references to Appendices
		2.20 pm	Battalion H.Q. moved up to the POMMIER LINE, to the junction of BRESLAU ALLEY, running a wire out from the night report centre. Bat. Scissors went forward to confer with O.C. 2. Buvings and to arrange the situation. He found the situation as follows:- A mixed force of all four Battalions holding MONTAUBAN ALLEY, through 2 frontage about 600 yards, amounting to about 100 rifles, 4 Vickers guns and 8 Lewis guns. They were in touch with the 30th Division on the right, but the left flank was in the air. The men were much exhausted, and S.A.A. and water urgently required. Tools and a carrying party were much needed	
		3 pm	Bat. Scissors returned to Bn. H.Q and sent this information to Bde H.Q	
		4.43 pm	After a further review of the situation, and consultation with O.C. 2 & 7th Buffs and T. Queens, report vide App. II (A.O.G.4) was sent to Brigade H.Q	App. II
		7.33 pm	Report Brentim joined Battn H.Q in the POMMIER LINE	
		7.30 pm	During the evening the Brigadier came forward and after consultation with O.C. Battalions decided that they should be re-organised at once and that it should be taken over by 7th R.W. Kent Regt as soon as possible. Therefore at 10 p.m. Battalion H.Q., "D" Co. and "B" Co. had 2 Platoons, moved forward via BRESLAU ALLEY, MILL TRENCH, and MINE ALLEY to a point in MINE ALLEY about 100 yards S. of the western known in MONTAUBAN where Capt. Waddington was over for his much Bat Scissors. After consultation with him, it was decided that it was impracticable to carry out the attempt by night owing to enemy shelling and the possibly being unknown all through the night. MINE ALLEY was heavily damaged, & telephone cable was run out from Battn. report centre as far as MILL trench, but was broken several times by shell fire. Each time it down, both a party went out to repair the breaks	

2449 Wt. W14957/M90 750,000 1/16 J.B.C. & A. Forms/C.2118/12.

Army Form C. 2118.

WAR DIARY or INTELLIGENCE SUMMARY
(Erase heading not required.)

Instructions regarding War Diaries and Intelligence Summaries are contained in F.S. Regs., Part II. and the Staff Manual respectively. Title Pages will be prepared in manuscript.

Place	Date	Hour	Summary of Events and Information	Remarks and references to Appendices
	2nd	2.30 am	2nd Summons went round the front line and made the arrangements about the relief. About 5 am "D" Coy. was moved up into MONTAUBAN Alley, with "B" Coy. in support. All troops of the Queens and E. Surreys were withdrawn, also two platoons of the Buffs.	
		9 am	Owing to the continuous heavy shelling round the portion RHINE Alley where Battalion H.Q. was, causing several casualties, the H.Q. was moved earlier without drees to the original place in POMMIER LINE. During the day MONTAUBAN Alley was intermittently shelled, and a slow barrage placed on approaches. Many Germans were seen in the then known BAZENTIN and MAMETZ woods, and were fired on by Lewis guns.	
		6 pm	The 2 Platoons of "B" Coy. engaged in carrying, reported at Battalion H.Q. and were sent up the line. They had suffered no casualties during the night. May was carrying 3. During 3rd & 4th July, the situation was much the same, and Minenwerfer of importance to mention. On the evening of the 4th, the Battalion was relieved by 8th Suff'k Regt. relief being complete about 12 midnight. Battalion marched to BRONTAY FARM. From the 1st to 4th July, the casualties were:— Killed 2/Lt. J.R. Hatter Wounded Capt. J.R. Bowden " 2/Lt. S. Bowman " (at duty) 2/Lt. J.A. Troussons " " J. Moston "	

Lt. S.H. Woodhouse

WAR DIARY or INTELLIGENCE SUMMARY

Army Form C. 2118.

(Erase heading not required.)

Place	Date	Hour	Summary of Events and Information	Remarks and references to Appendices
	5th to 7th		2nd Lieut D.G. Phipps Wounded " " H.J. Gregory " 1086 R.S.M. Pearson R. Killed 1068 " Unspronted R. Wounded Other ranks killed 37 " " wounded 135 " " missing 1 The behaviour of all ranks during the whole action was excellent in every respect. Many N.C.O.s exhibited marked qualities of leadership.	
	7th	12 noon	Battalion in billets and bivouac in an annexe BRONFAY FARM.	
		11 PM	Draft of 74 men arrived.	
	11th	7 AM	Marched to TRIGGER WOOD, South of BILLON WOOD, arriving at 11 AM: distance about 8½ miles.	
	12th	7 PM	Marched up through MARICOURT to the BRICQUETERIE and	

Army Form C. 2118.

WAR DIARY
or
INTELLIGENCE SUMMARY.
(Erase heading not required.)

Jan 17 7 Ruckens Vol 1

Instructions regarding War Diaries and Intelligence Summaries are contained in F. S. Regs., Part II. and the Staff Manual respectively. Title pages will be prepared in manuscript.

Place	Date	Hour	Summary of Events and Information	Remarks and references to Appendices
LAMOTTE.	1-1-17	to	Training.	
	8-1-17		Training.	
LE TITRE.	9-1-17.		GENERAL MAXSE bids farewell to Officers of Division, and present Medal Ribbons.	
LAMOTTE.	10-1-17.		Training. Boxing Contest with "BUFFS". All events won.	
			Move Orders received.	
"	11-1-17.		Left LAMOTTE at 11-35a.m. to march to DOMLEGER.	
			Arrived DOMLEGER 5-30p.m.	
DOMLEGER.	12-1-17.		Left DOMLEGER at 10-35a.m. to march to LE MEILLARD.	
			Arrived LE MEILLARD at 12-30p.m.	
LE MEILLARD.	13-1-17.		Days Rest. Cleaning up. Boxing Contests.	
LE MEILLARD.	14-1-17.		Left LE MEILLARD to march to RAINCHEVAL at 9-0a.m.	
			Arrived RAINCHEVAL at 4-45p.m.	
RAINCHEVAL.	15-1-17.		Days rest. Cleaning up etc.	
RAINCHEVAL.	16-1-17.		Left RAINCHEVAL to march to HEDAUVILLE at 9-0a.m.	
			Arrived at HEDAUVILLE at 12-30p.m. Battalion in huts.	
HEDAUVILLE.	17-1-17.		"B" "C" and "D" Coys attached to 53rd Brigade for Fatigue.	
"	18-1-17.		Training.	
"	19-1-17.		Training.	
"	20-1-17.		Training.	
"	21-1-17.		Training.	
"	22-1-17.		Training. Draft of 192 N.C.O's and men arrived 12-Midnight.	
"	23-1-17.		Training.	
"	24-1-17.		Training. "B" "C" and "D" Coys return from fatigue.	
"	25-1-17.		Training.	
"	26-1-17.		Training.	
"	27-1-17.		Training.	
"	28-1-17.		Training.	
"	29-1-17.		Training. About 120 men per Coy. "A" "B" "C" and "D" to MARTINSART for fatigues.	
			One platoon attached to 92nd Field Co. R.E. (now 174th Tunnelling Co.)	
"	30-1-17.		**Fatigues.**	
"	31-1-17.		Fatigues.	

Army Form C. 2118.

7 RW Kent
20/1/17

WAR DIARY
or
INTELLIGENCE SUMMARY.
(Erase heading not required.)

Instructions regarding War Diaries and Intelligence Summaries are contained in F. S. Regs., Part II. and the Staff Manual respectively. Title pages will be prepared in manuscript.

Place	Date	Hour	Summary of Events and Information	Remarks and references to Appendices
			HONOURS AND AWARDS.	
			The undermentioned Officer, and Warrant Officer Awarded the MILITARY CROSS.	The following is an Extract from a letter of a man of the draft which arrived on the 22nd.
			CAPTAIN C.G.TINDALL. R.S.M. A. TAPP.	"One thing I can be thankful for, and that is, that we have joined a smart Battalion; I guess it is one of the smartest in the British Army.
			OFFICERS JOINED THE BATTALION DURING THE MONTH.	Even just behind the line we have to clean our equipment, buttons etc., and as for changing the guard, I guess it would beat the Guard changing at Whitehall easy.
			LIEUT.COL.E.M.LIDDELL.(To Command Battalion). 5-1-17. CAPTAIN F.R. LATTER. Rejoined From England. 27-1-17. CAPTAIN J.B.MATTHEWS. " " 27-1-17.	The full band turns out every day at Guard Mounting and retreat. It looks great and personally I am very proud of them."
				-o-o-o-o-o-o-o-o-o-o-o-o-

A. G. Menfs [?]
Lt. Lieut. Col.
Commanding 7th Battalion Royal West Kent Regiment.

Army Form C. 2118.

WAR DIARY
or
INTELLIGENCE SUMMARY.
(Erase heading not required.)

7th Royal West Kents

Instructions regarding War Diaries and Intelligence Summaries are contained in F.S. Regs., Part II. and the Staff Manual respectively. Title pages will be prepared in manuscript.

Place	Date	Hour	Summary of Events and Information	Remarks and references to Appendices
HEDAUVILLE	1-2-17.		Training etc.	
"	2-2-17.		Training etc.	
"	3-2-17.		Training etc. Boxing Finals. (Light Heavy, Middle, and Featherweight Contests won)	
"	4-2-17.		"A" and "D" Coys. to WELLINGTON HUTS from MONMOUTH HUTS	
"	5-2-17.		Training and fatigues.	
"	6-2-17.		Training and fatigues.	
"	7-2-17.		Training and fatigues.	
"	8-2-17.		Training and fatigues.	
"	9-2-17.		Training and fatigues. Fatigues ended.	
"	10-2-17.		Received orders to proceed to ST PIERRE DIVION. Battalion in Dugouts.	
"	11-2-17.		First line Transport to MARTINSART. Battalion made up to 135 per Company fighting strength.	
ST PIERRE DIV -ION	12-2-17.		Battalion to Front Line relieving 12th Middlesex Regiment. Relief complete 11-0 p.m.	
	13-2-17.		Battalion in Front Line.	
	14-2-17.		Battalion in Front Line. Attack on Strong Point vide appendix. Apendix 19.	App:19.
	15-2-17.		Battalion Relieved from Front Line by Royal Berks. Battalion proceeded to MONMOUTH HUTS.	
	16-2-17.		At MONMOUTH HUTS. Moved to WELLINGTON HUTS at 12-30 p.m.	
	17-2-17.		At WELLINGTON HUTS.	
	18-2-17.		Battalion moved into Support. Head Quarters in SUDBURY TRENCH.	
	19-2-17.		Battalion moved from Support Position to the Front Line relieving the 8th EAST SURREY REGT.	
FRONT LINE.	20-2-17.		Battalion in Front Line.	
	21-2-17.		Battalion in front line. Enemy artillery Active. The relief of the 8th East Surrey Regt on the night of the 20th inst was successfully carried out by 6-30p.m.	
"	22-2-17.		Battalion in frontline. Enemy Artillery Active. Commanding Officer (Lieut.Col.E.M.Liddell) wounded.	
"	23-2-17.		Successfull patrol work carried/and direct observation of the enemy gained which led to the invalueable information of the enemy's retirement.	
			Patrol reports attaced. Appendix 20.	App:20.
	24-2-17.		Battalion relieved from front line by 8th East Surrey Regt. Battalion to Dug-outs in support.	
	25-2-17.		Battalion in dug-outs at MOQUET FARM. Battalion in Reserve.	
	26-2-17.		Battalion in Reserve in Dug-outs at MOQUET FARM.	
	27-2-17.		Battalion moved into support. One Company in SOUTH MIRAUMONT TRENCH, one Company in GRANDCOURT TRENCH, 2-Companies and Battalion Hd.Qrs. in BOOM RAVINE.	

Army Form C. 2118.

WAR DIARY
or
INTELLIGENCE SUMMARY.
(Erase heading not required.)

Place	Date	Hour	Summary of Events and Information	Remarks and references to Appendices
TRENCHES.	28-2-17.		Battalion in support. Disposition of Companies as on 27th instant.	
			OFFICERS JOINED DURING THE MONTH.	
			Captain. N.A. Charrington.	
			2/Lieut. R.P. Woodyear.	
			2/Lieut. E.L. Corley.	
			2/Lieut. E.M. Smith. F.H.F.	
			2/Lieut. G.H. Kinder.	
			CASUALTIES IN OFFICERS DURING MONTH.	
			Captain J.B.B. Ford. — Killed 16-2-17.	
			Captain J.B. Matthews. — Killed 17-2-17.	
			Lieut. Col. E.M. Liddell. — Wounded 22-2-17.	
			2/Lieut. E.L. Corley. — Killed 23-2-17.	
			2/Lieut. P.A. Beckett. — Killed 14-2-17.	
			2/Lieut. H.G. Dix M.C. — Killed 14-2-17.	

M.E. Phillips.
Major.
Commanding 7th Battalion Royal West Kent Regiment.

NARRATIVE OF OPERATIONS FEBRUARY 14th 1917.

APP 19

On receipt of orders for the attack on GRANDCOURT TRENCH from R.16.a.98. to R.16.b.48. by One Company of the 7th Battalion Royal West Kent Regt, I visited CAPTAIN FORD Commanding "A" Company which had been detailed for this attack, and spent some hours with him making a reconnaissance and handed him his orders framed exactly on the orders from 55th Infantry Brigade.

On the evening of the 13th a line for moving off was put out by Compass Bearing by CAPTAIN FORD himself from the EAST of SIXTEEN ROAD at R.16.a.73. extending EAST for 250 yards. This is almost exactly opposite the EAST end of FOLLY TRENCH.

In good time before ZERO the Company was drawn up along the taped line in two waves with 2/LIEUT. DIX.M.C. on the right and 2/LIEUT.BECKETT on the left of the leading wave, and CAPTAIN FORD in the centre of the second wave which followed at 60 yards distance.

Before ZERO I took up a position about R.15.b.45, which appeared the best position for observation, and was connected by telephone. At ZERO minus 5, the 4.5 Howitzers opened on POINT R.16.a.98, and at ZERO the 18-Pounder Barrage, which was to take the form of 3-Rounds Rapid from each gun, opened on the objective. This Barrage lasted for four minutes as Batteries did not appear to open simultaneously. Two Guns of the 55th Brigade Trench Mortar Battery co-operated from GRANDCOURT TRENCH, WEST of SIXTEEN ROAD. Four Guns of the 55th Machine Gun Company also co-operated by fire from the high ground in R.15.a. and b.

Almost immediately our barrage opened the enemy S.O.S, in the form of one golden star rocket, was sent up from SOUTH to NORTH from four points which appeared to me at GRANDCOURT TRENCH, EAST of SIXTEEN ROAD, and in the direction of BOOM RAVINE, COFFEE TRENCH, and TEA TRENCH. Enemy machine Guns and rifles at the same time opened fire from about R.16.a.98. and RUM TRENCH. It was too dark to observe the movements of our men; enemy barrage came down 7-minutes after ZERO. Hour of ZERO 5-45a.m.

I had previously ordered CAPTAIN MATTHEWS with 2-Platoons of "C" Company which had been holding GRANDCOURT TRENCH WEST of SIXTEEN ROAD, to co-operate with "A" Company, and told him that the point R.16.a.98. must be taken. As rifle fire continued and it appeared that there was a brisk fight, about 6-0a.m. I sent CAPTAIN HOLLAND to GRANDCOURT TRENCH to assist if necessary. This Officer passed through the barrage, and at 7-20a.m. I received a report from him timed 7-5a.m. that the objective was gained, but that CAPTAIN FORD was wounded and 2/LIEUT DIX.M.C. and 2/LIEUT.BECKETT were killed, and C.S.M. Keleher was wounded, and that he had sent CAPTAIN MATTHEWS to take over command of "A" Company with one platoon of "C" Company to assist.

By 8-0a.m. there was still some artillery activity and machine gun and rifle fire, so I went to GRANDCOURT TRENCH to ascertain the situation; I arrived at the bomb stop known as point 87, and as "A" Company were in the part of the trench beyond I felt sure that the objective had been gained, and reported to that effect to Brigade Headquarters by wire.

About 10-0a.m, I heard that CAPTAIN MATTHEWS was missing, probably killed, so I sent 2/LIEUT. JONES to command "A" Company with orders to consolidate the ground gained, to make a bomb stop at R.16.b.48. and to try to exploit success along the trench to the EAST. I received a message from this Officer to the effect that he found it impossible to work along the trench beyond R.16.b.48. owing to the activity of enemy snipers, and to the state of the trench, which was virtually non existent and afforded no cover of any description, so he was making a bomb stop at the farthest point gained, which he took to be 150 yards EAST of SIXTEEN ROAD,

About 3-30p.m. 2/LIEUT. SHATTOCK "C" Company who was commanding in GRANDCOURT TRENCH, WEST of SIXTEEN ROAD reported in person to Battalion Headquarters, and stated that he had discovered that our original bomb stop, known as point 87, was not at that point at all, but was in reality about 150 yards WEST of that point about R.16.a.86. and the line that "A" Company was holding was only from that point to POINT 87 where the new bomb stop had been erected. From this point the line of SIXTEEN ROAD was recognisable and it was therefore clear that the objective had not been gained, and that the sniping complained of was coming from the enemy's Strong Point at R.16.a.98. which was still intact.

It was impossible to communicate this news immediately by telephone as the line was broken, but about 5-0p.m. I was enabled to report ~~this~~ the situation to Brigade Headquarters.

On the evening and the night of the 14th I again reconnoitered the position, and by observation and by means of patrols it was discovered that the wire was quite intact round the Strong Point at R.16.a.98, therefore I decided that it was not adviseable to attempt a raid at once.

On talking with such N.C.O's as could give information, I am of opinion that during the attack, which was evidently not a surprise, "A" Company lost direction and edged away to the left, crossing SIXTEEN ROAD without knowing it; the left of the Company reached GRANDCOURT TRENCH between R.16.a.68. and 87, which was only occupied by an enemy outpost who ran away on the approach of our troops, and that the Strong Point at R.16.a.98. was only approached by the right of the leading wave who were stopped by the uncut wire, and the majority killed by enemy rifle and machine gun fire.

                                                          Lieut. Col.
Commanding 7th Battalion Royal West Kent Regt;

Field.
17-2-17.

APP: 20.

PATROL REPORTS.

22-2-17. This afternoon about 3-30p.m. LIEUT.LUCAS went out along WEST MIRAUMONT ROAD as far as R.11.a.90.35.(second A in damaged on 1:10,000 ANCRE VALLEY MAP. From this point he could see SOUTH MIRAUMONT TRENCH as far WEST as POINT 48. and North East about as Far as R.5. d. 05.15. This trench was wired, there was also wire across the W.MIRAUMONT ROAD. There was also wire in front of POINT 86 and along the trench running N.E. from that point.

He was unable to distinguish the junction of CREST TRENCH and W. MIRAUMONT ROAD; it appeared to be obliterated. LIEUT.LUCAS saw no signs of movement in the enemy's lines whatsoever except one man, who got out of the trench about R.11. b.20.98. and ran swiftly across the open and jumped into the trench about R.11.b.48. Snipers were firing occassionally from CREST TRENCH but he was unable to locate any.

He then looked back towards our own lines and could see all our men digging, carrying etc, from about R.11.a.90. as far as R.11. c.58. He judged they must have been in full view, and in direct enfilade from CREST TRENCH.

LIEUT.LUCAS returned at 4-30p.m. During the whole time he was out our 18-pounder shrapnel was bursting in rear of him.

I think it would be practicable to establish an observation post at the point where LIEUT.LUCAS was, provided that our artillery can be persuaded not to shell it, but there is practically no cover from view from the left flank.

I am convinced that the BOSCHE is not on the crest at all WEST of the WEST MIRAUMONT ROAD, but I do not recommend that our trench line be advanced further than it is at present, until CREST TRENCH is cleared of the enemy. It is extremely difficult to obtain observation on S.MIRAUMONT TRENCH from the centre or the left of our line for the following reaspns:-

1. There is no cover from view from the right flank, therefore a post so established would be inapproachable by day.
2. There is no marked guiding line made as WEST MIRAUMONT ROAD,to facilitate approach by night (a tape line could be used for this purpose).
3. It would be nesessary to go still further forward than on the WEST MIRAUMONT ROAD to re gain the required observation.

In any case patrols and posts will be pushed forward to such an extent that the ridge will be entirely denied to the enemy.

It is, however, impossible to get patrols and advanced groups to act with the necessary confidence with the present continual danger of being shelled by our own artillery.

23-2-17. At 4-30a.m. two observation and snipers posts were established about R.10.b.65. and R.10.b.75. from which points excellent observation can be had of S. MIRAUMONT TRENCH. Two snipers posts have also been established by the right Company about R.11.a.55. and R.11. a.65. Between 5-0a.m. and 8-0a.m. this morning LIEUT.LEWIN and LIEUT.LUCAS proceeded along WEST MIRAUMONT ROAD as far as R.11. a.77. right up to the wire in front of S. MIRAUMONT TRENCH; they waited there for about half an hour, and saw or heard no signs of the enemy. At R.11. a.86 there are two rows of Chevaux de frise across the road, and signs of a recently occupied post, fresh biscuits and a newspaper etc being found there.

These two Officers then proceed along the trench running N.E. to about R.11.a.90.75. and then they walked along CREST TRENCH to about R.11.a.95.55. but encountered no Germans in either of these trenches. They report wire to the WEST of CREST TRENCH. They then returned to point 92. and brought forward a Lance Corporal and Four men, who are now occupying Point 94.and will creep forward with a Lewis Gun to the wire at R.11.a.86. which will be held as a post day and night, and will be linked up by telephone if sufficient wire is forthcoming. I have given instructions for a Vickers gun to be placed at Point 92. which is at present known as "Z" Post from whence there is an excellent field of fire E.S.E. EAST and N.E.

(Continued over).

APP:.204

PATROL REPORTS (Continued).

    I consider it would be practicable to work down CREST TRENCH from N.W. to S.E. with a bombing party, Strength One Platoon, providing that there is sufficient fog or mist for it to move up the WEST MIRAUMONT ROAD without being seen.
Germans are seen accassionally in CREST TRENCH S.E. of R.11. b.23. from point 92. Corporal Luckman the best shot in the Battalion has claimed to have hit five during the last 36-hours.

Army Form C. 2118.

WAR DIARY
or
INTELLIGENCE SUMMARY.
(Erase heading not required.)

7/ R.W.Kents
March 17
Vol. 19

Instructions regarding War Diaries and Intelligence Summaries are contained in F. S. Regs., Part II. and the Staff Manual respectively. Title pages will be prepared in manuscript.

Place	Date	Hour	Summary of Events and Information	Remarks and references to Appendices
BOOM RAVINE	1-3-17.		Battalion in Reserve	
"	2-3-17.		Moved to E.MIRAUMONT ROAD.Relieved E.SURREYS.Relief completed 9-30 p.m.	
E.MIRAUMONT ROAD.	3-3-17.		Relieved by SUFFOLK REGT.Battalion moved back to WARWICK HUTS.	
WARWICK HUTS.	4-3-17.		Training.	
"	5-3-17.		Training and fatigues.	
"	6-3-17.		Training and fatigues.	
"	7-3-17.		Training and fatigues.	
"	8-3-17.		Training and fatigues.	
"	9-3-17.		Training and fatigues.	
"	10-3-17.		Training and fatigues.	
"	11-3-17.		Training and fatigues.	
"	12-3-17.		Battalion moved to SAINT PIERRE DIVION under canvas.	
St PIERRE DIVION.	13-3-17.		Training and fatigues.	
"	14-3-17.		Training and fatigues.	
"	15-3-17.		Battalion moved to HESSIAN TRENCH under canvas.	
HESSIAN TR:	16-3-17.		Fatigues in MIRAUMONT.	
"	17-3-17.		Fatigues in MIRAUMONT.	
"	18-3-17.		Battalion moves to LOUPART LINE,travelling via IRLES.Battalion in Dugouts.	
LOUPART LINE	19-3-17.		Officers mounted proceeded on reconoitring expedition."A" and "C" Coys to ACHIET-LE-GRAND."B" and "D" Coys in billets in BIHUCOURT. Orders received to move to BIHUCOURT.	
BIHUCOURT.	20-3-17.		Battalion moved back to KITCHENER HUTS,via IRLES.	
KITCHENER HUTS.	21-3-17.		Battalion marched to SENLIS.	
SENLIS.	22-3-17.		Battalion marched to VILLIERS BOCQUAGE.	
VILLIERS BOCQUAGE.	23-3-17.		Battalion moved to PONT NEUF by bus.Marched from there to FERRIERS.	
FERRIERS.	24-3-17.		Battalion at FERRIERS.Church Service.	
"	25-3-17.		Battalion marched to SALLEUX.Departed by rail at 5-20 p.m.	
"	26-3-17.		Detrained at STEENBECQUE. Marched to WITTES.	

Army Form C. 2118.

WAR DIARY
or
INTELLIGENCE SUMMARY.
(*Erase heading not required.*)

Instructions regarding War Diaries and Intelligence Summaries are contained in F. S. Regs., Part II. and the Staff Manual respectively. Title pages will be prepared in manuscript.

Place	Date	Hour	Summary of Events and Information	Remarks and references to Appendices
WITTES.	27-3-17.		Cleaning up etc.	
"	28-3-17.		Training. Route March.	
"	29-3-17.		Training.	
"	30-3-17.		Training. Firing on range.	
"	31-3-17.		Training.	
			OFFICERS JOINING THE BATTALION DURING THE MONTH.	
			LIEUT. L.H.COOPER.	
			2/LIEUT. E.W.DAY.	
			2/LIEUT. R.F.KNIGHT.	
			LIEUT. V.C.SEWELL.	
			2/LIEUT. R.P.MAGNUS.	
			2/LIEUT. W.J.NEWBERRY.	
			2LIEUT. D.E.M.WOODHOUSE.	
			OFFICERS' CASUALTIES DURING MONTH.	
			Captain.C.W.R.Knight. Sick To England.	
			Captain. E.Stopford Holland. " " "	
			Lieut. S.J.Pymm. " " "	
			2/Lieut. G.E.Neves. " " "	
			2/Lieut. F.N.Holt. " " "	
			2/Lieut. D.V.Sutherst. Taken on Establishment of T.M.B.	

Capt.
Captain.
Commanding 7th Battn.Royal West Kent Regiment.

Army Form C. 2118.

WAR DIARY
or
INTELLIGENCE SUMMARY
(Erase heading not required.)

Instructions regarding War Diaries and Intelligence Summaries are contained in F. S. Regs., Part II. and the Staff Manual respectively. Title pages will be prepared in manuscript.

Place	Date	Hour	Summary of Events and Information	Remarks and references to Appendices
WITTES.	1-4-17.		Training. Church Parades etc.	
WITTES.	2-4-17.		Training. Firing practises on Range at AIRE.	
WITTES.	3-4-17.		Training. Firing practises on Range at AIRE.	
WITTES.	4-4-17.		Training. Firing practises on Range at AIRE.	
WITTES.	5-4-17.		Training. Inspection by the Brigadier General. Football. 1st round Divisional Tournament 7th R.W.Kent Regt. 13-goals 7th Queens.1-goal.	
WITTES.	6-4-17.		Training. Firing practises. 2nd round Divisional Football Tournament 7th R.W.Kent Regt Nil. 7th Buffs. 4-goals.	
WITTES.	7-4-17.		Training.	
WITTES.	8-4-17.		Training. Ceremonial Parades etc.	
WITTES.	9-4-17.		Training. 5-Mile Cross Country Race.	
WITTES.	10-4-17.		Training.	
WITTES.	11-4-17.		Training.	
WITTES.	12-4-17.		Training.	
WITTES.	13-4-17.		Training.	
WITTES.	14-4-17.		Training.	
WITTES.	15-4-17.		Training.	
WITTES.	16-4-17.		Training.	
WITTES.	17-4-17.		Training.	
WITTES.	18-4-17.		Training. Orders received to make preparations for move to forward area vacated by the 46th Division. (Under 6-Hours notice to move).	
WITTES.	19-4-17.		Preparations for move.	
WITTES.	20-4-17.		Operation Orders for move received. Left WITTES at 10-10a.m. marching to HAM-EN-ARTOIS. Arrived at HAM-EN-ARTOIS at 12-30p.m.	
HAM-EN-ARTOIS.	21-4-17.		Orders received to march to BETHUNE. Left HAM-EN-ARTOIS at 9-15a.m. arrived BETHUNE at 1-30p.m. Battalion in Old French Barracks. Very Comfortable.	
BETHUNE.	22-4-17.		At BETHUNE. Reconnaisance of the Corps area.	
BETHUNE.	23-4-17.		At BETHUNE. -do-.	
BETHUNE.	24-4-17.		Training.	
BETHUNE.	25-4-17.		Training.	
BETHUNE.	26-4-17.		Training. Preliminary Orders received for move to Line.	
BETHUNE.	27-4-17.		Operation orders received for move to SAINS-LES-PERNES. Left BETHUNE at 9-15a.m. marched to SAINS-LES-PERNES arriving there at 4-45p.m. One hour halt for dinner was made.	

Army Form C. 2118.

WAR DIARY
or
INTELLIGENCE SUMMARY.
(Erase heading not required.)

Instructions regarding War Diaries and Intelligence Summaries are contained in F. S. Regs., Part II. and the Staff Manual respectively. Title pages will be prepared in manuscript.

Place	Date	Hour	Summary of Events and Information	Remarks and references to Appendices
SAINS-LES-PERNES.	28-4-17.		Orders received for move to line near ARRAS. Battalion marched to BRIAS and entrained at 7-30a.m. Transport proceeded by Road arriving at ARRAS at 7-20p.m. Battalion detrained at ARRAS at 4-0p.m. Battalion spent night in Old German trenches.	
	29-4-17.		Battalion moved into front line in front of CHERISY.	
	30-4-17.		Battalion in Reserve.	

OFFICERS JOINED DURING THE MONTH.

Lieut. Col. L.H.Hickson. (To Command Bn.).
2/Lieut. W.E.Arnold.
Captain H.B.Wheeler.
Lieut. I.Heaton.
2/Lieut. A.Godley.
2/Lieut. P.E.Rand.
2/Lieut. C.F.Fryer.
....

CASUALTIES IN OFFICERS DURING THE MONTH.

Lieut. F.L.Lucas.   Sick To England.
Captain T.W.Bell.   "   "   "
Captain. H.B.Wheeler. To Base as Draft Conducting Officer.
Captain.O.C.Johnsen. To 54th Bde (Staff Capt)
....

[signature]
Captain,
Commanding 7th Battalion Royal West Kent Regt;.

WAR DIARY
or
INTELLIGENCE SUMMARY.
(Erase heading not required.)

Army Form C. 2118.

Instructions regarding War Diaries and Intelligence Summaries are contained in F.S. Regs., Part II. and the Staff Manual respectively. Title pages will be prepared in manuscript.

Place	Date	Hour	Summary of Events and Information	Remarks and references to Appendices
TRENCHES.	1-5-17.		Battalion in Reserve. Relieved by the 53rd Brigade (6th Royal Berks). Moved back to Old German Lines.	
"	2-5-17.		Battalion moved into Support.	
"	3-5-17.		Attack on CHERISY vide appendix 21. and 22.	App: 21. 22.
"	4-5-17.		Battalion relieved by the 5th Royal Berkshire Regiment. Relief complete 12-Midnight.	
BEURAINS.	5-5-17.		Battalion proceed to bivouacs in BEURAINS.	
"	6-5-17.		Battalion at BEURAINS reorganising and refitting.	
"	7-5-17.		Training etc.	
"	8-5-17.		Training etc.	
"	9-5-17.		Training etc.	
"	10-5-17.		Training etc.	
"	11-5-17.		Training etc. Battalion Football Team played the 56th Divisional Train, Battalion Team won by 1-goal to Nil.	
"	12-5-17.		Training etc.	
"	13-5-17.		Training etc. Battalion Team played the 55th Brigade Headquarters, Battalion team won by 2-goals to Nil.	
"	14-5-17.		Orders received to move to new area. Battalion Left BEURAINS at 11-30a.m. arrived new camp (at S.17. Central Ref Map. Sheet 51.B. S.W. 1/40.000) at 1-0p.m.	
CAMP.S.16. central.	15-5-17. 16-5-17.		Training. Reconnaisance of new line by Officers.	
"	17-5-17.		Training, Rapid Marching etc. Rugby Match against 7th BUFFS. Battalion Rugby team won by 11-Points to 3-Points.	
"	18-5-17.		Training etc. Battalion Football Team played the 55th Infantry Brigade Headquarters, /Result won 1-Goal 55th Infantry Brigade Headquarters 1-Goal.	
"	19-5-17.		Training. Reconnaisance of the line by Officers. Battalion Rugger Team played the 55th Infantry Brigade Headquarters Rugger Team. Result:- Battalion Team 48-Points. 55th Infantry Brigade 0-Points.	
"	20-5-17.		Training. Preliminary Orders recieved to take over line. Cricket Match between the Battalion and 14th Northumberland Fusiliers. Result:- Draw.	
"	21-5-17.		Battalion took over the line relieving the 8th Suffolks. Relief complete 3-0p.m. "A" and "B" Companies in HINDENBURG LINE, "C" and "D" Companies in Support Trench Nr ROOKERY. No heavy shelling took place while taking over the line. Our artillery shelled heavily at 9-30p.m. Advantage was taken of the wind to send over a quantity of gas shells.	App: 23.

T/134. Wt. W708—776. 500000. 4/15. Sir J. C. & S.

WAR DIARY
or
INTELLIGENCE SUMMARY.
(Erase heading not required.)

Army Form C. 2118.

Instructions regarding War Diaries and Intelligence Summaries are contained in F. S. Regs., Part II. and the Staff Manual respectively. Title pages will be prepared in manuscript.

Place	Date	Hour	Summary of Events and Information	Remarks and references to Appendices
TRENCHES.	22-5-17.		Morning wet. Very quiet. Usual Counter Battery shelling.	
"	23-5-17.		Nothing of importance occured during the day, artillery very quiet.	
"	24-5-17.		Battalion mainly on fatigue duty such as making dug-outs, salving, and trench digging. Battalion still in Support. Working parties are formed, and various fatigues are carried out both by day and night. Last night a party of Germans evidently out on patrol lost their way and reached a part of the line the 7th QUEEN's were holding. One was taken prisoner, and the rest fired on one being wounded the rest apparently escaped untouched.	
"	25-5-17.		Since mid-day the Germans have been extraordinarily quiet scarcely firing a shell, our artillery has been worrying him all day. It is not possible to give the reason for the silence of the Germans. App:24. Very quiet, nothing of importance happened. The Battalion is still on fatigues such as Improving trenches, salving, making dug-outs. During the afternoon the Germans shelled with more regularity to which our artillery is replying.	
"	26-5-17.		This morning the Germans shelled GREY STREET with heavies. A slight red cloud swept across the line today; it took the form of a gas cloud but was at a great height. Sniping and observation, parties sent out. Preliminary orders recieved from Brigade to take over the front line.	
"	27-5-17.		Considerable artillery activity. Battalion took over the front line from the 7th.QUEEN'S. 8th. East Surreys Relief complete at 12-30a.m. Disposition of Companies as follows:- on left Bn. 7th.QUEEN'S on Right. App:25. "D" Company on the left, "A" Company on the right, "B" Company in support, "C" Company in Reserve.	
"	28-5-17.		Bosche shelled Battalion Headquarters from 4-30a.m. to 5-30a.m. very heavily.	
"	29-5-17.		Nothing of importance happened during the day. Bosche shelled rather heavily during the morning. Last night the Germans left their trenches and made their way to ours; they were soon "spotted" and our troops succeeded in dropping a Stokes Trench Mortar Bomb amongst them which stopped them from coming further. A few were seen crawling back to their lines wounded this morning.	
"	30-5-17.		Last night the enemy made a raid on No.4. Post. He was driven back, a Lewis Gun on the Post doing good work. The enemy again attacked and endeavoured to encircle the post, but failed. Afterwards our men retaliated by raiding the German line. This was not successful, we had a few casualties including one Officer. A few Germans were killed and a wounded prisoner taken. Reliefs have taken place between Companies and the dispositions are now as follows:- "D" Company on the right, "B" Company on the left, "C" Company in Support, and "A" Company in reserve.	

Army Form C. 2118.

WAR DIARY
or
INTELLIGENCE SUMMARY.
(Erase heading not required.)

Instructions regarding War Diaries and Intelligence Summaries are contained in F. S. Regs., Part II. and the Staff Manual respectively. Title pages will be prepared in manuscript.

Place	Date	Hour	Summary of Events and Information	Remarks and references to Appendices
TRENCHES.	31-5-17.		Battalion on fatigue cleaning and deepening trenches. Tonight Preparations are being made for an attack by "C" Company/tomorrow on a German Post. Zero 10-45 P.m. The enemy is sending over some gas shells.	App:26. App:27. App:28.
			HONOURS AND AWARDS.	
			The undermentioned Officers awarded the M.C:-	
			LIEUT. A.V. McDONALD. 2/LIEUT. D.V. SUTHERST. (attd T.M.B).	
			....	
			CASUALTIES IN OFFICERS DURING THE MONTH.	
			Lieut. Col. L.H.Hickson. Wounded.	
			Captain. F.R.Latter. Wounded and Missing.	
			Captain. H.Warren. Wounded.	
			2/Lieut. C.H.Grist. Killed.	
			2/Lieut. R.P.Magnus. Wounded.	
			2/Lieut. G.H.Kinder. Wounded.	
			2/Lieut. L.V.Barnes. Wounded.	
			2/Lieut. C.M.Francis. Shell Shock.	
			2/Lieut. D.E.M.Woodhouse. Wounded at Duty.	
			2/Lieut. F.H.F.Smith. " "	
			2/Lieut. T.P.Jones. Wounded.	
			....	
			OFFICERS JOINED DURING THE MONTH.	
			2/Lieut. C.W.A.Duffield. 2/Lieut. G.E.Neves.	
			....	
			LOCAL PROMOTIONS.	
			CAPTN. P.N.ANSTRUTHER.D.S.O.M.C. promoted Lieut. Col. pending confirmation by superior authority. (Whilst in Command) 19-5-17 CAPTAIN. T.T.WADDINGTON.M.C. promoted A/Major. pending confirmation by superior authority (Whilst second in Command) 19-5-17. The undermentioned promoted A/CAPTAINS whilst Commanding a Company 19-5-17;2/LIEUT. D.E.M.WOODHOUSE. 2/LIEUT. R.S.HEBBLETHWAITE.	

[signature] Lieut. Colonel.
Commanding 7th Battalion Royal West Kent Regiment.

APP: 21.

On the 3rd May 1917 the 55th Brigade were detailed to attack and capture BLUE LINE (first objective) and RED LINE (final objective), with the 41st. Brigade on its left and the 54th Brigade on its right.

  Assaulting Battalions :-

    7th Buffs   - Right.
    8th East Surrey Regt - Left.
    7th Royal West Kent Rgt-Support Battalion
    7th Queens - Brigade Reserve.

The 7th Royal West Kent Regt., was detailed to find one Company as Moppers up,(one platoon to Buffs, three platoons to East Surrey Regt.); this duty was allotted to "D" Company, Capt.F.R.LATTER; two Companies in close support,("A" Company, Capt.L.WARREN, - "B" Company, 2/Lieut. A.V.McDONALD), and one Company for carrying forward from Advanced Brigade Dump,("C" Company, Lieut. I.HEATON).

  Hour of Zero - 3.45 a.m.

At Zero minus 2 hours, the Battalion was disposed of as under :-

  "D" Company with assaulting Battalions as detailed.
  "A" Company at the Quarries near N.30.b.92.
  "B" Company in old German support trench in N.30.b.
  "C" Company at Adv. Brigade Dump at O.25.c.Central
  Battalion Head Quarters at the Quarries,about N.30.b.73.

Captain P.N.ANSTRUTHER.D.SO.,M.C., was detailed to act as liaison Officer at Advanced Brigade Report Centre at O.25.d.74.

At Zero minus 45 minutes, "A" Company moved forward to a position in rear of our support trench.

At Zero the attack commenced.

"A" Company occupied our forming up trenches as soon as they were vacated by assaulting Battalions.

At Zero plus 45 minutes, two platoons "B" Company moved up to original British front line, and at Zero plus 2 hours, i.e., 5.45 a.m. Battalion Head Quarters and "B" Company less two platoons moved up to original British support line; Head Quarters were subsequently established in old British front line. At this time reports from assaulting Battalions shewed that the BLUE LINE had been reached, but that the position on the right was obscure.

At 7.30 a.m., a message timed 7.6 a.m. and signed by Captain P.N.ANSTRUTHER was received through Advanced Brigade Report Centre that the East Surrey Regt., required support, and that "A" and "B" Companies were to be sent up to be placed at the disposal of Colonel IRWIN, 8th East Surrey Regiment. 2/Lieut. F.H.F.SMITH with two platoons "A" Company was sent up, and moving by NORTH end of CHERISY, arrived at BLUE LINE and extended the line to the left, being mixed up with elements of the 41st. Brigade. "D" Company had by this time been concentrated under the command of 8th East Surrey Regiment, and was put in on the left flank, this flank being considered at the time the dangerous flank.

About 7.30 a.m. this Company was ordered by Col. IRWIN to move across to the right flank, where the enemy were seen to be massing, which operation was most gallantly executed by Captain LATTER and his Company; Captain LATTER was wounded about this period, but remained in command of his Company.

Shortly after this the remaining two platoons of "A" Company and two platoons of "B" Company were moved up to CABLE TRENCH in order to be in closer support to the assaulting Battalions.

About 8.30 a.m. the Battalion was disposed of as under :-

```
"D" Company-------------------------------------BLUE LINE.
Two Platoons "A" Company------------------------BLUE LINE (in touch
                                                with elements of
                                                41st. Brigade.)
"A" Company, less 2 platoons--------------------CABLE TRENCH.
Two Platoons "B" Company------------------------CABLE TRENCH.
"B" Company, less 2 platoons--------------------BRITISH FRONT LINE.
"C" Company-------------------------------------Carrying.
```

At this time indefinite reports from the front tended to shew that a German counter attack was developing; the enemy's barrage was very heavy on our front and support line, and the attack of the 54th Brigade appeared not/to have succeeded, as enfilade Machine Gun fire from the right was playing on all troops moving about on the crest and the CHERISY slope.

Shortly after 9.0 a.m.,(as far as can be gathered), the enemy

APP: 22

The 7th Battalion Royal West Kent Regiment at Zero Hour was disposed as follows:-

"D" one Coy. Moppers Up.
"C" one Coy. Carriers.
"A" and "B" Supporting Coys.

"A" Company was extended in the open behind the British Support Trench and just after Zero Hour moved into the support trench.
Communication with this Company was lost until about 8-30a.m. when 2-Platoons were found in British Front Line. The other 2-Platoons with Company Headquarters had gone forward to CABLE TRENCH.
"B" Company was in the old German Support Line behind the QUARRIES. At Zero plus 45-minutes COL.HICKSON gave the order for this Company to move up. They had just started when I got on to him on the telephone and told him that the BRIGADIER'S orders were to stand by. 2-Platoons, however, had gone up to the British Support line and Battn Headquarters with 2-Platoons of "B" Company was all that COL.HICKSON had in hand henceforwards.
About 6-0a.m. when the order came to move up in support COL.HICKSON advanced with Headquarters and 2-Platoons of "B" Company.
He intercepted a runner of the 54th Brigade who gave him a verbal message that the Germans were Counter Attacking on the right.
In consequence of this he moved up behind 54th Brigade and sent a message back to "QUEEN'S" to that effect.
I went forward to reconnoitre the situation and found the ROYAL FUSILIERS and 12th MIDDLESEX occupying their front line. I returned to COL.HICKSON and reported to him whereupon he moved into the British front line.
He sent forward patrols to attempt to glean news of the situation, but they discovered little. He then met COL.RANSOM who told us that his Reserve Company was in CABLE TRENCH with a bomb stop on the right, the 54th Brigade not having advanced.
At 7-30a.m. a message from Brigade via CAPTAIN.ANSTRUTHER ordering "A" and "B" Companies to move up to support COL.IRWIN was shewn to COL.HICKSON. He ordered LIEUT.McDONALD with "B" Coy, all of which was then in front line, to wait further orders; and sent forward 2/LIEUT.SMITH with all of "A" Company that was available, viz:-
2-Platoons.
COL.HICKSON then went to Brigade forward Report Centre to try to get on the telephone to Brigade but the line was broken.
At about 8-45a.m. he received a message from Brigade telling him that COL.IRWIN with the 8th EAST SURREYS was at ST MICHAELS MONUMENT and that the Royal West Kent Regt were to go to his assistance taking Lewis Gun Drums, Water, and S.A.A.
A message was sent to the Dump to send forward the required stores to the left of our front line.
Immediately afterwards another message was received from Brigade ordering the Royal West Kent Regt to go to the right flank of the BUFFS.
As the order had been given to move to the left, and stores had been sent for COL.HICKSON decided to continue with the first order, and moving along the front line sat down to wait for the stores.
Before they arrived the EAST SURREYS came back and everyone remained in the British front line.

flanking movement began to cause our advanced troops to fall back.   As soon as it was clear that this was the case, Colonel L.H.HICKSON gave orders that the positions occupied by "A" and "B" Companies were to be manned and held on to, and a message was sent back for "C" Company to carry up Bombs and S.A.A. at once, and to bring their arms and equipment with them when they came.

According to the report of 2/Lieut. F.H.F.SMITH and of the senior N.C.O. left of "D" Company, the enemy succeeded in working round both the left and right flanks of our position on the BLUE LINE.

Orders were received from Col. IRWIN to fall back to a position on the slope WEST of CHERISY.   Several successive attempts to hold the enemy were made by "D" Company, who suffered heavily, Captain LATTER being wounded (it is feared, mortally) for the second time.   2/Lieut.F.H.F.SMITH rallied at the sunken road WEST of CHERISY, where a short stand was made. A considerable number of men belonging to the Brigades on our right and left converged on to the 55th Brigade frontage, and having no leaders and organisation, tended rather to add to the confusion, than to increase the prospects of being able to hold the enemy. A stand was made by units of the 55th Brigade in CABLE TRENCH, but a great number of men of all Units passed over this trench and went straight back to our original front line .

Captain H.WARREN with "A" Company less two platoons, and Lieut.V.C.SEWELL with two platoons "B" Company did not leave this trench until they were outflanked on either side by the enemy, to whom about this time considerable loss was occasioned by fire of Lewis Guns and some rapid fire, particularly on our left .   These units then withdrew to the original British front line; coming over the crest from CABLE TRENCH ~~to our front line,~~ they were fired on by some of our men in the front line, who mistook them for the enemy; but this was fortunately stopped by the Officers present when it was realised they were not the enemy.

Captain WARREN was wounded as he left CABLE TRENCH. By about 11.0 to 11.30 a.m. everyone was back in our original front line. The Germans made no attempt to advance further than CABLE TRENCH. "C" Company had in the meanwhile come up with S.A.A., bombs and water, and was retained to help garrison the line.

During the retirement, particularly when our original positions had been reached, and the disorganisation of units was very considerable the action of all Officers and of some N.C.O's (especially Lewis Gunners in rallying, encouraging and leading forward their men again, was most praiseworthy.

As soon as the probability of any further advance by the enemy became unlikely, the work of reorganisation of units was taken in hand.

Lieut. Col. HICKSON was wounded about mid-day by shrapnel, and Captain. P.N.ANSTRUTHER took over the command of the Battalion, leaving 2/Lieut. D.E.M.WOODHOUSE at Advanced Brigade Report Centre, he being also slightly wounded. After the completion of the work of reorganisation I established my Head-quarters on the left of the front line near O.26.b.93.

At 6.16 p.m., a message was received from Brigade Head Quarters that the 7th Queens would re-counter attack at 6.15, and that when they formed up in the front line, we were to move back to the support line. Zero hour was subsequently altered to 7.15 p.m., and by that time all four Companies were back in the support line.

As there were no definite orders as to the role of other Battalions I ordered "B" and "C" Companies to move up and occupy the front line as soon as the 7th Queens were clear of it. This was done. The attack did not succeed, and by about 8.30 p.m., they were back in our own lines again. At 11.0 p.m. the situation was reported to Brigade Head Quarters in my Q.O.C.187, copy as below :-

"Dispositions of the Unit under my command are as follows aaa Two Coys about 60 and 70 strong each in the front line, with East Surreys on their right, and two and a half platoons 7th Queens on their left aaa The left of these last is in direct touch with R.B.aaa One Company in Support Trench, and remains of "D" Coy (about 15 strong) in the same trench, both on left of E.Surreys aaa I have placed two Lewis Guns and three standing patrols from 80x to 100x in front of the line aaa My headquarters are at O.26.a.12. "

The 4th of May passed without any event of importance. According to arrangements made by Lt. Col.WATSON, Commanding 7th Queens, "C" and "D" Companies withdrew from the line after dark, and "B" and "A" Companies were lent temporarily to 8th East Surrey Regt., for purposes of the relief. Two Companies 6th Royal Berkshire Regt. relieved these two Companies, and the Battalion marched back to bivouacs near BEAURAINS, arriving at 2.30 a.m.

CASUALTIES :-

Killed - 2/Lieut. C.H.GRIST.
         2/Lieut. R.P.MAGNUS.

Other Ranks-------------------22.

Wounded - Lieut.Col.L.H.HICKSON.
          Capt. H. WARREN.
          2/Lieut. G.H.KINDER.
          2/Lieut. L.V.BARNES.

Other Ranks-------------------73.

Wounded)
& Missing) Capt. F.R.LATTER.

Other Ranks-------------------4.

Missing. Other Ranks-------------------46.

Shell Shock 2/Lieut. C.M.FRANCIS.

Other Ranks-------------------1.

Wounded,
(At Duty.) 2/Lieut. D.E.M.WOODHOUSE.
           2/Lieut. F.H.F.SMITH.

Other Ranks-------------------15.

---------------oOo---------------

Field.
7 May 1917.

Captain
Commanding 7th Battalion Royal West Kent Regt.

App 23

7th Battalion Royal West Kent Regiment.

ORDER No.57.

Ref. Map.Sheet 51.b.S.W.   21 May 1917.

The Battalion will relieve the 8th. Suffolks in the line to-day.

HOUR OF START :- 1.30 p.m.

ORDER OF MARCH :-   "D" Company.
                           "C"   "
                           Drums.
                           Headquarters.
                           "A" Company.
                           "B"   "

Stretcher Bearers will be with their Companies.

ROUTE :- Headquarters and two Companies via HINDENBURG LINE; two Companies via SUSSEX AVENUE.

GUIDES :- Guides for relieving Battalion will be at Starting Point, N.34.a.76 at 3.0 p.m.   From there, Platoons will move at 5 minutes interval.

DRESS :- Light fighting order, waterproof sheet folded under the flap of the haversack.

RUNNERS :- Two Battalion runners will be attached to "C" and "D" Coys., and will report at 1.15 p.m.

COMPLETION OF RELIEFS:- Completion of Company reliefs will be reported to Battalion Headquarters.

STORES AND WORK :- Lists of Stores and Work in hand will be taken over, and duplicate copies sent to Battalion Headquarters.

TACTICAL :- The Battalion is in support to the 7th Queens on the left and the 8th Buffs on the right.
"C" and "D" Coys are supporting Left Battalion
"A" and "B" Coys are supporting Right Battalion.
O.C."C" Coy., is the Senior Officer in charge of left support, and will report in person to O.C. Queens on completion of the relief.

BOX RESPIRATORS :- During the Relief Box Respirators will be worn at the "ALERT" position.

MOVEMENT :- No movement to take place outside communication trenches before 9.30 p.m.

(Signed:-)   H. E. SHATTOCK. Lieut.
A/Adjutant.

Ref. Map. (Trench). and
Aeroplane Photographs.

7th Royal West Kent Regiment Order No.59.

31st May 1917.

1. "C" Company will attack and Capture the two posts held by the enemy at O.31.b.9.1. and O.31.b.8.3. Two Platoons will attack the first mentioned, starting from LARK SAP, and building up an assaulting line in the clover patch, extending from about O.31. d. 85. 95. to O.31. d. 75. 98.
One Platoon will attack the last mentioned from STORK TRENCH, with its left on WREN LANE, and on a frontage of 80x.

2. The objectives have been treated by Artillery fire during the day. From ZERO minus 30-minutes 18-Pounders will fire on the objectives, and from ZERO plus 1-minute all artillery fire will lift from FONTAINE TRENCH, on which a steady rate of fire will be maintained.

3. The attack will be prepared by fire from 2-Stokes Mortars, four Vickers Guns and two Lewis Guns.
The Stokes Mortars will bombard the left objective intermittently from 7-0p.m. to 10-0p.m. At 10-45p.m. these guns will open with an increased rate of fire which will cease at 10-55p.m.
2-Vickers Guns firing from STORK TRENCH about O.3. b.2.2. will engage the right objective from ZERO minus 5. to ZERO plus 2, and from ZERO plus 2. to ZERO plus 11. these guns will switch on to the left objective.
2-Vickers Guns firing from STORK TRENCH near its junction with WREN LANE will engage the left objective from ZERO to ZERO plus 10, and will subsequently switch on to CABLE TRENCH, in the direction of CHERISY, and will engage any hostile Machine Guns which may be firing from this direction.
2-Lewis Guns of "A" Company will take up a position about O.31.d.60.50. and will engage the right objective in enfilade from ZERO minus 5. to ZERO plus 10.

4. The two platoons detailed for the right objective will leave our present front line at ZERO, forming two waves at 50x distance.
The platoon detailed for the left objective will be lent one rifle section by "D" Company, and will advance in two waves at 50x distance; this platoon will leave our front line at ZERO plus 10. Further details of regarding method of advance have been communicated verbally to all concerned.

5. Immediately the objective has been gained, Patrols will be pushed forward to the front and flanks to guard against surprise. Two Sections 7th QUEEN'S, who's assembly positions have already been notified, under an R.E. Officer and two R.E.N.C.O's will be sent forward to each of the objectives with wiring materials to wire in front of the objectives.
Covering parties will be provided for these by troops actually in the objectives.
2/LIEUT. AUZIER and 2/LIEUT. HARLEY are the two R.E.Officers detailed for the right and left objectives respectively.
The above parties 7th QUEEN'S will arrive at right and left front Company Headquarters at 9-0p.m; they will be shewn there wiring material dumps and put under cover until required.
At 12-Midnight, two platoons 7th QUEEN'S, with tools, will be at the head of WREN SAP, where they will meet 2/LIEUT. HARLEY, who will allot them the task of continuing WREN SAP forward as far as the left objective.
A covering party will be provided for them by O.C."D" Company.

6. The Signalling Officer will arrange to run out a wire to the right objective when gained.

7. Guides will be provided by Officer's Commanding "D" and "B" Companies, from amongst N.C.O's and men who have been out on patrol before, to take "C" Company out, and to see that assaulting parties get within view of their objectives.

X.
(Continued over).

Continued.

8. O.C."C" Company will arrange to have dumps made at the head of LARK and WREN LANES, consisting of the following articles:-
   - S.A.A.
   - Bombs.
   - L.G.Magazines.
   - Rations and Water.
   - Tools.
   - Very Lights.
   - Mess Tins.

   These will be carried forward by parties detailed by O.C."B" Company for right objective, and O.C."D" Company for left objective..

9. The L.G. of No.11. Platoon of "C" Company will be sent out to the left objective as soon as it has been gained.
   A Vickers Gun will be sent up to the right objective by O.C."C" Company as soon as he is assured that the situation is clear.
   The two Lewis Guns of "A" Company detailed in last part pf para 3, will face half right, i.e. Eastwards after ZERO plus 10, and will form a defensive right flank, remaining out until dawn.
   A tape will be run out by the supports of the right assaulting platoons

10. Watches will synchronised at 7-45p.m. and again at 10-0p.m.

11. Password "DAVY JONES".

12. Hour of ZERO is 10-45p.m.

    Issued at 6-30p.m.

    Copies to:-
    C.O.
    Diary.
    "A" Coy.
    "B" Co.
    "C" Co.
    "D" Co.
    O.C.Section M.G.Corps.
    O.C.Section. T.M.B.
    O.C.92nd Field Co. R.E.
    O.C. - Coy. 7th Queen's.
    55th Infantry Brigade Headquarters.

APP 24   Copy No. __

7th R.W.Kent Order No. 57.

Ref: Map Sheet.
CHERISY & ETERPIGNY.   May 31st, '17.

1. There are strong indications that the enemy is about to withdraw to the Switch System running S.E. from VIS-EN-ARTOIS.

To deal with such a withdrawal objectives & frontages have been allotted to Battns. of the Brigade & have been fully explained to O.S. C. Coys. & all concerned.

The disposition of the Brigade will be one of two alternatives:—

(a) 7th Queens on the left.
    7th Buffs   "   " right.
    7th R.W.Kents in Support.
    8th E. Surreys " Reserve.

(b) 7th R.W.Kents on the left.
    8th E. Surreys " " right.
    7th Queens in Support.
    7th Buffs " Reserve.

The disposition of the Batt. under 1(a) will be "A" & "B" Coys. on the right & "C" & "D" Coys. on the left, with Batt. Hd. Qrs. in the HINDENBURG SUPPORT at N.36.c.51.

The disposition of the Batt. under 1(b) will be "A" Coy. right front Coy., "B" Coy. right Support Coy, "D" Coy. left front Coy., & "C" Coy. left Support Coy.

3. Active patrolling will be carried out by leading Coys. of front Battalions with a view to discovering at once any withdrawal on the part of the enemy. Immediately any signs of a withdrawal are suspected close touch will be maintained with the enemy by strong fighting patrols, backed up by supports, boldly handled. Any such advance will take the form of the two front Coys. acting as two separate Van Guards moving on parallel lines, the two Support Coys. forming two Main Guards.

Advanced fighting patrols should number not less than eight. These patrols will make every effort to again send back all information, both of the enemy & also of our own troops on the right & left. Commanders of these patrols will demand reinforcements when they require them in order to deal quickly & effectively with situations which may arise.

4. If the enemy front system, i.e. FONTAINE TRENCH & YORK TRENCH, is found to be evacuated, orders will be issued from Batt. Hd. Qrs. for the occupation of this line.

The distribution of the Batt. would then be as follows:-

Under I(a):- "A" Coy. POG LANE.
"B" " BROWN TRENCH.
"D" " Trench joining
  sapheads in front of
  CURTAIN TRENCH.
"C" Coy. CURTAIN TRENCH.
Batt. H.Q. AVENUE TRENCH, about N.36.d.8.7. (H.Q. of left Coy. of right Battn.)

Under I(b):-
"A" Coy. patrolling as far as

first objective from U.2.c.30.80. to O.32.d.70.80.

"B" Coy. in support to "A" in FONTAINE TRENCH from its junction with WOOD TRENCH inclusive to O.32.c.60.75.

"D" Coy. patrolling through CHERISY VILLAGE to first objective from O.32.d.70.80. to the left boundary of the Brigade.

"C" Coy. in support to "D" in FONTAINE TRENCH from O.32.c.60.75. to the left of the Brigade.

BATT. H.Q. in the dugout reported in Sunken Road about O.32.a.4.7.

Upon orders being issued to occupy 1st, 2nd or 3rd Objectives, companies will act in the same manner as above, under 1(b), each successive objective being consolidated & made secure. Dividing line between Coys. on the 2nd Objective being about O.33.b.0.30., & on the 3rd Objective ORIENT LANE inclusive to the right Coy.

5. Under 1(a), orders to move from positions detailed in first part of para. 4, will be issued from Batt. H.Q.,

but this will not absolve O. C.
& sing Coys. from the responsibility
of keeping themselves well informed
of the movement of troops in front
of them & on their flanks.

6. The 14th Division will be operating
on the left of the 55th Brigade &
the importance of keeping continual
touch with the troops & of reporting
their movements from time to time
cannot be too strongly impressed
upon all ranks.

7. During the advance visual communication will be established
between Coys. & Batt. H. Q.

8. Nothing definite can be laid
down regarding the action of
Lewis Guns with leading Coys.
during the advance. It is suggested
that a Lewis Gun should be at
the head of a Van Guard immediately in rear of the patrols.

9. All ranks are to be warned
against falling victims to German

ruses & traps during the advance. The reports which have been circulated from time to time regarding the advance in February & March should give a sufficient idea of what is to be expected during an operation of this nature.

10. Issued at 5.45 pm 22-5-17

Copies to:
1   A Coy
2   B —
3   C —
4   D —
5   } Bde
6
7   R.E.?
8   ...
9   ...
10 ...

7TH ROYAL WEST KENT ORDER No 55

SECRET. **App: 25.** COPY No **9**

1. The Bn will relieve the 7th QUEENS in the front line this evening.
2. Dispositions will be as follows:—
   "D" Coy on the LEFT (relieving A Coy of QUEENS)
   A Coy — RIGHT (— — D Coy — —)
   B Coy in SUPPORT (— — B Coy — —)
   C Coy in RESERVE (— — C Coy — —)
3. Companies will commence moving at the following times & by the ROUTES detailed.
   "D" Coy at 9 p.m. via PELICAN & CURTAIN Tr. Guides will meet platoons where PELICAN LANE becomes a trench at 9.15 p.m.
   "A" Coy at 9.30 p.m. via VALLEY-TRACK in N.35 b & N.36 a — AVENUE Tr. Guides will be just beyond Junct. of AVENUE Tr & BROWN Tr at 10.15 p.m.
   "B" Coy at 10 p.m. route as for "A" Coy to dugouts in PELICAN LANE.
   "C" Co. by daylight to CUCKOO TR. at times to be arranged by O.C. Coys. concerned.
4. Guides will be as above.
5. Preparatory to relief each Co. will send an advance party consisting of 1 Officer, C.S.M., 1 N.C.O. per platoon & at least 1 runner per Co. to take over & they to be in their Co. sector by daylight.

over & they will be in their Coy. Sectors by)

6. For the purpose of relief y the QUEENS will take over from y the BUFFS the posts in Rotten Row & those in town will be taken over by O.C. "A" Co.

7. Completion of relief will be reported to BATT. H.Q. by the code word "CARROTS"

8. During the relief Box Respirators will be worn at the "Alert"

9. BATT. H.Q. will move to the ROOKERY at 10.30 p.m.

Ref. Trench maps issued.   Copy No 2

APP. 27.

7th R.W. Kent Order No 60.

1. The posts at present held by the Enemy at O.31.d.90.35. and O.31.d.8.8. known at present to the Battalion as Nos. 1 and 3 respectively, will be occupied by strong fighting patrols tonight. These tasks are allotted as under :–
   No 1 to "D" Coy (Two sections)
   No 3 to "B" Coy (One platoon).

2. Details regarding the strength & formation of these patrols have already been issued verbally to O's C. Coys concerned.

3.(a) The advance of D Coys patrol will be preceeded by a Stokes Mortar bombardment, the hour of commencement of which will depend on the report of the reconnoitring patrol, probably 11.30 p.m.

(b) The advance of B Coys patrol will be preceeded and covered by a Machine Gun and Lewis Gun barrage as detailed below:—

10.30 P.M to 10.45 P.M. 2 M.Gs and 2 L.Gs of 'A' Coy will engage the objective from STORK TRENCH.

10.45 P.M to 11.5 P.M. a Lewis Gun of B. Coy will engage the objective with enfilade fire from a point about O.31.d.65.50. to which it will be guided by the Corporal who took out 'A' Coys patrol last night.

This gun will take out a tape with it, and will remain in position until the objective is captured, keeping a special look-out for parties of the enemy who may be retiring or reinforcing from FONTAINE TRENCH.

NOTE. Nos 3 and 2 posts have been bombarded by our 4.5" howitzers this afternoon.

4. When the objectives have been captured they will at once be consolidated. Lewis Guns will be pushed forward into them, and O.C. Coy concerned will send up stores and material to them in the following order:— Bombs, S.A.A., Tools, Very lights, wiring material, water and rations.

a line will be run out to No 3 Post from LARK LANE.

2/Lt LEWIS (OC. platoon in WOOD TRENCH) will obtain touch with our troops in NO 3 POST when gained, by means of patrols.

5. 2/Lt KNIGHT (Batt. Intelligence Officer) will be attached to OC "B" Coy for liaison purposes and will remain with him until the situation is clear.

6. A tape will be run out to NO 3 Post in rear of the Supports.

7. Watches will be synchronised at 9PM.

8. All ranks taking part in the operations will be reminded that success depends upon their guile when approaching the objectives, and upon their dash and determination when in touch with the enemy.

Live Germans are not necessarily required for identification purposes.

The objectives once gained will be held onto at all costs, and

reinforcements demanded for their purpose
if required.

9 Issued by runner at 8 PM

      Copy No 1 — C.O
      —   2 — Diary
      —   3 — File
      —   4 — 'A' Coy
      —   5 — 'B' —
      —   6 — 'C' —
      —   7 — 'D' —
      —   8 — 2/Lt Lewis
      —   9 — Bde H.Q.
      —   10 — M.G.O.
      —   11 — N.C.O. i/c Stokes Gun.

App 28.

Operations against enemy posts in
O.31.b.

C Company, consisting of three platoons
only, under 2nd Lt H.T. GREGORY was
detailed to attack and capture the
objectives, and orders were consequently
issued at 6.30 PM (vide O.O. No 67
attached). The scheme had been
previously thoroughly explained verbally
to all concerned, and a conference
of officers taking part in the operation
was held after the issue of orders.

During the day, the objectives
had been subjected to a thorough
artillery preparation, and excellent
results were observed.

The preparation by the trench
mortars had been thoroughly started
according to programme, and at
ZERO (10.45 PM)

At 9.26 PM the Brigade Major brought
in person some information received
from 17th Balloon Section, to the
effect that a trench had been
dug joining up the right objective
with FONTAINE TRENCH, running
approximately through O.31.d.90.05

to O.32.a.80.10. It was therefore decided to attach one Platoon of 'A' Coy, which had been withdrawn from this line the previous night, to the two right platoons of 'C' Coy. Orders were issued for this platoon to move to the objective in rear of those of 'C' Coy, and, when the assault took place, to extend the line to the right and form a stop along the new reported trench towards FONTAINE TRENCH. This platoon only got into position just before Zero, actually at 10.55 A.M., and orders to it had to be given somewhat hastily.

The preparation by Machine guns, Lewis guns and Stokes Mortars opened according to programme.

At Zero the right party commenced moving forward from our front line. This party was under the command of 2nd Lt WOODYATT. The advance of this party was led by guides from men of 'A' Coy, who had been out on patrol on two previous occasions. The formation

2.

adopted was three lines of parallel columns in file as far as the clover patch; on arrival there and successive wave was to form a line in extended order on a frontage of 150x. This manoeuvre was carried out by the first and second waves, but the platoon of 'A' Coy. owing to the hurried orders had lost direction slightly, and a chance shell had caused them eight casualties.

2nd Lt. WOODYATT thereupon held a conference of his N.C.Os. in the clover patch & made arrangements to put matters straight. 2nd Lt. GREGORY who was in LARK SAP also noticed that a hitch had occurred somewhere, so he sent a sergeant out to ascertain the reason, and the reorganisation was soon effected.

The signal for the assault was one blast on the whistle, to be followed by one round fired by each man of the leading wave, and then charge. As they charged a dozen Germans jumped up and took to their heels. They were fired

at and chased, but it is not
known how many escaped.
This was about 11.45 PM.

In the meantime, the left platoon
of "C" Coy plus one section "D" Coy
left our front line at ZERO + 10,
and advanced in two waves
straight to its objective, which it
reached without opposition; one
German fled on their approach.

This party was fired at by
our own riflemen in CASINO
TRENCH, half left from them, but
sustained no casualties. The objective was gained about 11.15 PM.

The enemy put down a heavy
barrage on the whole of our front
line system, particularly on
CURTAIN TRENCH & WOOD TRENCH, at 11.15 PM, in
answer to Golden Rain Rockets
sent up from FONTAINE TRENCH.

I am rather of opinion that
the alarm was given by the
fact that the right party cheered
when they assaulted.

As soon as each objective had
been gained, wiring parties of the

7th Queens

under R.E. supervision were sent forward, and communication wiring covered by patrols pushed forward to the front and flanks.

Two platoons 7th Queens commenced joining up the left objective with WREN SAP about 4.30 PM, and dug a continuous trench averaging about 2'6" deep.

The Lewis gun of 11 platoon was sent forward into the left objective & the attached section of 'D' Coy withdrawn.

A line was run out to the right objective, and a Vickers gun sent up. The report from the Kite Balloon Section proved to be false, therefore the platoon of 'A' Coy & two sections of 'D' Coy were sent back.

Patrols from the two Companies holding the original front line moved backwards and forwards most of the night creeping forward as directed in para 8 of attached orders. These patrols passed several times through

6.

the enemy barrage, but suffered no casualties. Serjeant P.C.105 + men displayed great courage while engaged on this duty.

Lateral communication by means of patrols was established all along the new advanced line as far as WOOD TRENCH in a comparatively short time.

At 1.30 PM 2nd LT GREGORY visited his posts and found all correct.

At 4 AM I visited MAJOR WEBBERTON, who throughout the operation had been at advance Battalion report centre. and 2nd LT GREGORY, and self of and myself think the dispositions made were in accordance with requirements.

2nd LT NEVES, who took over the left objective reported after daylight that there were some twenty dead Germans in front of his position, but that he could not get them in until nightfall.

7.

The objectives were not so strongly held as they have been on previous nights. I am of opinion that the artillery, Stokes mortar and we own Machine gun fire prevented the night garrisons from getting up from FONTAINE TRENCH.

The German trench mortar which often fired on our left company was kept quiet by a Stokes mortar of ours, and also by one cooperating on the right of the 14th Division.

The behaviour of all ranks was all that could be desired, and the work of patrols and their leaders was particularly good.

We suffered twelve casualties, all from shell-fire.

R.H. Anstruther Lieut Col.
Commdg 7th Rl. Irish Regt.

1 - VI - 17

ANNEX TO Operation Order No.60.
─────────────────────────────────

1. It has now been reported ~~that~~ by the Kite Ballon Section that the right objective has been extended as shewn on attached map.

2. O.C. "A" Company will therefore detail one platoon to go over in close support to the two right platoons of "C" Company. This Platoon will conform to the orders issued to the two right platoons of "C" Company, and will move 30x in rear of the 2nd wave. At the moment of assault this platoon will ease off to the right in order to conform to the new line of trench shewn, and will establish a block in the direction of FONTAINE TRENCH. This platoon will carry bombs, and rifle grenades (as many as available).

3. This added information increases the importance of the enterprise, since if the enemy is allowed to dig further the post wouldpossibly not be captured without a larger operation.

....

Army Form C. 2118.

WAR DIARY
or
INTELLIGENCE SUMMARY.
(Erase heading not required.)

7 R W Kent Regt June 17

Instructions regarding War Diaries and Intelligence Summaries are contained in F. S. Regs., Part II. and the Staff Manual respectively. Title pages will be prepared in manuscript.

Place	Date	Hour	Summary of Events and Information	Remarks and references to Appendices
Trenches.	1-6-17.		Battalion in front line. The day has been very quiet.	
"	2-6-17.		Morning fairly quiet. Enemy snipers very active. Battalion relieved by 6th Northamptonshire Regiment. During relief the enemy made a raid on our Advanced Post. Relief complete 5-45a.m. 3rd instant.	App:29. App:30.
Camp.	3-6-17.		In Camp at S.17. Central. Ref: Map.Sheet.51.B.S.W. Cleaning up etc. refitting.	
"	4-6-17.		Training,Range Practices etc.	
"	5-6-17.		Training. Football match. Regimental Team v 7th Queen's. Result:- Regtl.Team 1-goal.7thQueen's 1-Goal.	
"	6-6-17.		Training. Range Practices etc. Football match. Officers v Sergts. Result:- Officers 2-goals Sgts.1-goal.	
"	7-6-17.		Training. Cricket Match. Officers v Rest of Battn. Result:- Draw.	
"	8-6-17.		Training.	
"	9-6-17.		Training.	
"	10-6-17.		Training.	
"	11-6-17.		Training.	
"	12-6-17.		Training. Football Match Regimental Team v 7th Queen's.Result:- Regtl. Team 1-goal. 7th Queen's Nil.	
"	13-6-17.		Training. Warning orders for relief of Division, and move back to rest area received	
"	14-6-17.		Training. Cricket Match. Headquarters v Rest of Battn. Result:- Win for Bn. Headquarters by 1-run which was scored from a byé.wide.	
"	15-6-17.		Operations received for move to COIGNEUX. Battalion left Camp at S.17.Central. at 4-25a.m. and arrived at Camp at COIGNEUX at 11-30a.m. One hours halt was made during the march, the distance of which was 15-miles.	
Camp. COIGNEUX.	16-6-17.		Training.	
"	17-6-17.		Church Services.	
"	18-6-17.		Training.(Bathing.	
"	19-6-17.		Training.(	
"	20-6-17.		Training.(Medal Ribbands presented by Corps-Commander.	
"	21-6-17.		Training.(Vide App: 31.	
"	22-6-17.		Training.(	
"	23-6-17.		Training.(Party of Officers visited the Somme Battlefields.	
"	24-6-17.		Church-Services. 1st Round Divisional Football Tournament. 7th R.W.K. v 12th Middlesex.Result:- 7th R.W.K. Nil.Middlesex 1.	
"	25-6-17.		Training.(	
"	26-6-17.		Training.(App: Divisional Relay Race.10-miles Cross Country, took 4th place	
"	27-6-17.		Training.(32.	
"	28-6-17.		Training.(	

Army Form C. 2118.

WAR DIARY
or
INTELLIGENCE SUMMARY.
(Erase heading not required.)

Instructions regarding War Diaries and Intelligence Summaries are contained in F. S. Regs., Part II. and the Staff Manual respectively. Title pages will be prepared in manuscript.

Place	Date	Hour	Summary of Events and Information	Remarks and references to Appendices
Camp. COIGNEUX.	28-6-17.		Brigade Sports. Parchment letters presented to recipients by the Brigadier General.	
"	29-6-17.		Training.	
"	30-6-17.		Training. Divisional Sports. Bn. took 4-First Prizes and 1-Second Prize.	
			HONOURS AND AWARDS.	
			2201. Sgt. Coleman A. Military Medal.	
			24793 Cpl. Yeoman C.F. " "	
			5949 Pte. Skelton W. " "	
			2438 " Fittall G. " "	
			6552 " Fairbrother E. " "	
			1050 C.S.M. Gozens L. MEDAILLE MILITAIRE.	
			60. C.S.M. Summerfield G. Parchment Letter.	
			1201 Sgt. Coleman A. " "	
			3883 C.Q.M.S. Nobles. J. " "	
			24575 Sgt. Conway G. " "	
			1278 Sgt. Morris H. " "	
			3489 Sgt. Hamblin C. " "	
			18058 Sgt. Alexander A. " "	
			23598 Cpl. Hooper F.W. " "	
			23581 Cpl. Roberts F.C. " "	
			24793 Cpl. Yeoman C.F. " "	
			6066 Sgt. Igard F. " "	
			8542 L/S. Medhurst A.E. " "	
			6552 Pte. Fairbrother E. " "	
			2438 " Fittall G. " "	
			5949 " Skelton W.C. " "	
			CAPTAIN. H. WARREN. MILITARY CROSS.	
			A/CAPTN. D.E.M. WOODHOUSE. MILITARY CROSS.	
			OFFICERS JOINED DURING THE MONTH.	
			LIEUT.COL.C.H.L. CINNAMOND. To Command. 9-6-17.	
			MAJOR.V.M. FITZHUGH. To 2nd in Command. 13-6-17,	
			2/Lieut. W.H. Cousins. 20-6-17.	
			2/Lieut. C.P. Wyatt. 20-6-17.	
			2/Lieut. C.L. Miskin. 20-6-17.	
			OFFICERS CASUALTIES DURING THE MONTH.	
			2/Lieut. C.L. Miskin. To England Sick. 20-5-17.	
			2/Lieut. G.E. Neves. Wounded. 2-6-17.	
			CM2 Command	
			Commanding 7th Battalion Royal West Kent Regt.	

OPERATION REPORT FOR NIGHT 2nd and 3rd June 1917.

APP: 29

The HORSESHOE POST was garrisoned by Two Lewis Guns, One Vickers Gun, and 2-Sections. About 9-30p.m. the enemy put over several "Pineapple" Bombs into this post, and about 9-45p.m. commenced shelling it, paying particular attention to the right portion of it. As the hostile artillery fire was kept up at a normal rate for that time of day over the rest of the Sector, this was not particularly noticeable from other parts of the line, and was not reported by the N.C.O. in charge of the post.

An officer of this Company was wounded by a "Pineapple" Bomb in No.1. Post about 9-0p.m.

About 10-30p.m. the shelling became more intense on HORSESHOE POST. One Lewis Gun and team, the Vickers Gun and about 6-men were knocked out. The remainder of the garrison stood to, and suddenly a shower of bombs were thrown into the post from the right, and a large party of the enemy, estimated at 40, rushed it. The remaining Lewis Gun emptied all its magazines at close range, confusion arose, hand to hand fighting ensued, and our men were driven back to No.1. Post.

A bombing party was hastily organised by SERGT. WOODGATE, which worked up the trench and attempted to drive the enemy out, but failed.

The position in the remainder of the Sector was at this time as follows:-
"B" Company on the right had been relieved by "A" Company 6th Northants, and "A" Company in Reserve, and one platoon "D" Company in support had also been relieved; these units were on their way out of the line, but CAPTAIN. LEWIN M.C. of "B/ Company had still remained at right Company Headquarters. "D" Company less one platoon, CAPTAIN. HEBBLETHWAITE, had been relieved by one platoon "D" Company 6th Northants on the left, but remained standing to in CURTAIN TRENCH; "D" Company 6th Northants less one platoon had just arrived to relieve our "C" Company, and CAPTAIN ROBERTS was already at left Company Headquarters. I did not receive definite news that HORSESHOE POST had been rushed until after 11-10p.m. but I had already called for artillery support through liason Officer R.A. The first definite news from 2/LIEUT. GREGORY Commanding "C" Coy. was to the effect that HORSESHOE POST had been lost, and that the immediate Counter Attack had failed to retake it. I then ordered CAPTAIN HEBBLETHWAITE to take the platoon of "D" Company which was standing to in CURTAIN TRENCH up WREN LANE, and lauch a determined bombing attack up the trench to recover the lost post. This he did. Hearing no information for a long time, I sent CAPTAIN LEWIN forward to clear up the situation. This was about 1-0a.m. to 1-30a.m. CAPTAIN LEWIN went forward with Sergt. Dungay, and found the attack of "D" Company progressing, but "sticky", so he with Sergt. Dungay led them forward in person with great gallantry, throwing bombs himself, and succeeded in driving the enemy back along the new communication trench, to within a few yards of its junction with HORSESHOE TRENCH, but was unable to make any further progress. He therefore established a bomb stop at the furthest point reached, under heavy fire from German Bombs, and posted a strong bombing party behind it. He then came back to left Company Headquarters and reported to me. I then gave orders for the remaining platoon of "C" Company with a few "oddments" that could be collected, to make an attack from the right across the clover patch.

This attack commenced from LARK LANE just before dawn, and the platoon was backed up by one platoon 6th Northants under LIEUT. FROST. A combined bombing attack was to take place simultaneously from the left by "D" Co supported by another platoon 6th Northants under 2/LIEUT. WARNER.

The attack on the right succeeded in reaching and charging the enemy's position but was driven off by bombs.

2/LIEUT. WARNER was killed during this attack.

Having no more troops to deal with the situation, I was ordered by the Brigadier to hand over the Sector as it was to the 6th Northants, and withdraw the remainder of the 7th Royal West Kent Regiment.

This was done by 6-45a.m. 3rd inst.

<u>NOTE.</u> Casualties occurred during the operation amounted to:-

        3-Lewis Guns.
        32-Other ranks.
        1-Officer Slightly wounded at duty.

        (sd) P.N.Anstruther. Lieut.Col.
      Commanding 7th Battn. Royal West Kent Regt.

SECRET   APP.30   Copy No 8

7th Royal West Kent Order No. 61

Ref: Map 51B SW   2nd June 1917

1. The Battalion will be relieved by the 6th Northamptonshire Regt. tonight
And after relief will proceed to our old camp at S.17.

2. The incoming Bn will be disposed as under:-
Two Coys. front line. 'A' Coy on the right. 'D' Coy on the left. Dividing line STORK POST inclusive to left Coy.
'C' Coy. in CUCKOO TR.
'B' Coy in PELICAN LANE.
Headquarters of the right coy. will be those at present occupied by 'C' Coy.
Headquarters of left Coy, which will take over from 'C' and left platoon of 'D' will be in present left coy. headquarters.

3. Guides will be provided by Coys as under.

2.

'B' Coy - two guides (one for ROTTEN ROW and one for WOOD TR.)
'C' Coy - three guides (one for LARK POST which although at present held by 'C' Coy will be in the right coy. area, - one for STORK POST, - one for WREN POST.)
'D' Coy - one for left platoon sector
'A' Coy - four guides for PELICAN LANE. The guides will all report to Bn. H.Q. at 9.15 pm. This scale of guides has been arranged with O.C. 6th Northants in order to get all advanced posts relieved quickly. Therefore any supplementary guides will be met at Coy. HQrs.

4. The advanced parties from incoming unit will arrive about 6pm this evening and take over and lists of trench stores &c., will be signed and countersigned, will be made out and forwarded to the Adjt. by 2 pm on 3rd inst.

3.

5. Completion of relief will be reported to Bn. H.Q. by the code words ONIONS.

6. The Bn. will march to the Camp by platoons, or where this is not possible by small closed up parties under an officer or N.C.O.; the choice of route left entirely to the discretion of those concerned, men are to be warned that march discipline is maintained, and no straggling allowed (the excellence of the march discipline when the Bn. came out of the line last time was remarked on by several senior officers).

7. Advanced parties ~~should~~ will go down early, consisting of a N.C.O. and a few other ranks up to about six will report to Bn HQ. ~~at~~ by 5 P.M.

8. All packs, mess gear &c. unable to be carried will be at

the transport dump by 9 p.m. and one man per coy. will be detailed to accompany these down to the Camp with the transport.

Two more limbers for Lewis Guns and mounted officers chargers will be at the cross roads ST MARTIN sur COJEUL M 33 a 77. at 12 midnight.

9. During relief Box Respirators will be worn at 'ALERT'

    Copies 1   CO
             2   OC. A
             3   " B
             4   " C
             5   " D
             6   S. O. & I. O.
             7   Diary.
             8   Spare
             9   Bde

APP. 31

7th Battalion Royal West Kent Regiment.

Date.	Hour.	Nature of Training.	Location.	Remarks.
1917. MONDAY. 18th. June.	7.0--7.45 a.m.	Adjutant's Parade	Vicinity of Camp.	
	9.0--12.30 a.m. p.m.	Musketry, Bayonet Fighting, Attack formations.	--do--	
	2.30-5.30 p.m.	Instruction of Officers and N.C.O's under Company arrangements. Instruction of Specialists.	--do--	
	4.15p.m.	Conference of Company Commanders.	--do--	
TUESDAY. 19th.June.	7.0--7.45 a.m.	Rapid Marching.	Along Roads in Vicinity of Camp.	
	7.0--1.30 a.m. p.m. 5.0--7.0 p.m.	Range Practices	"B" Rifle Range.	
	9.0--11.0 a.m.	Wiring.	Vicinity of Camp.	
	9.0-12.30 a.m. p.m.	Digging.	--do--	
	11.30 a.m. --12.45 p.m.	Training of Specialists.	--do--	
	2.30-5.30 p.m.	Instruction of Officers and N.C.O's under Company arrangements. Instruction of Specialists.	--do--	
	4.15 p.m.	Conference of Company Commanders.	--do--	

7th Battalion Royal West Kent Regiment.

Date.	Hour.	Nature of Training.	Location.	Remarks.
1917. WEDNESDAY. 20th June.	7.0 –7.45 a.m.	Bayonet Fighting, Close Order Drill, Rapid Marching.	Vicinity of Camp.	
	9.0–11.0 a.m.	Digging, Wiring.	–do–	
	11.30 a.m.––12.45 p.m.	Musketry, Instruction of Specialists.	–do–	
	12.0 noon–12.45 p.m.	Bayonet Fighting.	–do–	
	2.30–3.30 p.m.	Tactical problems for Officers and N.C.O's.	–do–	
	4.15 p.m.	Conference of Company Commanders.	–do–	
THURSDAY. 21st June.	7.0 –7.45 a.m.	Close Order Drill, Rapid Marching.	Vicinity of Camp.	
	9.0 a.m.––1.0 p.m.	} Range Practices.	"B" Rifle Range.	
	5.0––7.0 p.m.	}		
	9.0––10.15 a.m.	Musketry.	Vicinity of Camp.	
	9.0––12.45 a.m. p.m.	Instruction of Specialists.	–do–	
	10.30 a.m.––12.30 p.m.	Wiring.	–do–	
	2.30––3.30 p.m.	Instruction of Officers and N.C.O's under Company arrangements. Instruction of Specialists.	–do–	
	4.15 p.m.	Conference of Company Commanders.	–do–	

7th Battalion Royal West Kent Regiment.

1917. Date.	Hour.	Nature of Training.	Location.	Remarks.
FRIDAY. 22nd. June.	7.0 — 7.45 a.m.	Close Order Drill.	Vicinity of Camp.	
	9.0 a.m. — 12.30 p.m.	Battalion Attack Formation.	Place to be notified later.	
	2.30 — 3.30 p.m.	Examination of Officers and N.C.O's.	Camp.	
	4.15 p.m.	Conference of Company Commanders.	-do-	
SATURDAY. 23rd. June.	7.0 — 7.45 a.m.	Rapid Marching, Bayonet Fighting.	Vicinity of Camp.	
	9.0 a.m. — 12.30 p.m.	Revision.	-do-	
	2.30 p.m.	Conference of Company Commanders.	Camp.	

App: 32

7th Battalion Royal West Kent Regiment.

Date.	Hour.	Nature of Training.	Location.	Remarks.
1917. MONDAY. 25th June.	7-0 – 7-45 9-0 – 10-0. 10-0 – 11-0. 11-15 – 12-30. 2-30 – 3-30 4-15.	Rapid Marching. Musketry, including firing from the hip whilst on the move. Bayonet Fighting. Attack formations. Instruction of Officers and N.C.O's in wiring under Bn. arrangements. Instructions of Specialists. Conference of Company Commanders.	Roads in Vicinity of Camp. Vicinity of Camp. " " " "	
TUESDAY. 26th June.	6-0 a.m. – 6-0 p.m. 7-0 – 7-45. 7-30 – 1-30. 9-0 – 10-0. & 2-30 – 3-30. 4-15.	Range Practice. Close Order Drill. Range practice for Lewis Gun Teams. Instruction of Officers and N.C.O's in fire direction and control under Company arrangements. Conference of Company Commanders.	"A" Range. Vicinity of Camp. "B" Range. Vicinity of Camp.	
WEDNESDAY. 27th June.	7-0 – 7-45. 9-0 – 10-0. 9-0 – 11-0. 10-15 – 12-30. 11-30 – 12-45. 2-30 – 3-30. 4-15.	Close Order Drill. Instruction of Specialists. Digging. Wiring. Musketry. Instruction of Officers and N.C.O's in bombing tactics under Company arrangements. Instruction of Specialists. Conference of Company Commanders.	Vicinity of Camp. " " " " "	

7th Battalion Royal West Kent Regiment.

Date.	Hour.	Nature of Training.	Location.	Remarks.
THURSDAY. 28th June.	7-0 — 7-45.	Rapid Marching.	Vicinity of Camp. J.16.b.	
	7-0 — 1-0.	Range practice.	" " "	
	9-0 — 11-0.	Digging.	" " "	
	10-30 — 12-30.	Wiring.	" " "	
	11-30 — 12-30.	Bayonet Fighting.	" " "	
	2-30 — 3-30.	Tactical problems for Officers and N.C.O's. Instruction of Specialists.	" " "	
	4-15.	Conference of Company Commanders.	J.16.b.	
	5-0. — 7-0.	Range practice.		
FRIDAY. 29th June.	7-0 — 7-45.	Close Order Drill.	Vicinity of Camp.	
	9-15 — 12-30.	Battalion attack formations.	Place to be notified later.	
	2-30 — 3-30.	Instruction of Officers and N.C.O's in Map reading, use of Compass etc. Instruction of Specialists.	Vicinity of Camp. " " "	
	4-15.	Conference of Company Commanders.	" " "	
SATURDAY. 30th June.	7-0 — 7-45.	Bayonet Fighting.	Vicinity of Camp.	
	9-0 — 12-30.	Revision.	" " "	
	2-30.	Conference of Company Commanders.	" " "	

Field. 22nd June 1917.

Lieut. Col.
Commanding 7th Battalion Royal West Kent Regt.

WAR DIARY or INTELLIGENCE SUMMARY.

Army Form C. 2118.

Place	Date	Hour	Summary of Events and Information	Remarks and references to Appendices
COIGNEUX	1-7-17.		Preliminary orders for move received.	
"	2-7-17.		Orders received for march to HALLOY. Battalion left COIGNEUX at 8-35a.m. arrived at HALLOY at 11-30a.m.	App: 33.
HALLOY.	3-7-17.		Orders received that Battalion would entrain at DOULLENS for North. Battalion left HALLOY at 8-45p.m. entrained at DOULLENS at 11-30p.m. "A" Company was detached for this move; see App: 34.	App: 34.
"	4-7-17.		Detrained at HOPOUTRE siding near POPERINGHE at 7-30a.m. and marched to camp near ABEELE arriving there at 9-0a.m.	
Nr ABEELE.	5-7-17.		Received warning order that the Battalion would relieve a Battalion of the 90th Infantry Brigade.	
"	6-7-17.		Battalion left Camp Nr ABEELE at 2-0a.m. and marched to PALACE CAMP Nr.DICKEBUSCH arriving at 3-45a.m.	App: 35,36.
PALACE CAMP.	6-7-17.		Battalion moved into Support relieving the 2nd Bedfords West of DICKEBUSCH. Battalion in Support, providing Working Parties for Royal Engineers. Work consisting of carrying for Mining Work etc.etc.	
TRENCHES.	7-7-17.		Battalion still on fatigues, and working parties.	
"	8-7-17.		Working parties still being provided for work in conjunction with Royal Engineers. Places of work:- ZILLEBEKE; ZILLEBEKE BUND; ZILLEBEKE DUMP, DORMY HOUSE T.18. a. 65. 20.	
"	9-7-17.		Working Parties as for previous day. Enemy shelled our positions very heavily, but little damage was done. Composite Platoon formed consisting of 1-Officer and 25-Other Ranks, and proceeded to join the 92nd Field Company Royal Engineers.	
"	10-7-17.		Orders received that the Battalion would relieve the 7th QUEEN's in the front line. Operation orders issued to Companies by 12-noon. Message received from Brigade that this was cancelled. Companies notified accordingly.	App;37.
"	11-7-17.		During the day a Bosche aeroplane came over and destroyed two of our captive balloons, our A.A.gunfire destroying a third. Five minutes later one of our planes flew over the German Lines and destroyed his 2-balloons which were up.	
"	12-7-17.		Working Parties provided as previously.	
"	13-7-17.		Enemy shelled our positions rather heavily again today. Damage slight. Working Parties still provided.	
"	14-7-17.		Working Parties still being found. Two Platoons of "B" Company have been attached to the Canadian Tunnelling Company today for carrying in conjunction with mining work.	
"	15-7-17.		Working Parties still being found. "B" Company's working party was caught in enemy barrage on their way to rendezvous, several casualties resulting. The Officer in charge of the party was wounded and 5-Other Ranks killed. Warning orders received that the relief of the 7th QUEEN's would take place on the 17th instant.	
"	16-7-17.		Working parties finished today.	

Army Form C. 2118.

WAR DIARY
or
INTELLIGENCE SUMMARY.
(Erase heading not required.)

Instructions regarding War Diaries and Intelligence Summaries are contained in F. S. Regs., Part II. and the Staff Manual respectively. Title pages will be prepared in manuscript.

Place	Date	Hour	Summary of Events and Information	Remarks and references to Appendices
TRENCHES.	17-7-17.		Orders issued to Companies re relief of 7th QUEEN's in the front line. Battalion relieved the 7th QUEEN's in the front line Companies dispositions as under. "A" Company in the front line. "C" Company in Close Support. "D" Company in Support. "B" Company in Reserve.	App: 38.
"	18-7-17.		Enemy batteries shelled very heavily during the relief, Mustard Oil and Gas Shells were also used. Several casualties occurred.	
"	19-7-17.		Enemy guns less active, weather very dull, and observation bad.	
"	20-7-17.		RITZ STREET system of trenches and vicinity of ZILLEBEKE very heavily shelled throughout the day. Enemy shelled our sector throughout the day Battalion Headquarters at DORMY HOUSE, also Brigade Headquarters at BEDFORD HOUSE were also shelled.	
"	21-7-17.		During the day our Sector was subjected to very heavy shelling, the trenches being badly damaged and many casualties occurring. Enemy aircraft was very active during the day flying very low over our trenches, firing into them with their machine guns. About 7-0p.m. several of our planes were up but did not engage the low flying enemy machines. Our patrols reconnoitred the enemy front line between 10-30p.m. and 12-15a.m. and found it unoccupied.	
"	22-7-17.		Artillery on both sides was very active throughout the day. Enemy strong points and wire being engaged by our fire. Our patrols went out to reconnoitre enemy wire and front line during the night, The front line was found to be unoccupied and his wire badly damaged presenting little obstacle.	
"	23-7-17.		Enemy bombardment of our lines extremely intense, our front line being very badly damaged. Counter battery work reduced the enemy shelling about 11-30a.m. During the day one of the Battle Dumps were blown up by enemy fire. Gas shells fell in the vicinity of WELLINGTON CRESENT and ZILLEBEKE at 1-0a.m. Battalion relieved by the 19th KINGS LIVERPOOLS. Relief completed by 4-0a.m. During the relief enemy shelled very heavily with Gas, and H.E. shells. On relief Battalion proceed to CANAL RESERVE CAMP Near DICKEBUSCH.	App;39
CANAL RESERVE CAMP.	24-7-17.		Day spent in resting in Camp. During the day 29-men were sent to hospital suffering from gas poisoning contracted during the relief. Battalion proceeded to OTTAWA CAMP in the evening.	
OTTAWA CAMP.	25-7-17.		Battalion in Camp Resting. Baths. 70-Reinforcements arrived today.	
"	26-7-17.		Battalion resting.	
"	27-7-17.		Battalion resting. Orders with reference to the part the Battalion would take in the Coming Offensive issued.	App;40.

T2134. W1. W708—776. 500000. 4/15. Sir J. C. & S.

App. 33

7th ROYAL WEST KENT REGIMENT ORDER No. 58.

Ref: Map. Sheet.
LENS.11.
Ed.2. 1/100,000.

1st July 1917.

1. The Battalion will march to HALLOY tomorrow.

2. STARTING POINT:- LEVEL CROSSING on the SAILLY-AU-BOIS – COIGNEUX Road.

3. ROUTE:- COIGNEUX - AUTHIE - THIEVRES.

4. HOUR OF START:- 8-0a.m.

5. ORDER OF MARCH:- Headquarters "A" Echelon less Stretcher Bearers.
   "C" Company.
   Drums.
   "D" Company.
   "A" Company.
   "B" Company.
   Headquarters "B" Echelon.
   Stretcher Bearers.
   1st Line Transport.

6. DRESS:- FULL MARCHING ORDER.

7. All Lewis Guns, Officers Kits, Orderly Room Boxes and Drummers Packs will be stacked at the Q.M.Stores ready for loading by 7-0a.m. under arrangements to made between the Q.M. and Transport Officer. Mess Boxes will be ready for loading not later than 7-30a.m.

8. Rations for consumption on 3rd Instant will be delivered direct to Q.M.Stores in the New Area on the afternoon of July 2nd.

9. LIEUT. HARLEY, 16-Other Ranks, and 2-Horses 92nd Field Coy.R.E's. will be attached to the Battalion for Discipline, Billets, and Rations from tomorrow the 2nd Instant.
The N.C.O's and men will be rationed and Billeted by "A" Company.

10. A rear party, consisting of the Orderly Officer, Sanitary Sergeant, and one Sanitary man per Coy, and Headquarters will remain behind to clear up the Camp, and will proceed independently to HALLOY in rear of the Brigade.
Huts, Lines, Latrines, Cookhouses and Incinerators will be left scrupulously clean and will be inspected by the 2nd in Command before the Battalion moves off.

11. The packs of N.C.O's and men certified by the M.O. as unable to carry them will be dumped at the Q.M.Stores at 7-30a.m. punctually.

(SD). P.N.ANSTRUTHER. CAPTAIN.

ADJUTANT.

7th ROYAL WEST KENT REGIMENT ORDER No.59.

Ref:- Map .Sheet.
    Lens.11.
    Ed.2.1/100,000.

3rd July 1917.

1. (a). The Battalion less "A" Company, "A" Company Cooker and Team, and attached Section 92nd Field Company Royal Engineers, will entrain at DOULLENS (SOUTH) today in Train No.11. timed to start at 23-19.

    STARTING POINT:- Railway Crossing ½-mile North of Church HALLOY.
    HOUR OF START:- 8-45p.m.
    ORDER OF MARCH:- Headquarters "A" Echelon less stretcher bearers.
(b).   "D" Company.
                                 Drums.
                                 "B" Company.
                                 "C" Company.
                                 "Headquarters" "B" Echelon.
                                 Stretcher Bearers.

(c). "A" Company, attached 92nd Field Coy. R.E. and one cooker and team will entrain at the same place in Train No.17. timed to start at 7-19. on the 4th instant.
This party will be under the Command of CAPTAIN.D.E.M.WOODHOUSE.M.C.

(d). Hour of Start for Troops proceeding by No.17. Train will be 4-45a.m. on the 4th instant.
Starting Point:- Railway Crossing ½-mile North of Church HALLOY.

ROUTE:- L'ESPERANCE ——— LE MARAIS SEC ——— DOULLENS STATION (leaving the main ARRAS ——— DOULLENS Road, and taking the 2nd Class Road leading N.W. just EAST of the Railway Bridge ¼-mile N.W. of the D in DOULLENS).

2. All Transport will be at the Station 3-Hours before the hour of departure of the trains.
HOUR OF START for 1st Line Transport less one cooker will therefore be 6-45p.m. on the 3rd.
HOUR OF START for "A" Company's cooker will be 2-45p.m. on the 4thinst.

3. Lewis Guns, and Officers Messes will be loaded at Company Headquarters by 6-15p.m. Officers Kits, Drummers packs, and all other baggage for loading will be sent to Q.M.Stores not later than 4-0p.m.

4. Rations for consumption on the 4th instant will be carried on the man. Rations for consumption on the 5th instant will be carried to the New Area by the Divisional Supply Column and dumped at the detraining Stations.
(Rations for "A" Company and attached R.E's. for consumption on 4th and 5th instant will be drawn at HALLOY today (3rd instant) and carried on the man.

5. Billets, Latrines, Cookhouses and Incinerators will be left scrupulously clean and will be inspected by the 2nd in Command before the Battalion moves off.

6. Steel Helmets and Box Respirators will be carried by dismounted Officers, and mounted Officers will ensure that these articles are available at short notice any time after entraining.

                                       (sd). P.N.Anstruther. Captain.
                                                 ADJUTANT.

ADDENDA TO

7th ROYAL WEST KENT REGIMENT ORDER No.59.

(a). With Reference to para 2. The Mess Cart will call at the Orderly room at 8-0p.m. for one Officers Mess Box per Company. Any Boxes arriving after that hour will be left behind.

(b) Exact entraining strength by Officers and Other Ranks will be submitted to the Orderly Room by 9-0p.m.

(c) All water bottles will be filled before starting.

(d) On arrival at the Station men will be told off to carriages or trucks; the entrainment will not commence until the "Advance" is sounded on the bugle.

(e) O.C.Companies will report to the Adjutant when their men are in the train

(sd) P.N.Anstruther, Captain.
ADJUTANT.

SUPPLY ARRANGEMENTS.

1. The Battalion less "A" Company and attached 92nd Field Coy. R.E. details entraining on 3rd July will draw rations on the 2nd inst for consumption on the 3rd and 4th instant.

2. Rations for 3rd instant will be carried on the man, and rations for consumption on the 4th instant will be carried on the Supply Wagons.

3. "A" Company and attached 92nd Field Coy, R.E. details entraining on the 4th instant will draw rations on the 3rd instant for consumption on the 4th and 5th instant.

4. Rations for consumption on the 4th instant will be carried on the man and cookers.

5. Rations for consumption on 5th instant will be carried to the New Area by the Divisional Supply Column and dumped at detraining Stations.

6. Divisional Supply Column Lorries for these units will proceed empty to forward area on 3rd/4th instant and draw from new railhead on 4th inst and dump at detraining station.

7. 55th Infantry Brigade moving to BAILOY FAMECHON Area on 2nd instant will draw from new refilling point to be selected by Senior Supply Officer.

7th ROYAL WEST KENT REGIMENT ORDER No. 60.

APP.35

Ref: Map.   5th July 1917.
HAZEBROUCK 5A.
Ed.2. 1/100,000.

1. The Battalion will relieve a Battalion of the 90th Infantry Brigade in Support WEST of DICKEBUSCH about 200x S.E. of the second R. in SCHERPENBERG.R. tonight.

2. STARTING POINT:- Cross Roads on the FRANCO – BELGIAN FRONTIER 400x S. of Battalion Headquarters.
   HOUR OF START:-   2-0a.m. (6th inst).
   ROUTE:-   RENINGHELST – OUDERDOM.
   ORDER OF MARCH:-   Headquarters "A" Echelon & Drums, less Stretcher Brs.
                      "A" Company.
                      "B" Company.
                      "C" Company.
                      "D" Company.
                      Headquarters "B" Echelon.

                      1st Line Transport.

   Companies will pass the Starting Point 200x distance, and will maintain that distance throughout the march.
   Halts will be at for 10-minutes at 10-minutes to each clock hour.
   Watches will be synchronised at the Starting Point.
   Touch will be maintained with Companies in front during the march.
   Guides will be met at Cross Roads OUDERDOM.

3. All Transport to be parked on the ABEELE – RENINGHELST Road, West of the Starting Point, by 2-0a.m.
   Lewis Gun Limbers for Lewis Guns and Messes will be loaded at Company Headquarters by 10-0p.m. tonight, and will then return to Transport Lines.
   Mess Cart and Maltese Cart to be at Battalion Headquarters by 10-0p.m.
   Q.M. Stores to be loaded at a time to be mutually arranged between the Q.M. and Transport Officer.
   Men whose packs are to be carried will retain their steel helmets and carry them slung from the left hook of the tunic.

4. Advance Party composed as under will meet CAPTAIN WADDINGTON. at the Starting Point at 5-0p.m. tonight:-

        C.Q.M.S's of "A" and "C" Coys.   (On Bicycles.)
        One Sgt.   of "B" and "D" Coys.
        One N.C.O. of "HQ" Coy.   (On Bicycle).
        One Other Rank per Coys.& "HQ".
        One Battalion Runner.   (On Bicycle.)

N.B. The ABEELE – RENINGHELST Road is continuous and there is no break ¾-mile East of Starting Point as there appears to be on the HAZEBROUCK Map.

                (sd) P.N.Anstruther. Captain.
                     ADJUTANT.

App. 36.

7th ROYAL WEST KENT REGIMENT ORDER No. 61.

Ref: BELGIUM.
Sheet.28.N.W.   8th July 1917.

1. The 7th Royal West Kent Regiment will relieve the 2nd Bedfordshire Regiment, Reserve Battalion of the 89th Infantry Brigade at CHATEAU SEGARD tonight.
Companies will relieve corresponding Companies of the 2nd Bedfordshire Regiment.
Battalion Headquarters will be at H.30.c.16.

2. STARTING POINT:- OUDERDOM – DICKEBUSCH Road outside the Camp.
   HOUR OF START:- 10-30p.m.
   ORDER OF MARCH:- Headquarters "A" Echelon.
   "A" Company.
   "B" Company.
   "C" Company.
   "D" Company.
   Headquarters "B" Echelon.
   1st Line Transport.

   Distance of 200x between Companies will be observed.

   ROUTE:- To be notified later.

   DRESS:- Full Marching Order, and Steel Helmets.
   Box Respirators to be carried at the "ALERT" position.

3. Working parties will be found as per attached table.
Routes and rendezvous will be reconnoitred before dark.

4. Completion of relief will be reported to Battalion Headquarters by the code word "BUNNUM".

5. All Dumps, Stores, etc, will be taken over from outgoing Companies, and lists signed and countersigned forwarded to the Orderly Room by 12-noon the 7th instant.

(sd) P.N.Anstruther. Captain.

ADJUTANT.

11 JUL 1917

2/E. ROYAL WEST KENT REGIMENT ORDER No 62.

1. The Bn will relieve the 7th Bn. Queen's in the Left Subsector on the night 11/12th July.

APP. 37

2. Companies will parade so as to pass the starting point (X roads at H.30.c.3.8) as follows:—

    A Co. — 9-0 pm
    C Co. — 9-10 pm
    D Co. — 9-20 pm
    Hd. Qrs. — 9-25 pm
    B Co. — 9-30 pm

At least 200x distance will be maintained between platoons and companies.

3. ROUTE — H.30.b.03.65. — track to I.25.a.36.55. — Canal Bridge at I.19.d.5.7 — Corduroy Road — TROIS ROIS — under railway to communication trench at S.W. end of ETANG du ZILLEBEKE — ZILLEBEKE — VINCE STREET.

4. Companies relieve Coys of 7th Queen's as under:—
    A Co. relieves B Co. in FRONT LINE.
    C Co.   "   A Co. " STANLEY STREET.
    D Co.   "   C Co. " WELLINGTON CRESCENT.
    B Co.   "   D Co. " RITZ ST., NORMAN ST., and KITE ST.

5. Guides from the 7th QUEENS on a scale of one per Coy. H.Q. and one per platoon, i.e. (A.5,- C.4,- D.3,-B.4,) will meet Coys. at junction of RITZ ST., and VINCE ST., at 10.15 p.m.

6. An advance party composed as under will parade at Orderly Room at 2.30 p.m. & proceed to the trenches to reconnoitre & take over sectors, trench stores, dumps, etc.—

    Signalling Officer. ⎫
    3 Signallers.   ⎬ Per Bn. H.Q.
    R.S.M.   ⎭
    3 O.R.

    1 Officer.   ⎫
    1 N.C.O.   ⎬ Per Company.
    2 Signallers.   ⎭

    1 N.C.O.   ⎫
    1 O.R.   ⎬ Per Platoon.

7. Packs will not be taken up to the line, but will be stacked by Coys. ready for removal to 1st Line Transport, at S. end of the trench at present occupied, by 2-0 p.m. Officers' kits not required in the trenches will be dumped at the same place by 6-0 p.m.

6 JUL 1917   **APP. 38**

Amendments and Addenda to
the ROYAL WEST KENT REGT ORDER No. 62.

(a) Throughout this order all dates
will be postponed five days
i.e. for 11th read 16th and
12th read 17th etc.

(b) Reference para 2. Amend as
under:—
     A Co   —   2.30 am on 17th
     C Co   —   2-40 am "
     H.Q.   —   2-50 am "

(c) Reference para 3.:— Route
will be by track pointed
out verbally to OC. Coys.

(d) Reference para 5:— For
10-15 pm read 4-0 am 17th

(e) Reference para 6:— For
2-30 pm read 4-0 pm 16th

(f) Reference para 7:— Officers
kits will be dumped by
2-0 am 17th instead of 6-30 pm

and Mess Boxes by 8-30 p.m.

8. Officers kits and mess gear acquired in the line will be dumped at N. end of the trench at present occupied by 9.15 p.m. N.B. Kits must not exceed Pack, Blanket and W/P Sheet. Mess gear should be in Sandbags.

9. During the relief and at all times in the trenches, Box Respirators will be worn at the "ALERT" position.

10. Lists of Dumps and Trench Stores taken over, signed and countersigned will be forwarded to the Adjt. by 7.a.m. on 12th inst.

11. Reports in the trenches will be as laid down in W.K.300 of 10th inst.

12. Completion of relief will be wired by the code word "BUNBUM"

-ness boxes and pry kit etc required in the line should be dumped overnight.

(g) B. B and D Companies and their Hd. Qrs. will proceed independantly to the trenches, and will arrange for their reliefs to be complete by 3.30AM. 2/LT. ARNOLD and DAY. will make arrangements direct with OC. 7th Queen's for all details regarding the relief of these two Companies, and also for detailing ~~arrangement of~~ of advance parties.

(h) Each Company will take over 60 magazines in 15 buckets from 7th QUEENS and will take up 36 magazines in 8 buckets with them.

R. Arbuthnot Capt.
adjt
7th R.W.K.

Table of Working Parties issued with 7th Royal West Kent Regiment Order No.61.

UNIT.	STRENGTH.	TIME.	RENDEZVOUS.	TO REPORT TO.	WORK.
"A" Company.	1-Officer. 1-Platoon.	5-30a.m.	ZILLEBEKE BUND.	Sgt. Birtles. 201 Field Co. R.E.	Upkeep of Communication Trenches.
"A" Company.	1-Officer. 2-Sections.	10-3p.m.	DOTT DOUBE.	Officer of 2nd Guardian Tunnelling Company R.E.	Look on Bew Brigade Headquarters.
"B" Company.	1-Officer. 2-Platoons.	12-Midnight.	ZILLEBEKE.	Representative of 171 Tunnelling Co. Royal Engineers.	Carrying for Mining work.
"B" Company.	1-Officer. 2-Sections.	11-0p.m.	I.16.d.85.20.	-do-	-do-

N.B.— Platoons will consist of 65-Other Ranks, including N.C.O's. Sections will consist of 6-Other Ranks, including N.C.O's.

DRESS for Fatigues:— Rifles, Bandoliers, and Box Respirators at the "ALERT".

7th ROYAL WEST KENT REGT. ORDER No 63.

APP: 39.

23-VII-

1. The battalion will be relieved by the 19th KINGS LIVERPOOL REGT tonight. Companies of the relieving battalion will be disposed as under:—

   'C' Coy relieves 'B' Coy
   'B'   "   "   'C' "
   'A'   "   "   'D' "
   'D'   "   "   'A' "

2. Guides as under will report to the adjutant at Bn. HQ. QIS. at at 6.30 PM:—
   4 per company under an officer to be detailed by O.C. 'A' Coy.
   N.B. 'A' Coy will supply 3 guides to act as 'B' Coy guides. 'B' Coy will consequently only send one guide.

3. On relief, the battalion will march by platoons to CANAL RESERVE CAMP. H.27.a.52. 800X N.W of DICKEBUSCH

2

An advance party consisting of one
N.C.O. and one or two men may be
sent down to this Camp this
afternoon if desired, to act as
guides.

4. Relieving Companies may be expected
to arrive shortly after 10.30 PM.

5. Kits & mess boxes to be sent to the
R.S.M's dump by midnight.

6. Lists of dumps & stores handed over
signed & countersigned, to be sub-
-mitted to the Adjutant by 6 PM
24th

7. Completion of relief to be reported
by the code word "BOOBAH".

8. Acknowledge.

R.H. Anstruther Capt.
Adjt
7th R.W.F.

PRELIMINARY ORDER.

APP:40.

7th. Battalion Royal West Kent Regiment ---- ORDER No. 63. 64

1. GENERAL PLAN.

(a) On "Z" day the II Corps, consisting of the 8th, 18th, 24th, 25th and 30th Divisions, will attack with three Divisions in the Front Line, viz:-
    24th Division on the Right.
    30th Division in the Centre.
    8th Division on the Left.
The 18th. Division will support the 30th Division.
The 25th Division will support the 8th Division.
The Objectives of Divisions are marked on the special maps already issued to Companies.
    FIRST Objective---------BLUE LINE.
    SECOND Objective--------BLACK LINE.
    THIRD Objective---------GREEN LINE.
    FOURTH Objective--------RED LINE.
Whether or not the advance to the RED LINE will be made on "Z" day, depends on the amount of opposition encountered.

(b) The 18th Division will attack the GREEN LINE on a One Brigade Front with the 53rd. Infantry Brigade.
The 53rd. Infantry Brigade will pass through the 30th. Division, forming up on the BLACK LINE ready to advance at, approximately, Zero plus six hours 20 minutes, and act as follows:-

(i) After the capture of the GREEN LINE, the 53rd. Infantry Brigade will send out strong patrols to seize any ground or tactical points evacuated by the enemy.

(ii) The first objectives of these patrols will be on the general line of the road junction at J.4.d.13 - Fork Roads J.4.b.16.

(iii) If the line referred to in sub-para (ii) is reached, the 53rd. Infantry Brigade is to push troops further forward with a view to ascertaining if that portion of the enemy defences running from West of MOLENAARELSTHOEK to the East of ZONNEBEKE, which are within the boundaries of the 18th Divisional attack, are held, and in the event of these defences being found unoccupied, troops are to be pushed still further forward to establish themselves on the RED LINE.
The boundaries of the 18th Division and between Battalions of the 54th Infantry Brigade in the attack, are shewn on the special map issued to Companies.

(c) For the purpose of these operations, the 7th Battalion Royal West Kent Regiment, the 7th Battalion Queens Royal West Surrey Regt., and the 80th Field Coy., R.E., are placed under the orders of the G.O.C., 54th Infantry Brigade.
About 1½ hours after Zero on "Z" day, the 54th Infantry Brigade and attached troops will commence to move forward from the CHATEAU SEAGARD Area to the RITZ Area (just East of ZILLEBEKE)
The 54th Infantry Brigade is not to move forward from the assembly trenches in the RITZ Area without orders from Divisional Head Quarters, but is to be prepared to adopt either of the following courses :-

(i) After Zero plus 8 hours 40 minutes, to send forward the 11th Royal Fusiliers to form a Right flank, and the 7th Queens and 12th Middlesex Regiments to garrison certain strong points in support of the 53rd Infantry

(2).

(c) (i) Brigade if the Lines mentioned in sub-paras. (ii) or
(Continued) (iii) of para.1 (b) above, are reached by that Brigade.
In the event of the situation developing as favourably as to admit of troops of the 53rd. Brigade gaining the RED LINE, the remainder of the 54th Brigade will be moved forward to relieve the assaulting Battalions of the 53rd Infantry Brigade and to continue the consolidation of the ground gained.

In the event of the enemy being found to be holding the line West of MOLENAARELSTHOEK and East of ZONNEBEKE (or some other line in this vicinity), it is not intended to attack this line on "Z" day or before sufficient artillery support is available.

The 53rd. Infantry Brigade, in such an eventuality, is to establish itself on a line within assaulting distance of the enemy.

(ii) To pass through the 53rd Infantry Brigade and attack the RED LINE on "Z" plus 1 day.

If the 54th Brigade are required to attack, on "Z" plus 1 day, the RED LINE from the GREEN LINE, (or from any line between them, which may have been reached by the 53rd. Brigade), - the action to be taken by it will be as follows:-

The 3 assaulting Battalions will be ordered to move forward from the RITZ Area to the Western edge of POLYGONE WOOD in the following order :-

11th Royal Fusiliers (Right Attack) leading,
followed by 6th Northamptonshire Regt.(Centre Attack),
followed by 7th Bedfordshire Regt.,(Left Attack).
They will each be accompanied by such troops as are allotted to them for the attack.

The route to be taken by these Battalions from the RITZ Area to POLYGONE WOOD will be the A.T.N.TRACK (See special map.)

On arrival at Western edge of POLYGONE WOOD, they will deploy into attack formation between the boundaries allotted to them (shewn in yellow on special map).

When all three Battalions have deployed into attack formation they will move forward simultaneously until they arrive at the line which has been reached by the 53rd. Brigade, where they will halt until the Zero hour notified for the 54th Brigade attack.

(d) Role of Units of 54th Infantry Brigade and attached troops.

(i) The 11th Royal Fusiliers will be responsible for the protection of the Right flank of the attack on the RED LINE, whether it is made by the 53rd Brigade on "Z" day, or by the 54th Brigade on "Z" plus 1 day.

In the event of the attack being made by the 54th Brigade, this Battalion will be responsible for the capture of the RED LINE between its junction with the GREEN LINE at J.d. 9.30 and Strong Point No.26 at J.5.c.15 (exclusive) including the high ground on which Strong Points 20, 21, and 22 are situated. "D" Company less ½ Company, 7th Battalion Royal West Kent Regt., is attached to this Battalion to act as mopping-up parties.

In the event of the attack on the RED LINE being made by the 53rd Brigade, special instructions will be issued to this Battalion by the G.O.C. 53rd Infantry Brigade.

(ii) The 6th Northamptonshire Regiment will be responsible for the capture of the high ground on which Strong Points F.,G.,27, 28, and 33 are situated and for the capture of the RED LINE between Strong Points 26., and 33.,(both inclusive.)

It will also, if possible, make good the ground on which Strong Points 30.,31.,and 32 are situated.

(3).

(d) (Continued)

(ii) "A" Company, 7th Battalion Royal West Kent Regt., is allotted to this Battalion for mopping-up purposes in the area South West of the road which runs from J.4.d.95 to J.4.b.45.00.

North East ~~xxxxxxxxxxx~~ and East of that road the 6th Northamptonshire Regt., will be responsible for providing their own mopping-up parties.

(iii) The 7th Bedfordshire Regt., will be responsible for the capture of the Village of MOLENAARELSTHOEK (North West of Point J.5.a.05), the high ground in D.29.c., on which Strong Point H is situated, and the RED LINE between Strong Point 33. (exclusive) and Strong Point 36.(inclusive), including the sites of Strong Points 34., and 35.

"B" Company, 7th Battalion Royal West Kent Regiment is allotted to this Battalion for "mopping-up" purposes in the Area South West of the road from J.4.b.45.00 to J.4.b.16.

East and North East of this road the 7th Bedfordshire Regt., will be responsible for providing their own "mopping-up" parties.

(iv) The 7th Queens Royal West Surrey Regt will provide garrisons of 1 Officer and 1 platoon each, for Strong Points E., and Nos. 13., to 27.(inclusive).

(v) The 12th Middlesex Regt., will provide garrisons of 1 Officer and 1 platoon each, for Strong Points F.,G.,H., and Nos., 28., to 36. (inclusive.)

(vi) The 54th M.G.Coy will be distributed as follows :-
1½ Sections attached to the 3 assaulting Battalions,
1 Section to go forward, when required, to Strong Points E.,F.,G.,and H.,
1½ Sections in Brigade Reserve.

(vii) 54th. T.M.Battery :-
1 Section 4 Mortars with all personnel in Brigade Reserve.

(viii) 80th. Field Coy.,R.E.
4 Sections with their affiliated Infantry Platoons will be held in readiness to go forward to construct and occupy Strong Points E.,F.,G., and H. (One Section to each).

(e) "Mopping-up" Parties.
"D" Coy less ½ Coy., 7th Battalion Royal West Kent Regt., is attached to the 11th Royal Fusiliers for "mopping-up" during the attack.
"B" Coy ~~xxxxxxxxxx~~, 7th Battalion Royal West Kent Regt., is attached to the 7th Bedfordshire Regt., for "mopping-up" during the attack.
"A" Coy., 7th Battalion Royal West Kent Regt., is attached to the 6th Northamptonshire Regt., for "mopping-up" during the attack.

These "mopping-up" parties will join the Battalions to whom they are attached after the arrival of the 54th Brigade in the RITZ Area.

In the attack they will not proceed East of the line of the road which runs from J.4.d.95 to J.4.b.16.

As soon as they have completed the task of "mopping-up" allotted to them, they will rejoin their Battalion in Sq. J.4.c., or in such other position as it may be in at the time.

(4).

1. (f). Carrying Party.
"C" Company and ½ "D" Company, 7th Battalion Royal West Kent Regiment, are detailed to act as a carrying party, under Captain A.R.HOGG. Detailed instructions will be issued to the Officer Commanding Carrying Party.
The Officer Commanding Carrying Party will be required to furnish guides for the Pack Animal Train, and Guards for Advanced Dumps as may be required.

2. TANKS.
1 Company (12 Tanks) have been detailed to co-operate with the 54th Brigade in attack on the RED LINE.
The distribution will be :-
    7th Bedfordshire Regt.----------- 4 Tanks.
    6th Northamptonshire Regt.------- 4 Tanks.
    Brigade Reserve.----------------- 4 Tanks.

3. DUMPS.
A Brigade Bomb Store has been formed at I.22.d.89.
As soon as circumstances permit, the Brigade Dump will be moved forward along the line of the A.T.N. TRACK.
Brigade Dump will be established in Trenches crossing Track at J.9.a.55., and an Advanced Dump at J.4.b.50.

4. CAPTURE OF MATERIAL.
The capture of guns, ammunition dumps and trench mortars, and their nature, will be reported without delay; the report should state where they are to be found.
On no account are any of the spare parts etc., of the guns to be removed by the Infantry.

5. AMMUNITION AND BOMBS ETC., TO BE CARRIED.
Details will be communicated later.

6. RATIONS AND WATER. Details will be communicated later.

7. LOCATION OF UNITS AND TIME OF MOVES.
Details will be communicated later.

8. SURPLUS KIT AND PACKS.
Instructions will be communicated later.

9. MEDICAL ARRANGEMENTS.
Will be communicated later.

10. REPORTING CASUALTIES.
Instructions will be communicated later.

---------------oOo---------------

7th ROYAL WEST KENT REGIMENT ORDER NO. 64.   APP: 41.

30th July 1917.

1. The 7th Battalion Royal West Kent Regiment will march to NEW DICKEBUSCH CAMP, H.33.a.4.0. tonight.

   STARTING POINT:- Road Junction at G.4.d.15.00.

   HOUR OF START:- 11-5p.m.

   ROUTE:- Road Junction at G.30.c.5.9. - ST. HUBERTUSHOEK - MAIN DICKEBUSCH Road.

   ORDER OF MARCH:-   Headquarters.
   "A" Company.
   "B" Company.
   "C" Company.
   "D" Company.
   Transport as detailed in para 3.

   A distance of 100-yards between Platoons and Companies will be observed during the march.

   DRESS:- Light Fighting Order.

2. Packs, and Officers kits will be dumped at the Q.M.Stores as detailed below:-
   "A" Company.   6-0p.m.
   "B" Company.   6-30p.m.
   "C" Company.   7-0p.m.
   "D" Company.   7-30p.m.
   Hd.Qrs.   8-0p.m.

   Surplus Officers Mess Stores to be dumped at the same place by 10-0p.m.

3. The following Transport will accompany the Battalion to the New Area:-

   2-Field Kitchens.
   1-Water Cart.
   2-Limbers for Lewis Guns.
   Mess Cart.
   2-Limbers for Officers Baggage, and Mess boxes.
   Maltese Cart.
   1-Limber for rations.

4. Officers kits must not exceed 35-lbs; there will be an opportunity of sending articles back to the Transport Lines from the New Area, in the event of the Battalion being moved forward.

5. Rations for the 31st July and 1st August will be carried on the man with the exception of one Limber load which will accompany the Battn. to NEW DICKEBUSCH CAMP and will be issued there.

6. All articles for loading with the exception of Officers Messes will be taken to the Transport Lines between 7-0p.m. and 9-0p.m. N.C.O's incharge of parties will report to the Transport Sgt. for instructions as to loading. Officers Messes to be loaded by 10-0p.m.

(sd) P.F.Anstruther. Captain.

Adjutant.

O.C'S. Coys.

APP' 42

1. The Battalion will relieve the 20th. KINGS and 17th. KINGS in the front line tonight. Frontage:- From Strong Point at J.19.b.75.65. inclusive to CLAPHAM JUNCTION inclusive. Four Companies willbe in the front linein alphabetical order from right to left.

    "A". Coy. 7th.R.W.K. relieves "A". & "D". Coys.20th.KINGS.
    "B". Coy.   "   "   --------- --------"B". &"C". ------------------
    "C". Coy. ---------- --------"A". & "D". ------17th.KINGS.
    "D". Coy. ---------- --------"B". & "C". ------------------
    H.Q. Coy. ---------- --------H.Q. ------------------
at J.19.a.85.95.

2. Guides will be met at J.19.a.8595. O'S.C. Coys. must arrange to lead thier own Companies from present positionmto that point.

"C" Company will arrive at J.19.a.85.95. at 9-30p.m. "D" Company at 9-45p.m. "A" Company at 9-50p.m. and "B" Company at 10-0p.m.
"A" Company with one platoon,Coy HeadQuarters, and 4-Lewis Guns will arrive in the strong point at J.19.b.75.65.
Advance parties consisting of 2-N.C.O's per Company will take over sectors dumps etc during daylightThese N.C.O's must be in possession of full details regarding the relief. No smoking or talking will be allowed during the relief. The Signalling Officer will arrange to take over Stations. The Regimental Aid Psot will be in WINNEPEG STREET about I.24.d.65. Completion of relief will be reported in the code word BOOHAH.

                                                  (Sd) Captain P.N.Anstruther.
                                                         ADJUTANT.

Army Form C. 2118.

WAR DIARY
or
INTELLIGENCE SUMMARY.
(Erase heading not required.)

Instructions regarding War Diaries and Intelligence Summaries are contained in F.S. Regs., Part II. and the Staff Manual respectively. Title pages will be prepared in manuscript.

Place	Date	Hour	Summary of Events and Information	Remarks and references to Appendices
OTTAWA CAMP.	28-7-17.		Battalion resting.	
"	29-7-17.		Battalion resting. Working party consisting of 1-Officer and 100-Other Ranks proceed to DICKEBUSH to erect new camp.	
"	30-7-17.		Battalion moved to NEW DICKEBUSH CAMP. Complete by 12-Midnight.	App:41.
NEW DICKEBUSH CAMP.	31-7-17.		Battalion standing by, but did not take part in the Offensive commenced today.	
			OFFICERS JOINED DURING THE MONTH.	
			2/Lieut. A.B.Cullerne.	
			2/Lieut. C.R.Addison.	
			Rev: Captain. G.C.R.Cooke. C.F.	
			CASUALTIES AMONG OFFICERS DURING MONTH.	
			"2/Lieut. G.R.Addison. Wounded.	
			2/Lieut. W.H.Cousins. Wounded.	
			2/Lieut. C.P.Wyatt. Wounded.	
			A/Captain. D.E.M.Woodhouse M.C. WOUNDED.	
			2/Lieut. W.J.Newberry. Wounded.	
			2/Lieut. W.E.Arnold. Wounded. (Shell Shock).	
			Captain. T.T.Waddington M.C. Struck Off Strength to Senior Officers Course England	
			2/Lieut. N.A.Charrington. Sick to England.	
			Lieut. A.A.Eason. Sick to England.	
			A/Captain. R.S.Hebblethwaite. Sick to England.	
			Lieut. C.E.Longley. Appointed Draft Conducting Officer and Struck Off.	
			2/Lieut. F.G.Rand. Sick to England.	

CM Command
Lieut. Col.
Commanding 7th Battalion Royal West Kent Regiment.

WAR DIARY
or
INTELLIGENCE SUMMARY.

Army Form C. 2118.

(Erase heading not required.)

Place	Date	Hour	Summary of Events and Information	Remarks and references to Appendices
NEW DICKEBUSCH CAMP.	1-8-17.		Battalion left New Dickebusch Camp at 6-0a.m. arrived at OTTAWA CAMP 7-30a.m. Left OTTAWA CAMP at 7-0p.m. arrived New Dickebusch Camp at 8-45p.m. Battalion standing by.	
NEW DICKEBUSCH CAMP.	2-8-17.		Battalion Standing by during the day. Left New Dickebusch Camp at 7-15p.m. for trenches to relieve 18th King's Liverpool Regiment. Relief Complete 2-30a.m. on 3rd. "GOING" very bad and much shelling.	
TRENCHES.	3-8-17.		Distribution of Companies:- "A" Company. JAM ROW. "B" Company. JAM SUPPORT. "C" Company. JAM.RESERVE. "D" Company. JACKDAW RESERVE. Battn.Hd.Qrs. CRAB CRAWL TUNNELL.	
"	4-8-17.		Relief of 20th and 17th King's in the front was immediately undertaken. Commenced at 9-30a.m. completed at 1-45a.m. on the 4th. Weather still very bad. Distribution of Companies:- all 4-Companies in front about STIRLING CASTLE. Headquarters in Mine Crater at EAST end of SANCTUARY WOOD. 2-Prisoners of the 246th R.I.Rgt. 54th R.Division were captured by the Commanding Officer during the evening.	app.42.
"	5-8-17.		Enemy quiet during the day, between 9-30p.m. to 10-30p.m. enemy put down heavy barrage behind the front line. Our artillery replied effectively. No casualties.	
"	6-8-17.		2-Germans of the 239th R.I.Rgt, who had lost their way were shot by "D" Coy, at 4-30a.m. 10-Patrols were sent out during the night. 2/LT.LEWIS and 3-Other Ranks engaged a German Post Cpl.RAWLINGS and 2-Other Ranks accounted for a patrol of 10-Germans killing one, wounding 3, and dispersing the remainder. Dead German belonged to the 239th R.I.Rgt.	
"	7-8-17.		Quiet morning. In afternoon three enemy aeroplanes patrolled sector for several hours at a very low altitude, firing signals, and machine guns. They were entirely unmolested by our own planes or A.A.Batteries. Battalion relieved by the 7th QUEEN's. Commenced at 9-0p.m.	

Army Form C. 2118.

WAR DIARY
or
INTELLIGENCE SUMMARY.
(Erase heading not required.)

Instructions regarding War Diaries and Intelligence Summaries are contained in F.S. Regs., Part II. and the Staff Manual respectively. Title pages will be prepared in manuscript.

Place	Date	Hour	Summary of Events and Information	Remarks and references to Appendices
CHATEAU SEGARD.	8-8-17.	2-0p.m.	Relief Complete. Relief very slow owing to shell fire and mistakes on part of guides.	
"	9-8-17.		Battalion established at CHATEAU SEGARD. 5'9.M.V. Gun shelled area in afternoon.	
"	10-8-17.		In Reserve to 55th Infantry Brigade.	
NEW DICKEBUSCH CAMP.	11-8-17.		In Reserve to 55th Infantry Brigade. Moved to New Dickebusch Camp.7-30p.m.	
Nr.ABEELE.	12-8-17.		Battalion left New Dickebusch Camp at 2-30p.m. to entrain at OUDERDOM for ABEELE. Arrived at ABEELE 4-15p.m. and proceeded to very scattered billets 3-Miles WEST of ABEELE.	
"	13-8-17.		Re-organisation.	
"	14-8-17.		Re-organisation and training.	App:43.
"	15-8-17.		Training. Orders received in evening to entrain on the 15th for ZEGGERS CAPPEL. Battalion marched to ABEELE arriving at 8-30a.m. Entrained at 12-noon. Detrained at ESQUELBECQ and marched to billets in vicinity of ZEGGERS - CAPPEL. move complete by 4-15p.m.	
Nr. ZEGGERS CAPPEL.	16-8-17.		Training.	
"	17-8-17.		Training.	
"	18-8-17.		Training. A bombing accident occurred in morning, 2/Lt.JUDD and 2-Other Ranks were killed.	
"	19-8-17.		Church Services. Funeral of 2/LT.JUDD and 2-other ranks took place in afternoon in Cemetery 1½-miles S. of ST OMER on WOZERNES Road.	app:44.
"	20-8-17.		Training and Company Football.	
"	21-8-17.		Training and Company Football.	
"	22-8-17.		Training. Football match versus 8th E.Surrey Regiment, result 7th R.W.K.1. 8th E.Surreys.1.	
"	23-8-17.		Training. Football match Officers versus Sergeants. Officers.1. Sergeants. 1.	
"	24-8-17.		Training.	
"	25-8-17.		Training, Party of 75-Other Ranks visited SEASIDE by lorry.	
"	26-8-17.		Church Services. Battalion 2nd Anniversary Dinner at Transport Lines.	app:45.
"	27-8-17.		Training.	
"	28-8-17.		Training.	
"	29-8-17.		Battalion fired on Fifth Army Range "B".	
"	30-8-17.		Training.	
"	31-8-17.		Training. Football Match versus 8th E.Surrey Rgt. Result:- 7th R.W.K. 1. 8th E.Surrey Rgt. 1.	

Army Form C. 2118.

WAR DIARY
or
INTELLIGENCE SUMMARY.
(Erase heading not required.)

Place	Date	Hour	Summary of Events and Information	Remarks and references to Appendices
			OFFICERS JOINED DURING THE MONTH.	
			2/Lt. M.Edwards. Joined 14-8-17.	
			2/Lt. G.Tirbutt. " 14-8-17.	
			2/Lt. F.N.Holt. Rejoined 16-8-17.	
			2/Lt. H.G.Chandley. Joined 16-8-17.	
			2/Lt. S.Allchin. " 16-8-17.	
			2/Lt. R.V.Keyworth " 17-8-17.	
			2/Lt. G.J.Allen. " 17-8-17.	
			2/Lt. A.L.Dupont. " 17-8-17.	
			2/Lt. R.W.Coles. " 17-8-17.	
			2/Lt. E.Grethe. " 18-8-17.	
			2/Lt. H.S.Peglar. " 18-8-17.	
			2/Lt. W.F.Chapman. " 18-8-17.	
			2/Lt. G.T.M.Lewis. Rejoined 25-8-17.	
			2/Lt. M.Buffee. 29-8-17.	
			2/Lt. A.C.Michell. Joined. 3-8-17.	

			THE UNDERMENTIONED AWARDED THE DIVISIONAL COMMANDERS PARCHMENT CERTIFICATE FOR DEVOTION TO DUTY AND GALLANT CONDUCT IN THE FIELD.	
			2158 Sgt. Baldwin. C.F.	
			1808 L/S. Balls W. (Since Wounded)	
			3380 L/C. McDonald A. (Since Wounded)	
			24785 Pte. Logan R. (Since Wounded).	
			1638 " Breed S.	
			2340 C.S.M.Wicken J.	

			CASUALTIES IN OFFICERS DURING THE MONTH.	
			2/Lt.P.G.Rand. Sick to England 23-7-17.	
			2/Lt.R.V.Keyworth. Accidentally wounded 18-8-17.	
			2/Lt. W.E.Arnold. (Wounded To England) 18-8-17.	
			Lieut. V.C.Sewell. Sick to England. 20-8-17.	
			Lieut. L.M.Cooper Sick To England. 21-8-17.	
			2/Lieut. M.S.Judd. Accidentally Killed 18-8-17.	

			HONOURS AND AWARDS.	
			The undermentioned granted The DISTINGUISHED CONDUCT MEDAL for Gallantry in the field:-	
			24785 Pte. LOGAN. R. (Since Wounded)	

			HONOURS AND AWARDS.	
			The undermentioned Awarded the MILITARY MEDAL for Gallantry in the Field:-	
			2158 Sgt. C.F.Baldwin.	
			3380 L/C. McDonald A. (Since Wounded)	
			1808 L/S. Balls W. (Since Wounded).	

			A letter of Appreciation of the services rendered by 2-N.C.O's and runners who were attached temporarily to Bde Hd.Qrs. for the operations of the 10th Aug:1917	App:

M Cummerwd Lieut. Col.
Commanding 7th Bn.Royal West Kent Regt.

WAR DIARY or INTELLIGENCE SUMMARY

Army Form C. 2118.

7th R.W. Kents

Place	Date	Hour	Summary of Events and Information	Remarks and references to Appendices
Near ZEGGERS CAPPEL.	1-9-17.		Training.	
	2-9-17.		Training. Football Match versus 8th E.Surrey Regt. Result:- 7th R.W.K. 3; 8th E.Surrey.1.	
	3-9-17.		Training. Box Respirators refitted and tested.	
	4-9-17.		Training. -do- -do- -do-	
	5-9-17.		Training. Firing on Fifth Army Range.	App.47½
	6-9-17.		Training. Battalion attack scheme.	
	7-9-17.		Training.	
	8-9-17.		Training.	
	9-9-17.		Training. Church services.	
	10-9-17.		Training.	App.48
	11-9-17.		Training. Battalion attack scheme.	
	12-9-17.		Training. Firing on Fifth Army Range.	
	13-9-17.		Training. Brigade attack scheme.	
	14-9-17.		Training. Football match versus 8th.East Surrey Regt. Result:- 7th R.W.Kent.4; 8th E.Surrey.nil.	
	15-9-17.		Training.	
	16-9-17.		Church services. Football match versus 10th Essex Regt. Result:- 7th R.W.Kent.2; 10th Essex. nil.	App.49½
	17-9-17.		Training. Draft of 126 N.C.O's and men arrived as Reinforcements.	
	18-9-17.		Brigade Assault-at-Arms. The Battalion secured 7-Firsts and 5-Seconds.	
	19-9-17.		Training. Football match versus 110th Regt. French Infantry. Result:- 7th R.W.K.2; 110th Regt.1.	App.50.
	20-9-17.		Battalion Route March.	
	21-9-17.		Training.	
	22-9-17.		Training.	
	23-9-17.		Battalion left ZEGGERS CAPPEL Area 7.15 a.m. to entrain at ESQUELBEC Station for POPERINGHE. Arrived POPERINGHE 2.15 p.m. and marched to SCHOOL CAMP (late "K" Camp) near ST.JAN TER BIEZEN 3.0 p.m. First Line Transport moved by road.	
near ST.JAN TER BIEZEN.	24-9-17.		Training. Firing on Range.	App.51.
	25-9-17.		Training.	
	26-9-17.		Training.	
	27-9-17.		Training.	
	28-9-17.		Training.	
	29-9-17.		Training. Raid by hostile aircraft. No casualties.	
	30-9-17.		Church Services. -do- -do- No casualties.	

Army Form C. 2118.

WAR DIARY
or
INTELLIGENCE SUMMARY.
(Erase heading not required.)

Instructions regarding War Diaries and Intelligence Summaries are contained in F. S. Regs., Part II. and the Staff Manual respectively. Title pages will be prepared in manuscript.

Place	Date	Hour	Summary of Events and Information	Remarks and references to Appendices
			OFFICERS JOINED DURING THE MONTH.	
			2/Lt.P.T.STANLEY. Joined 6-9-17.	
			2/Lt.G.F.JOHNSTONE. " 8-9-17.	
			2/Lt.H.T.RAPSON. " 6-9-17.	
			2/Lt.H.G.J.HINES. " 9-9-17.	
			2/Lt.J.A.HORTON. " 9-9-17.	
			2/Lt.J.H.GLADWELL. " 11-9-17.	
			Lieut.A.A.EASON. Rejoined.12-9-17.	
			2/Lt.P.D.BERTRAM. Joined.17-9-17.	
			Captain.T.T.WADDINGTON.M.C. Rejoined 30-9-17.	
			2/Lt.H.J.HILLMAN. Joined 30-9-17.	
			2/Lt.W.H.CANDY. " 30-9-17.	
			2/Lt.G.SKOTTOWE. " 30-9-17.	
			2/Lt.C.JORDAN. " 30-9-17.	
			CASUALTIES IN OFFICERS DURING THE MONTH.	
			2/Lt.T.M.LEWIS transferred to R.F.C.17-9-17.	
			HONOURS AND AWARDS.	
			The undermentioned awarded the DISTINGUISHED CONDUCT MEDAL for Gallantry and Devotion to Duty in Action:-	
			11699.L/C.Scammell.G. (Since promoted Corporal.)	
			7504.L/C.Goldsmith.P. (Since promoted Corporal.)	
			23650.Cpl.Rawlings.R. (Since wounded)	
			The undermentioned awarded the MILITARY MEDAL for Gallantry and Devotion to Duty in Action:-	
			10421.Pte.Stacey.F.	
			6172. " Gayton.H.	
			4947. " Elliott.G.	
			1959. " Pierce.H.	
			15263. " Yates.A.	
			2414.L/C.Barber.G.	
			10178.L/C.Ursell.S.	
			1286.L/C.Greengrass.D.	
			1962.Pte.Payliss.F.	
			3217. " Swift.A.	
			PARCHMENT LETTER IN RECOGNITION OF GALLANT CONDUCT AND DEVOTION TO DUTY AWARDED BY DIVISIONAL COMMANDER TO THE UNDERMENTIONED :-	
			7504. Cpl.Goldsmith.P.	
			11699. Cpl.Scammell.G.	
			10421. Pte.Stacey.F.	
			4947. " Elliott.G.	
			1959. " Pierce.H.	
			6172. " Gayton.H.	
			15623. " Yates.A.	

CR Emmand
Lieut.Col.
Commanding 7th Battalion Royal West Kent Regiment.

7th ROYAL WEST KENT REGIMENT ORDER No. 65.

APP: 43.

Ref: Map. Sheet.
HAZEBROUCK 5a.

14th August 1917.

1. The 7th Royal West Kent Regiment will move to the ERINGHEM area tomorrow 15th instant.

    The Battalion less 1st Line Transport will proceed from ABEELE by train.

    The 1st Line Transport will march by road in accordance with para 3.

2. The Battalion will march to ABEELE STATION tomorrow:-

    STARTING POINT:- Junction of the 2nd Class Road, and the STEENVOORDE - ABEELE Road, 400x East of the 7-Kilometre milestone.

    HOUR OF START:- 6-40a.m.

    ORDER OF MARCH:- Headquarters.
    "C" Company.
    "D" Company.
    "A" Company.
    "B" Company.
    Stretcher Bearers.

    DRESS:- Full Marching Order.

3. The 1st Line Transport will proceed by Road, and will be brigaded under orders of the O.C. 153rd Company A.S.C.

    STARTING POINT:- CROSS ROADS where WATOU - GODEWAERSVELDE Road crosses ABEELE - STEENVORDE Road.

    HOUR OF START:- 7-15a.m.

    ORDER OF MARCH:- 7th Royal West Kent Regt; followed by 8th East Surreys.

4. All Baggage will be loaded by 6-30a.m. Officers kits and Mess Boxes of H.Q. and "A" and "B" Coys will be sent over to the Transport Lines before that hour.
    Officers kits, and Mess Boxes of "C" and "D" Coys. will be called for by limber at 6-0a.m. sharp, and will be taken to the Q.M.Stores for reloading in accordance with arrangements to be made by the Q.M. and T.O.

5. One lorry will report at Bde. H.Q. at 8-0a.m. The Q.M. will arrange for a guide to meet this lorry at that hour to conduct it to his store. Men unable to march will parade at the Q.M.Stores at that hour, and the packs of men certified by the M.O. as unable to carry them will be dumped at the Q.M.Stores by 6-0a.m.
    There will be a special "SICK PARADE" with reference to the above at 5-30a.m.
    A.Motor Ambulance will call at Battn. Hd.Qrs. at 7-0a.m. for collection of sick for evacuation.

(sd) P.N.Anstruther. Captain.

ADJUTANT.

TRAINING PROGRAMME - Week Ending 25th August 1917.

"A" Company 7th Battalion Royal West Kent Regiment.

APP 4A.

1917.		
Monday 20th Aug:	9-0 - 12-30p.m.	Range Practice, Judging distances etc.
	2-30 - 3-30p.m.	Instruction in Proficiency at Arms, Instructions of N.C.O's in writing reports.
	4-0p.m.	Conference of Company Commanders.
Tuesday 21st Aug:	9-0 - 12-30p.m.	Bayonet Fighting, Musketry, Close Order Drill, and Physical Training.
	2-30 - 3-30p.m.	Instruction in Proficiency at Arms, Instruction of N.C.O's in Map Reading and use of Compass.
	4-0p.m.	Conference of Company Commanders.
Wednesday 22nd Aug:	9-0-12-30p.m.	Bayonet Fighting, Musketry, Extended Order Drill, and Physical Training.
	2-30 - 3-30p.m.	Instruction in Proficiency at Arms, Instruction of N.C.O's in Bombing Tactics.
	4-0p.m.	Conference of Company Commanders.
Thursday 23rd Aug:	9-0-12-30p.m.	Bayonet Fighting, Musketry, Platoon Attack Formations, and Physical Training.
	2-30 - 3-30.	Instruction in Proficiency at Arms, Instruction of N.C.O's in patrolling and writing reports.
	4-0p.m.	Conference of Company Commanders.
Friday.24th Aug:	9-0 - 12-30p.m.	Range Practice, Judging Distances etc.
	2-30 - 3-30p.m.	Instruction in Proficiency at Arms, Instruction of N.C.O's in Map Reading and use of Compass.
	4-0p.m.	Conference of Company Commanders.
Saturday 25th Aug:	9-0 - 12-30p.m.	Musketry, Bayonet Fighting, Platoon Attack formations, Instruction in Proficiency at Arms.
	2-30 p.m.	Confernec of Company Commanders.

TRAINING PROGRAMME - Week Ending 26th August 1917.

"B" Co. 7th Battalion Royal West Kent Regiment.

1917.		
Monday. 20th Aug.	9-0a.m.-12-30p.m.	Bayonet Fighting, Musketry, Close Order Drill, and Physical Training.
	2-30 - 3-30p.m.	Instruction in Proficiency at Arms, Instruction of N.C.O's in writing reports.
	4-0p.m.	Conference of Company Commanders.
Tuesday. 21st Aug:	9-0a.m.- 12-30p.m.	Range Practice, Judging Distances etc.
	2-30 - 3-30p.m.	Instruction of N.C.O's in Map Reading, and use of Compass.
	4-0p.m.	Conference of Company Commanders.
Wednesday. 22nd Aug:	9-0 - 12-30p.m.	Bayonet Fighting, Musketry, Extended Order Drill, and Physical Training.
	2-30 - 3-30p.m.	Instruction in Proficiency at Arms, Instruction of N.C.O's in Bombing Tactics.
	4-0p.m.	Conference of Company Commanders.
Thursday. 23rd Aug:	9-0 - 12-30p.m.	Bayonet Fighting, Musketry, Platoon Attack formations, and Physical Training.
	2-30 - 3-30p.m.	Instruction in Proficiency at Arms, Instruction in N.C.O's in Patrolling and writing reports.
	4-0p.m.	Conference of Company Commanders.
Friday. 24th Aug:	9-0 - 12-30p.m.	Musketry, Bayonet Fighting, Platoon Attack formations, and Physical Training.
	2-30 - 3-30p.m.	Instruction in Proficiency at Arms, Instruction of N.C.O's in Map Reading, and use of compass.
	4-0p.m.	Conference of Company Commanders.
Saturday. 25th Aug:	9-0 - 12-30p.m.	Range Practice,
	2-30p.m.	Conference of Company Commanders.

TRAINING PROGRAMME - Week Ending 25th August 1917.

"C" Company 7th Battalion Royal West Kent Regiment.

1917.
Monday
20th Aug:
- 9-0 – 12-30p.m. — Bayonet Fighting, Close Order Drill, Physical Training.
- 2-30 – 3-30p.m. — Instruction in Proficiency at Arms, Instruction of N.C.O's in writing reports.
- 4-0p.m. — Conference of Company Commanders.

Tuesday.
21st Aug:
- 9-0 – 12-30p.m. — Bayonet Fighting, Musketry, Extended Order Drill, and Physical Training.
- 2-30 – 3-30p.m. — Instruction in Proficiency at Arms. Instruction of N.C.O's in Bombing Tactics.
- 4-0p.m. — Conference of Company Commanders.

Wednesday.
22nd Aug.
- 9-0 – 12-30p.m. — Range Practice, Judging distances etc.
- 2-30 – 3-30p.m. — Instruction in Proficiency at arms. Instruction of N.C.O's in Map Reading, and use of Compass.
- 4-0p.m. — Conference of Company Commanders.

Thursday.
23rd Aug:
- 9-0 – 12-30p.m. — Bayonet Fighting, Musketry, Platoon attack formations, and Physical Training.
- 2-30 – 3-30p.m. — Instruction in Proficiency at arms. Instruction of N.C.O's in Patrolling and writing reports.
- 4-0p.m. — Conference of Company Commanders.

Friday.
24th Aug:
- 9-0 – 12-30p.m. — Musketry, Bayonet Fighting, Platoon attack formations, and Physical Training.
- 2-30 – 3-30p.m. — Instruction in Proficiency at arms, Instruction of N.C.O's in Map Reading and use of Compass.
- 4-0p.m. — Conference of Company Commanders.

Saturday.
25th Aug:
- 9-0 – 12-30p.m. — Musketry, Bayonet Fighting, Platoon and Company attack formations. Instruction in Proficiency at arms.
- 2-30. — Conference of Company Commanders.

TRAINING PROGRAMME – Week Ending 25th August 1917.

"D" Company   7th Battalion Royal West Kent Regiment.

1917.		
Monday 20th Aug:	9-0 – 12-30p.m.	Bayonet Fighting, Physical Training, Musketry, Close Order Drill.
	2-30 – 3-30p.m.	Instruction in Proficiency at arms. Instruction of N.C.O's in writing reports.
	4-0p.m.	Conference of Company Commanders.
Tuesday. 21st Aug:	9-0 – 12-30p.m.	Bayonet Fighting, Physical Training, Musketry, Extended order drill.
	2-30 – 3-30p.m.	Instruction in Proficiency at arms, and use of Compass.
	4-0p.m.	Conference of Company Commanders.
Wednesday. 22nd Aug:	9-0 – 12-30p.m.	Bayonet Fighting, Musketry, Platoon Attack formations, Physical Training.
	2-30 – 3-30p.m.	Instruction in Proficiency at arms. Instruction of N.C.O's in Bombing Tactics.
	4-0p.m.	Conference of Company Commanders,
Thursday. 23rd Aug:	9-0 – 12-30p.m.	Range Practices, Judging distances etc.
	2-30 – 3-30p.m.	Instruction in Proficiency at arms. Instruction of N.C.O's in Patrolling and writing reports.
	4-0p.m.	Conference of Company Commanders.
Friday. 24th Aug:	9-0 –12-30p.m.	Musketry, Bayonet Fighting, Physical Training Platoon attack formations.
	2-30 – 3-30p.m.	Instruction in Proficiency at arms. Instruction in N.C.O's in Map Reading and use of compass.
	4-0p.m.	Conference of Company Commanders.
Saturday. 25th Aug:	9-0 – 12-30p.m.	Musketry, Bayonet Fighting, Physical Training, Platoon and Company Attack formations. Instruction in Proficiency at arms.
	2-30p.m.	Conference of Company Commanders .

7th Battalion Royal West Kent Regiment.

WEEK ENDING 25th AUGUST 1917.

Allotment of Assault Course (B.13. d.5.8.) and Bombing Pits. (B.20. a. 7.3.)

DATE.	ASSAULT COURSE.		BOMBING PITS.	
Mon:20th.	9-0 - 11-0a.m. 11-0 - 1-0p.m.	"B" Co. A "C" Co.		
Tues:21st.	9-0 - 11-0a.m. 11-0 - 1-0p.m.	"D" Co. "A" Co. B	9-0 - 11-0a.m. 11-0 - 1-0p.m. 2-0 - 4-0p.m.	"C" Co. "D" Co. "B" Co.
Wed:22nd.	9-0 - 11-0a.m. 11-0 - 1-0p.m.	"B" Co. "C" Co. C		
Thurs:23rd.	9-0 - 11-0a.m. 11-0 - 1-0p.m.	"D" Co. "A" Co. D	9-0 - 11-0a.m. 11-0 - 1-0p.m. 2-0 - 4-0p.m.	"A" Co. "B" Co. "C" Co.
Frid:24th.	9-0 - 11-0a.m. 11-0 - 1-0p.m.	"B" Co. "C" Co. A		
Sat:25th.	9-0 - 11-0a.m. 11-0 - 1-0p.m.	"D" Co. "A" Co. B	9-0 - 11-0a.m. 11-0 - 1-0p.m. 2-0 - 4-0p.m.	"C" Co. "D" Co. "A" Co.

A44a

7th Battalion Royal West Kent Regiment.

Programme of Training for week ending the 25th August 1917.

DATE	HOUR	NATURE OF TRAINING.	LOCATION.	REMARKS.
1917.				
Mon:20th Aug:	9-0a.m. - 12-30.	Range Practises. Bayonet Fighting, Physical Training, Musketry, Close Order Drill.	B.13. d. 5.8.	
	2-30 to 3-30p.m.	Instruction in Proficiency at Arms, and Instruction of N.C.O's in writing reports.	Vicinity of Billets.	
	4-0p.m.	Conference of Company Commanders.	Battalion Headquarters.	
Tues: 21st Aug:	9-0a.m.-12-30p.m.	Range Practises. Bayonet Fighting, Physical Training, Close order drill, extended order drill, Musketry.	B.13. d. 5.8.	
	2-30 - 3-30p.m.	Instruction in Proficiency at Arms. Instruction of N.C.O's in Map reading and use of Compass.	Vicinity of Billets.	
	4-0p.m.	Conference of Company Commanders.	Battalion Headquarters.	
Wed:22nd Aug:	9-0a.m.-12-30p.m.	Range Practises. Bayonet Fighting, Physical Training, Musketry, Extended order drill, Platoon Attack formations.	B.13. d. 5.8.	
	2-30 - 3-30p.m.	Instruction in Proficiency at Arms. Instruction of N.C.O's in Bombing tactics.	Vicinity of Billets.	
	4-0p.m.	Conference of Company Commanders.	Battalion Headquarters.	
Thurs:23rd Aug:	9-0 - 12-30p.m.	Range Practises. Bayonet Fighting, Physical Training, Platoon attack formations, Musketry.	B.13. d.5.8.	
	2-30 - 3-30p.m.	Instruction in Proficiency at Arms.	Vicinity of Billets.	
	4-0p.m.	Conference of Company Commanders.	Battalion Headquarters.	

DATE.	HOUR.	NATURE OF TRAINING.	LOCATION.	REMARKS.
1917.				
Frid: 24th Aug.	9-0 - 12-30p.m.	Range Practises. Musketry, Bayonet Fighting, Physical Training, Platoon Attack formations.	B.13. d. 5.8.	
	2-30 - 3-30p.m.	Instruction in Proficiency at Arms, Instruction of N.C.O's in Map reading and use of Compass.	Vicinity of Billets.	
	4-0p.m.	Conference of Company Commanders.	-do- Battalion Headquarters.	
Sat: 25th Aug:	9-0 - 12-30p.m.	Range Practises. Musketry, Bayonet Fighting, Platoon and Company attack formations, Proficiency at Arms.	B.13. d. 5.8. Vicinity of Billets.	
	2-30p.m.	Conference of Company Commanders	Battalion Headquarters.	

Field. 17th August 1917.

Lieut.Col.
Commanding 7th Battalion Royal West Kent Regiment.

7th Battalion Royal West Kent Regiment.

WEEK ENDING 1st SEPTEMBER 1917.

Allotment of Bombing Pits. at (B.20.a.?.)

DATE	TIME		COMPANY
1917.			
Tues: Aug: 28th.	9-0a.m.	to 11-0a.m.	"A" Company.
	11-0a.m.	to 1-0p.m.	"B" Company.
	2-0p.m.	to 4-0p.m.	"D" Company.
Thurs: Aug: 30th.	9-0a.m.	to 11-0a.m.	"C" Company.
	11-0a.m.	to 1-0p.m.	"A" Company.
	2-0p.m.	to 4-0p.m.	"B" Company.
Sat: Sept: 1st.	9-0a.m.	to 11-0a.m.	"D" Company.
	11-0a.m.	to 1-0p.m.	"C" Company.

ADJT

TF

APP 45

COPY OF LETTER FROM BRIGADIER GENERAL
Commanding 55th Inf. Brigade.

The Brigade Commander wishes to express his gratitude to your Battalion for the excellent services rendered by the N.C.O. and 14-Runners who were sent up at the last moment to man a supplementary system of relay posts for the recent operations. In spite of the fact that these men had only come out of the line the day before, and had rightly expected a few days rest, they thoroughly appreciated the importance of their task and shewed the greatest keeness in carrying it out. In spite of frequent heavy shelling they maintained swift communication for over 24-hours before they were relieved. He would like the men to know that their work was of the greatest assistance to him personally. He considers that the manner in which they carried it out reflects great credit on their Battalion. The following is a list of the N.C.O's and men who carried out the duties mentioned in the above:-

10178	L/C.	Ursell J.	"HQ".
18633	"	Humphries H.	"B" Co.
18868	Pte.	Adams C.	"C" Co.
10543	"	Thornton C.	"C" Co.
19439	"	Martin F.	"A" Co.
205633	"	Hayward F.	"B" Co.
337	"	Beale F.	"HQ".
19440	"	Morton E.L.	"D" Co.
19513	"	Howitt	"D" Co.
18862	"	Eager W.	"B" Co.
4740	"	Mayger A.	"A" Co.
3217	"	Swift J.	"C" Co.
24806	"	Grimley J.	"C" Co.
2297	"	Wright P.	"HQ".

(sd) J. Mitchell. Captain.
Staff Captain. 55th Infantry Brigade.

WEEK ENDING 8th SEPTEMBER 1917.

Allottment of Bombing Pits at (B. 20. a. 7. 3.)

Tuesday. 4th September.	9-0 a.m. to 11-0 a.m.	"A" Company.
	11-0 a.m. to 1-0 p.m.	"B" Company.
	2-0 p.m. to 4-0 p.m.	"C" Company.
Thursday. 6th September.	2-0 p.m. to 4-0 p.m.	"D" Company.
Saturday. 8th September.	9-0 a.m. to 11-0 a.m.	"C" Company.
	11-0 a.m. to 1-0 p.m.	"D" Company.
	2-0 p.m. to 4-0 p.m.	"A" Company.

APP. 47

TRAINING PROGRAMME – Week Ending 1st September 1917.

"A" Company 7th Battalion Royal West Kent Regiment.

1917. Monday 27th Aug:	9-0a.m. to 12-30.	Bayonet Fighting, Platoon Attack Formations, Box Respirator Drill, Musketry and Physical Training.
	2-30p.m. to 3-30.	Proficiency at Arms, N.C.O's patrolling (Day and Night) writing reports.
	4-0p.m.	Conference of Company Commanders.
Tuesday Aug: 28th.	9-0a.m. to 12-30.	Bayonet Fighting, Platoon Attack Formations, Platoon Attacks on Strong Points.
	2-30p.m. to 3-30.	Proficiency at Arms, N.C.O's Map Reading, duties on outposts.
	4-0p.m.	Conference of Commanders.
Wednesday Aug: 29th.	8-30a.m.	Range Practice on 5th Army Range.
Thursday Aug: 30th	9-0a.m. to 12-30.	Bayonet Fighting, Musketry, Platoon Attack Formations. Platoon Attack on Strong Points. Company attack formations.
	2-30p.m. to 3-30.	Proficiency at Arms, N.C.O's fire direction and control, indication of targets. Range finding (Barr and Stroud).
Friday Aug; 31st	9-0a.m. to 12-30.	Company attack formations forming defensive flank, Mopping up. Battalion attack formations, Box Respirator drill.
	2-30p.m. to 3-30.	Proficiency at arms, N.C.O's simple tactical problems under Company arrangements.
	4-0p.m.	Conference of Company Commanders.
Saturday. Sept: 1st.	9-0a.m. to 12-30. 2-30p.m	Revision. Conference of Company Commanders.

TRAINING PROGRAMME - Week Ending 1st September 1917.

"B" Company 7th Battalion Royal West Kent Regiment.

1917.

Monday 27th Aug:
- 9-0a.m. to 12-30. — Bayonet Fighting, Platoon Attack Formations, Box Respirator Drill, Musketry and Physical Training.
- 2-30p.m. to 3-30. — Proficiency at arms, N.C.O's patrolling (Day and Night) writing reports.
- 4-0p.m. — Conference of Company Commanders.

Tuesday 28th Aug:
- 9-0a.m. to 12-30. — Bayonet Fighting, Platoon Attack formations, Platoon attacks on Strong points.
- 2-30p.m. to 3-30. — Proficiency at arms, N.C.O's Map Reading, Duties on outposts.
- 4-0p.m. — Conference of Company Commanders.

Wednesday 29th Aug.
- 8-30a.m. — Range Practice on Fth Army Range.

Thursday 30th Aug:
- 9-0a.m. to 12-30. — Bayonet Fighting, Musketry, Platoon attack formations, Platoon Attacks on Strong Points.
- 2-30p.m. to 3-30. — Proficency at arms, N.C.O's fire direction and control, indication of targets. Range Finding (Barr and Stroud).

Friday 31st Aug:
- 9-0a.m. to 12-30. — Company attack formations, forming defensive flank, Mopping up. Battalion attack formations, Box Respirator drill.
- 2-30p.m. to 3-30. — Proficiency at arms, N.C.O's simple Tactical Problems under Company arrangements.
- 4-0p.m. — Confernec of Company Commanders.

Saturday. 1st Sept.
- 9-0a.m. to 12-30. — Revision.
- 2-30p.m. — Conference of Company Commanders.

TRAINING PROGRAMME. – Week Ending 1st September 1917.

"C" Company 7th Battalion Royal West Kent Regiment.

1917.
Monday. Aug:27th.
- 9-0 a.m. to 12-30. — Range Practices, Bayonet Fighting, Box Respirator Drill.
- 2-30 to 3-30. — Proficiency at arms, N.C.O's patrolling (Day and Night) writing reports.
- 4-0 p.m. — Conference of Company Commanders.

Tuesday; Aug:28th.
- 9-0 a.m. to 12-30. — Bayonet Fighting, Platoon Attack formations, Platoon attacks on Strong Points.
- 2-30 p.m. to 3-30. — Proficiency at arms. N.C.O's Map Reading, Duties on outposts.
- 4-0 p.m. — Conference of Company Commanders.

Wednesday. Aug:29th
- 8-30 a.m. — Range Practice on 5th Army Range.

Thursday. Aug:30th.
- 9-0 a.m. to 12-30. — Bayonet Fighting, Musketry, Platoon attack formations, Platoon attacks on Strong Points. Company attack formations.
- 2-30 p.m. to 3-30. — Proficiency at arms. N.C.O's fire direction and control, indication of targets. Range Finding (Barr and Stroud).

Friday Aug 31st.
- 9-0 a.m. to 12-30. — Company attack formations, forming defensive flank. Mopping up. Battalion attack formations. Box Respirator drill.
- 2-30 p.m. to 3-30. — Proficiency at arms. N.C.O's simple tactical problems under Company arrangements.
- 4-0 p.m. — Conference of Company Commanders.

Saturday. Sept. 1st.
- 9-0 a.m. to 12-30. — Revision.
- 2-30 p.m. — Conference of Company Commanders.

TRAINING PROGRAMME - Week Ending 1st September 1917.

"D" Company 7th Battalion Royal West Kent Regiment.

1917.

Monday Aug: 27th.
- 9-0 a.m. to 12-30. — Bayonet Fighting, Platoon attack formations, Platoon attacks on strong points. Box Respirator drill, Musketry.
- 2-30 p.m. to 3-30. — Proficiency at arms, N.C.O's patrolling (Day and Night) writing reports.
- 4-0 p.m. — Conference of Company Commanders.

Tuesday Aug: 28th.
- 9-0 a.m. to 12-30. — Range Practice, Bayonet Fighting.
- 2-30 p.m. to 3-30. — Proficiency at arms, N.C.O's Map Reading, Duties on outposts.
- 4-0 p.m. — Conference of Company Commanders.

Wednesday Aug: 29th.
- 8-30 a.m. — Range Practice on 5th Army Range.

Thursday 30th Aug.
- 9-0 a.m. to 12-30. — Bayonet Fighting, Musketry. Platoon attack formation, Platoon Attacks on Strong Points. Company Attack Formations.
- 2-30 p.m. to 3-30. — Proficiency at arms. N.C.O's fire direction and control, indication of targets. Range Finding (Barr and Stroud).

Friday 31st Aug.
- 9-0 a.m. to 12-30. — Company attack formations, forming defensive flank, Mopping up. Battalion Attack formations. Box Respirator drill.
- 2-30 p.m. to 3-30. — Proficiency at arms. N.C.O's Simple Tactical problems under Company arrangements.
- 4-0 p.m. — Conference of Company Commanders.

Saturday 1st Sept.
- 9-0 a.m. to 12-30. — Revision.
- 2-30 p.m. — Conference of Company Commanders.

TRAINING PROGRAMME WEEK ENDING 8th SEPTEMBER 1917.

"A" Company. 7th Battalion Royal West Kent Regiment.

1917.		
Monday 3rd Sept:	9-0 – 12-30p.m.	Range Practice, Bayonet Fighting.
	2-30 – 3-30p.m.	Proficiency at arms, N.C.O's fire direction, and control, Indication of targets.
	4-0p.m.	Conference of Company Commanders.
Tuesday 4th Sept.	9-0 – 12-30.	Platoon attack formations, Company in attack (Tactical Scheme) including consolidation and meeting Counter attack.
	2-30 & 3-30p.m.	Proficiency at arms, N.C.O's patrolling and writing reports.
	4-0p.m.	Conference of Company Commanders.
Wednesday 5th Sept.	8-30. – 12-30p.m.	Attached to 8th E.Surrey Regt (Details will be issued later).
	2-0 to 3-30p.m.	Wiring.
	4-0p.m.	Conference of Company Commanders.
Thursday 6th Sept.	9-0 – 12-30p.m.	Battalion in attack (Tactical Scheme) including consolidation and meeting Counter attack.
	2-30 – 3-30p.m.	Proficiency at arms, N.C.O's Judging distance, and range taking. (Barr and Stroud).
	4-0p.m.	Conference of Company Commanders.
Friday Sept.7th	9-0 – 12-30	Battalion in Attack (Tactical Scheme) including consolidation and meeting Counter attack.
	2-30 – 3-30p.m.	Proficiency at arms, N.C.O's patrolling and writing reports.
	4-0p.m.	Conference of Company Commanders.
Saturday 8th Sept.	9-0 – 12-30.	Revision.
	2-30p.m.	Conference of Company Commanders.

TRAINING PROGRAMME FOR WEEK ENDING 8th SEPTEMBER 1917.

"B" Company 7th Battalion Royal East Kent Regiment.

1917.
Monday 3rd Sept.   9-0 - 12-30.   Platoon attack formations, Company
                                       in attack (Tactical Scheme) including
                                       consolidation and meeting counter attack.
                      2-30 - 3-30p.m. Proficiency at arms, N.C.O's patrolling
                                       and writing reports.
                      4-0p.m.   Conference of Company Commanders.

Tuesday 4th Sept.   9-0 - 12-30.   Range Practice, Bayonet Fighting.
                      2-30 - 3-30p.m. Proficiency at arms, N.C.O's fire
                                       direction and control, Indication of
                                       targets.
                      4-0p.m.   Conference of Company Commanders.

Wednesday 5th Sept.   8-30 - 12-30.   Attached to 9th E. Surrey Rgt. (Details
                                       will be furnished later)
                      2-0 3-30.   Firing.
                      4-0p.m.   Conference of Company Commanders.

Thursday 6th Sept.   9-0 - 12-30.   Battalion in attack (Tactical Scheme)
                                       including consolidation and meeting
                                       Counter attack.
                      2-30 - 3-30.   Proficiency at arms, N.C.O's Judging dist-
                                       ance and range taking (Barr and Stroud).
                      4-0p.m.   Conference of Company Commanders.

Friday 7th Sept.   9-0 - 12-30.   Battalion in attack, (Tactical Scheme)
                                       including consolidation and meeting
                                       counter attack.
                      2-30 - 3-30.   Proficiency at arms, N.C.O's patrolling
                                       and writing reports.
                      4-0p.m.   Conference of Company Commanders.

Saturday 8th Sept.   9-0 - 11-30.   Revision.
                      4-30p.m.   Conference of Company Commanders.

TRAINING PROGRAMME WEEK ENDING 8th SEPTEMBER 1917.

"C" Company 7th Battalion Royal West Kent Regiment.

1917.

Monday 3rd Sept.	9-0 – 12-30.	Platoon attack formations, Company in attack (Tactical Scheme) including consolidation and meeting counter attack.
	2-30 – 3-30.	Proficiency at arms, N.C.O's patrolling and writing reports.
	4-0 p.m.	Conference of Company Commanders.
Tuesday 4th Sept.	9-0 – 12-30.	Company in attack (Tactical Scheme) including consolidation and meeting counter attack. Musketry, Bayonet Fighting.
	2-0 – 3-30.	Wiring.
	4-0 p.m.	Conference of Company Commanders.
Wednesday 5th Sept.	8-30 – 12-30.	Attached to 8th E. Surrey Rgt. (Details will be furnished later).
	2-30 – 3-30.	Proficiency at arms, N.C.O's fire direction and control, Indication of Targets.
	4-0 p.m.	Conference of Company Commanders.
Thursday 6th Sept.	9-0 – 12-30.	Battalion in attack (Tactical Scheme) including consolidation and meeting counter attack.
	2-30 – 3-30.	Proficiency at arms, N.C.O's Judging distance and range taking (Barr and Stroud).
	4-0 p.m.	Conference of Company Commanders.
Friday 7th Sept.	9-0 – 12-30.	Battalion in attack (Tactical Scheme) including consolidation and meeting counter attack.
	2-30 – 3-30.	Proficiency at arms, N.C.O's Patrolling and writing reports.
	4-0 p.m.	Conference of Company Commanders.
Saturday 8th Sept.	9-0 – 12-30.	Revision.
	2-30 p.m.	Conference of Company Commanders.

TRAINING PROGRAMME WEEK ENDING 8th SEPTEMBER 1917.

"D" Company 7th Battalion Royal West Kent Regiment.

1917.

Monday 3rd Sept.	9-0 – 12-30.	Platoon attack formations, Company in attack (Tactical Scheme) including consolidation and meeting counter attack.
	2-30 – 3-30.	Proficiency at arms, N.C.O's patrolling and writing reports.
	4-0p.m.	Conference of Company Commanders.
Tuesday 4th Sept.	9-0 – 12-30.	Company in attack (Tactical Scheme) including consolidation and meeting counter attack. Musketry, Bayonet Fighting.
	2-0 – 3-30.	Firing.
	4-0p.m.	Conference of Company Commanders.
Wednesday 5th Sept.	9-0 – 12-30	Musketry, Firing, "Mopping Up," Box Respirator Drill
	2-30 – 3-30.	Proficiency at arms, N.C.O's fire direction and control, Indication of targets.
	4-0p.m.	Conference of Company Commanders.
Thursday 6th Sept.	9-0 – 12-30.	Battalion in attack, (Tactical Scheme) including consolidation and meeting Counter Attack.
	2-30 – 3-30.	Proficiency at arms, N.C.O's Judging distance and range taking (Barr & Stroud)
	4-0p.m.	Conference of Company Commanders.
Friday 7th Sept.	9-0 – 12-30.	Battalion in attack (Tactical Scheme) including consolidation and meeting counter attack.
	2-30 – 3-30.	Proficiency at arms, N.C.O's Patrolling and writing reports.
	4-0p.m.	Conference of Company Commanders.
Saturday 8th Sept.	9-0 – 12-30.	Revision.
	2-30p.m.	Conference of Company Commanders.

APP 48

7th Battalion Royal West Kent Regiment.

Training Programme for week ending 15th September 1917

DATE	HOUR	NATURE OF TRAINING	Location of training	REMARKS
Mon.10 Sept.	9.0—12.30	Range practice. Bayonet fighting. Coy.,attack practice including consolidation.	B.13.d.40.90 Training area	Instruction daily in NIGHT PATROLING, vide 18.Div. No.G.660, as under, viz:—
	2.30—3.50	Proficiency at arms. N.C.O's patrolling and writing reports. Map reading.	Vicinity of billets.	
	4.0 p.m.	Conference of Company Commanders.	Battn.Hd.Qrs.	
Tues.11 Sept.	9.0—12.30	Battalion attack practice.	Training area.	Date. Place. Hour.
	2.30—3.30	Proficiency at arms. N.C.O's Fire direction and control; indication of targets.	Vicinity of billets.	"A" Company. B.15.c.80.70
	4.0 p.m.	Conference of Company Commanders.	Battalion Hd.Qrs.	10th to 12th Sept. 3.0 p.m. 13th to B.21.b.45.90. and 9.0 p.m. 15th Sept.
Wed. 12 Sept.		——RANGE PRACTICE——	5th Army Range.	"B" Company. B.14.a.20.10 10,12,14 Sept. 5.30 p.m. 11,13,15 B.13.b.8.c. and 8.45 p.m. Sept.
Thurs. 13 Sept.	9.30—1.30	Brigade Training.	Training Area.	"C" Company. B.14.a.central 10th to 4.0 p.m. 15th Sept. and 9.0 p.m.
	2.30—3.30	Proficiency at arms. N.C.O's examination in pamphlet 18 Div.G.600	Vicinity of billets.	
	4.0 p.m.	Conference of Company Commanders.	Battalion Hd.Qrs.	
Fri.14 Sept.	9.0—12.30	Range practice. Bayonet fighting. Coy.,attack practice including consolidation.	B.13.d.40.90. Training Area.	"D" Company. v.14.c.3.9. 10th to 12th Sept. 5.0 p.m. 13th to B.14.d.5.7. and 9.15 p.m. 15th Sept.
	2.30—3.30	Proficiency at arms. N.C.O's patrolling and writing reports. Map reading.	Vicinity of billets.	
	4.0 p.m.	Conference of Company Commanders.	Battalion Hd.Qrs.	
Sat.15 Sept.	9.0—12.30	Revision.	Training area.	
	2.30 p.m.	Conference of Company Commanders	Battalion Hd.Qrs.	

Field.
7-9-17.

Lieut.Col.
Commanding 7th Battalion Royal West Kent Regiment.

APP 49

TRAINING PROGRAMME – Week Ending 22nd Sept: 1917.

"A" Company. 7th Battalion Royal West Kent Regiment.

Mon: Sept:17th.	9-0 12-30p.m.	Platoon attacks on Strong Points. Construction of Strong Points.
	2-30 3-30	Proficiency at arms, N.C.O's Map Reading and writing reports.
	4-0p.m.	Conference of Company Commanders.
Tues: Sept:18th.	10-0a.m.	Brigade Assault at Arms.
Wed: 19th Sept.	9-0 12-30.	Range Practice, Bayonet Fighting.
	2-30 3-30.	Proficiency at arms, N.C.O's organisation and tactics of Bombing squads.
	4-0p.m.	Conference of Company Commanders.
Thurs: 20th Sept.	----8-15a.m.	Brigade Training.
	2-30 3-30p.m.	Proficiency at arms, N.C.O's method of organising consolidation parties, and allotment of tasks.
	4-0p.m.	Conference of Company Commanders.
Frid: 21st Sept.	9-0 12-30.	Route March.
	2-30 3-30.	Proficiency at arms, N.C.O's judging distance and use of the range finder.
	4-0p.m.	Conference of Company Commanders.
Sat: 22nd Sept.	9-0 12-30.	Revision.
	2-30p.m.	Conference of Company Commanders.

N.B.

Nightly Training in Patrolling in accordance with programme rendered.

TRAINING PROGRAMME.- Week Ending 22nd. September 1917.

"B". Company. 7th. Battalion Royal West Kent Regiment.

Mon.: Sept:17th.	9-0 12-30p.m.	Platoon attacks on Strong Points. Construction of Strong Points.
	2-30 3-30p.m.	Proficiency at Arms, N.C.O's. Map Reading and writing reports.
	4-0p.m.	Conference of Company Commanders.

Tues: Sept:18th.	10-0a.m.	Brigade Assault at Arms.

Wed: Sept:19th.	9-0 12-30p.m.	Company Attack Practice, including consolidation. Mopping Up.
	2-30 3-30p.m.	Proficiency at Arms. N.C.O's, method of organising consolidation parties and allotment of tasks.
	4-0p.m.	Conference of Company Commanders.

Thurs: Sept:20th.	8-15a.m.	Brigade Training.
	2-30 3-30p.m.	Proficiency at Arms. N.C.O's, methods of organisation and tactics of Bombing Squads.
	4-0p.m.	Conference of Company Commanders.

FRID; Sep t:	9-0 12-30.	Route March.
	2-30 3-30p.m.	Proficiency at arms, N.C.O's Judging distance and use of the Range finder.
	4-0p.m.	Conference of Company Commanders.

Sat: 22nd Sept.	9-0 12-30.	Revision.
	2-30p.m.	Conference of Company Commanders.

N.B.
Nightly Training in Patrolling in accordance with programme rendered.

TRAINING PROGRAMME. Week Ending 22nd Sept: 1917.

"C" Company. 7th Battalion Royal West Kent Regiment.

Mon: Sept. 17th.	9-0 12-30.	Platoon attacks on Strong Points, construction of Strong Points.
	2-30 3-30.	Proficiency at arms, N.C.O's Map reading and writing reports.
	4-0p.m.	Conference of Company Commanders.
Tues: 18th Sept.	10-0a.m.	Brigade Assault at arms.
Wed: 19th Sept.	9-0 12-30.	Company attack practice including consolidation and Mopping up.
	2-30 3-30.	Proficiency at arms, N.C.O's organisation and tactics of Bombing squads.
	4-0p.m.	Conference of Company Commanders.
Thurs: 20th Sept.	8-15a.m.	Brigade Training.
	2-30 3-30.	Proficiency at arms, N.C.O's organisation of consolidation parties, and allotment of tasks.
	4-0p.m.	Conference of Company Commanders.
Frid: 21st Sept.	9-0 12-30.	Route March.
	2-30 3-30.	Proficiency at arms, N.C.O's Judging distance and use of the range finder.
	4-0p.m.	Conference of Company Commanders.
Sat: 22nd Sept:	9-0 12-30.	Revision.
	2-30p.m.	Conference of Company Commanders.

N.B.
Nightly training in patrolling in accordance with programme rendered.

TRAINING PROGRAMME. Week Ending 22nd Sept: 1917.

"D" Company. 7th Battalion Royal West/Kent Regiment.

Mon: 17th Sept.	9-0 12-30,	Range Practice, Bayonet Fighting.
	2-30 3-30,	Proficiency at arms, N.C.O's organisation and tactics of Bombing Squads.
	4-0p.m.	Conference of Company Commanders.

| Tues: 18th Sept. | 10-0a.m. | Brigade Assault at arms. |

Wed: 19th Sept.	9-0 12-30,	Platoon attacks on Strong Points, Construction of Strong Points.
	2-30 3-30,	Proficiency at arms, N.C.O's Map reading and writing reports.
	4-0p.m.	Conference of Company Commanders.

Thurs: 20th Sept.	8-15a.m.	Brigade Training.
	2-30 3-30,	Proficiency at arms, N.C.O's method of organising consolidation parties, and allotment of tasks.
	4-0p.m.	Conference of Company Commanders.

Frid: 21st Sept.	9-0 12-30,	Route March.
	2-30 3-30,	Proficiency at arms, N.C.O's Judging distance and use of the range finder.
	4-0p.m.	Conference of Company Commanders.

| Sat: 22nd Sept. | 9-0 12-30 | Revision. |
| | 2-30p.m. | Conference of Company Commanders. |

N.B. Nightly training in patrolling in accordance with programme rendered.

APP 50

7th Battalion Royal West Kent Regiment.

PROGRAMME OF TRAINING. — 20th -23rd September 1917.

Date.	Time	Nature of Training.	Location.	Remarks.
Thursday 20th Sept.	9.0 p.m.	Forming up by night for ATTACK	B.15.c. B.13.b. B.14.a. B.14.b.	Night patrolling in accordance with programme rendered.
Friday 21 Sept.	9.0 a.m. to 12.30 p.m.	(a) Preliminary practice in forming up for night Attacks. (b) Platoon attacks on Strong Points. (c) Intensive digging.	Training Area.	Night patrolling in accordance with programme rendered.
	2.30 to 3.30 p.m. 4.0 p.m.	As per Programme rendered.		
	9.0 p.m.	Forming up by night for ATTACK.	B.15.c. B.13.b. B.14.a. B.14.b.	
Saturday 22 Sept.	11.0 a.m. to 1.0 p.m.	Throwing Live Bombs.	B.20.a.7.3.	Draft only.
	9.0 a.m. to 12.30 p.m.	Company Attack Practice.	Training Area.	

Field
20-9-17.

Lieut-Col.
Commanding 7th Battalion Royal West Kent Regiment.

App. 51

7th Battalion Royal West Kent Regiment.

PROGRAMME OF TRAINING ———————— 29th September 1917.

Date.	Time.	Nature of Training.	Location.	Remarks.
1917. Wednesday 26th Sept.	9.0 a.m. onwards 9.0 — 12.30 2.30—3.30.	Range Practice. Musketry, Patrolling, Bayonet Fighting, Physical Training. Intensive digging* proficiency at arms. N.C.O's organisation and tactics of bombing parties.	"A" Range., No.1.Area. No.1.Area.	All SIGNALLERS under the Signal Officer, daily. ————— * Organisation and allotment of tasks only.
Thursday 27th Sept.	9.0 — 12.30. 2.30— 3.30.	Musketry, Bayonet Fighting, Physical Training. Preliminary instruction in forming-up at night. Proficiency at arms. N.C.O's map reading and use of compass.	No.2.Area. No.2.Area.	
Friday 28th Sept.	9.0 a.m. onwards. 9.0 — 12.30 2.30—3.30. 4.0p.m.	Range practice. Musketry, Bayonet Fighting, Preliminary instruction in forming-up at night. Platoon attack formations. Deployments from column of route. Proficiency at arms/ Fire direction and control (N.C.O's) Conference of Company Commanders.	"A" Range. No.3.Area. No.3.Area. Battalion Hd.Qrs.	
Saturday 29th Sept.	9.0—12.30 2.30 — 3.30	Revision. Conference of Company Commanders.	No.4.Area. Battalion Hd.Qrs.	

Field.
25-9-17.

Lieut.Col.
Commanding 7th Battalion Royal West Kent Regt.

SECRET.

7TH BUFFS ORDER NO.81.

22nd September 1917.

REFERENCE MAP. SHEET 27, Edn.2.1/40,000.

1. 55th Infantry Brigade will move to-morrow to ST.JAN TER BIEZEN Area.

2. 7th Buffs will entrain at ESQUELBECQ Station at 9.20 a.m.

      Hour of Start.   7.50 a.m.

      Starting Point. Cross Roads Eastern end of ERINGHEM.

      Order of March. Headquarters, C.B.D.Bums, A.B.Draft.

      Route.   ZEGGERS CAPPEL.

3. "B" Company will join the Battalion during line of march at Road Junction D.3.a.5.7. at 8.15 a.m.

4. First Line Transport will be Brigaded and march under separate orders.

5. MAJOR L.WOOD and 2 representatives per Company, 1 from Battalion Headquarters and 1 from Transport will report to Staff Captain at 8th E.Surrey R.Headquarters, D.9.b.9.1. at 8.0 a.m. and proceed by lorry to the new Area.

6. Rations for the day will be carried on each man.

7. On march from POPERINGHE to destination, Companies will maintain a distance of 200 yards.

8. Companies and Headquarters will render an entraining State to Battalion Orderly Room by 7.15 a.m.

9. ACKNOWLEDGE.

                                                            Captain.
                            A/Adjutant, 7th Battalion, THE BUFFS.

Issued at 7.40 p.m.
Copies to:-
  "A" Company.
  "B" Company.
  "C" Company.
  "D" Company.
  2nd in Command.
  Transport Officer.
  Quartermaster.
  Medical Officer.
  Regt.Sgt.Major.
  Office.
  Diary.

ADMINISTRATIVE INSTRUCTIONS TO ACCOMPANY 7TH BUFFS ORDER NO.81.

1. Officers valises will be dumped outside Company Headquarters at 6.15 a.m. except "B" Company which must be dumped before 5.45 a.m. as the baggage wagon must leave "B" Company at 6.0 a.m. punctual.

2. Officers Mess property will be ready for loading as under and in each case the driver has been given definite orders (as well as the correct signal time) that he is to move off at the time stated and anything not ready will be left behind.

       "B" Company.   6.0 a.m.

       "A" Company.   6.30 a.m.

"C" and "D" Companies will send all Mess property to Quartermaster's Stores before 7.0 a.m.

3. Food required for the journey must be sent by Company Messes to Headquarters Mess by 6.45 a.m. for conveyance to ESQUELBECQ Station.

4. The Quartermaster will send two guides to the Office of the Area Commandant, LEDGERS CAPPEL before 8.0 a.m. to guide the two lorries to his stores.

5. All stretchers in possession of officers must be sent to the Quartermaster's Stores by 6.0 a.m.

6. On arrival in new Area the draft will be attached in equal numbers to each Company.

7. No.17 Platoon will be billeted separately on arrival in new Area, (except 2/LIEUT. S.A.HARVEY), and will be attached to "D" Company for rations.

8. Officers riding their chargers will instruct grooms to report at ESQUELBECQ Station to Pte. CHICK, who will be in charge of the chargers until they join up with the Transport.

9. Breakfast at 5.30 a.m.

10. All Companies will report in writing to the Adjutant by 7.0 a.m. that all billets have been inspected and found to be clean.

                      (Signed) C.K.BLACK. Captain.

22.9.17.   A/Adjutant, 7th Battalion, THE BUFFS.

Army Form C. 2118.

WAR DIARY
or
INTELLIGENCE SUMMARY.
(Erase heading not required.)

Instructions regarding War Diaries and Intelligence Summaries are contained in F. S. Regs., Part II. and the Staff Manual respectively. Title pages will be prepared in manuscript.

Place	Date	Hour	Summary of Events and Information	Remarks and references to Appendices
SCHOOL CAMP near ST.JAN-TER-BIEZEN.	1-10-17.		Training.	
	2-10-17.		Training.	
	3-10-17.		Training. Battalion Attack Scheme.	
	4-10-17.		Training.	
	5-10-17.		Training.	
	6-10-17.		Training.	
	7-10-17.		Divine Services.	
	8-10-17.		Training.	
	9-10-17.		Battalion left SCHOOL CAMP 6.55 a.m., and marched to DIRTY BUCKET CAMP. Arrived 10.0 a.m.	App. 52.
DIRTY BUCKET CAMP.	10-10-17.		Battalion moved at 10.5 a.m. for KEMPTON PARK, by 'busses. At 8.0 p.m. moved to relieve 6th Battn. Yorkshire Regt., in the front line. Relief complete at 4.0 a.m. 11th Oct.	
LINE.	11-10-17.		Battalion holding front line. Disposition of Coys: "B" and "C" Coys----Front Line. "A" and "D" Coys----In support.	
	12-10-17.		Enemy artillery active. Battalion attacked. Zero 5.25 a.m. Enemy shelling exceptionally heavy.	App. 53. App. 54.
	13-10-17.		Battalion relieved by 8th Battalion Suffolk Regiment. Relief complete 11.0 p.m.	
GOURNIER FARM.	14-10-17.		Battalion bivouacked for remainder of night at GOURNIER FARM. Battalion moved by Lorries to DIRTY BUCKET CAMP. Move complete 4.0 p.m. As Battalion were entering Lorries at CANAL BANK s everal casualties were caused by hostile aircraft.	
DIRTY BUCKET CAMP.	15-10-17.		Resting and cleaning-up.	
	16-10-17.		Resting and cleaning-up.	
	17-10-17.		Resting.	
	18-10-17.		Training.	
	19-10-17.		3-Officers and 200- O.R. detailed for carrying ammunition to the front line. Hd.Qrs. CANE TRENCH and HURST PARK. Lieut.A .GODLY in command of party.	
	20-10-17.		Training.	
	21-10-17.		Voluntary Church Services. Fatigue party returned at 10.0 p.m.	
	22-10-17.		Training.	
	23-10-17.		Training. Inspection of Companies in Marching Order by Commanding Officer.	

T2134. Wt. W708-176. 50r000. 4/15. Sir J. C. & S.

WAR DIARY
or
INTELLIGENCE SUMMARY.
(Erase heading not required.)

Army Form C. 2118.

Place	Date	Hour	Summary of Events and Information	Remarks and references to Appendices
DIRTY BUCKET CAMP.	24-10-17.		Battalion left DIRTY BUCKET CAMP at 12.0 noon for POPERINGHE. Arrived 1.30 p.m.	App.55.
POPERINGHE.	25-10-17.		Training (under Company arrangements.)	
	26-10-17.		Battalion left POPERINGHE at 2.30 p.m. Marched to PARROY CAMP, arriving 4.30 p.m. Relieved 17th Division at work on roads in vicinity of LANGEMARCK.	App.56.
PARROY CAMP	27-10-17.		Working on roads North of ST.JULIEN. Parties worked in two shifts - 2-Companies commencing work at 6.30 a.m. and 2-Companies at 9.30 a.m.	
	28-10-17.		Work on roads. Hostile aircarft bombed vicinity of camp. No casualties.	
	29-10-17.		Work on roads. Hostile aircraft bombed vicinity of camp. No casualties.	
	30-10-17.		Work on roads.	
	31-10-17.		Work on roads. 2- O.R. wounded.	
			OFFICERS JOINED DURING THE MONTH.	
			2/Lt.W.F.ROBERTS. Joined 2-10-17.	
			Capt. G.F.STALLARD.M.C. Joined 5-10-17.	
			2/Lt.W.U.C.TAYLER Re-joined 22-10-17.	
			2/Lt.E.A.THOMAS. Joined 29-10-17.	
			2/Lt.E.J.CURTIS. Joined 29-10-17.	
			OFFICERS CASUALTIES DURING MONTH.	
			2/Lt.J.A.HORTON. To 55th T.M.B. 5-10-17.	
			2/Lt.P.T.STANLEY. (To England for permanent Commn	
			(Indian Army. 7-10-17.	
			Capt.G.F.STALLARD.M.C. To 12th Bn.E.Surrey Regt. --- 13-10-17.	
			2/Lt.H.BUFFEE. Sick to England. 5-10-17.	
			Capt.F.H.LEWIN.M.C. Killed in Action 12-10-17.	
			2/Lt.A.C.MICHELL. -do- -do-	
			2/Lt.R.W.COLES. -do- -do-	
			2/Lt.J.H.GLADWELL. -do- 14-10-17.	
			Lieut.H.T.GREGORY. Died of Wounds. 12-10-17.	
			2/Lt.G.J.ALLEN. -do- 12-10-17.	
			Capt.I.HEATON. -do- 14-10-17.	
			Capt.P.N.ANSTRUTHER.DSO.MC. Wounded. 12-10-17.	
			Capt.F.H.F.SMITH. -do- -do-	
			Capt.A.R.HOGG. -do- 14-10-17.	
			Lieut.R.D.KENT.M.C. -do- 12-10-17.	
			OFFICERS CASUALTIES DURING MONTH.(Continued)	
			2/Lt.E.GRETHE. Wounded in Action. 12-10-17.	
			2/Lt.H.S.PEGLAR. -do- -do-	
			2/Lt.G.F.JOHNSTONE. -do- -do-	
			2/Lt.A.L.DUPONT. -do- -do-	
			2/Lt.H.T.RAPSON. -do- -do-	
			2/Lt.E.W.DAY. -do- 14-10-17.	

Lieut.Col.

Army Form C. 2118.

WAR DIARY
or
INTELLIGENCE SUMMARY.

(Erase heading not required.)

Instructions regarding War Diaries and Intelligence Summaries are contained in F.S. Regs., Part II. and the Staff Manual respectively. Title pages will be prepared in manuscript.

Place	Date	Hour	Summary of Events and Information	Remarks and references to Appendices
SCHOOL CAMP near ST. JAN-TER-BIEZEN.	1-10-17.		Training.	
	2-10-17.		Training.	
	3-10-17.		Training. Battalion Attack Scheme.	
	4-10-17.		Training.	
	5-10-17.		Training.	
	6-10-17.		Training.	
	7-10-17.		Divine Services.	
	8-10-17.		Training.	
	9-10-17.		Battalion left SCHOOL CAMP 6.55 a.m., and marched to DIRTY BUCKET CAMP. Arrived 10.0 a.m.	App. 52.
DIRTY BUCKET CAMP.	10-10-17.		Battalion moved at 10.5 a.m. for KEMPTON PARK, by 'busses. At 8.0 p.m. moved to relieve 6th Battn. Yorkshire Regt., in the front line. Relief complete at 4.0 a.m. 11th Oct.	
LINE.	11-10-17.		Battalion holding front line. Disposition of Coys: "B" and "C" Coys----Front Line. "A" and "D" Coys----In support.	
	12-10-17.		Enemy artillery active. Battalion attacked. Zero 5.25 a.m. Enemy shelling exceptionally heavy.	App 53. App. 54.
	13-10-17.		Battalion relieved by 8th Battalion Suffolk Regiment. Relief complete 11.0 p.m.	
GOURNIER FARM.	14-10-17.		Battalion bivouacked for remainder of night at GOURNIER FARM. Battalion moved by Lorries to DIRTY BUCKET CAMP. Move complete 4.0 p.m. As Battalion were entering Lorries at CANAL BANK's ever a 1 casualties were caused by hos tile aircraft.	
DIRTY BUCKET CAMP.	15-10-17.		Resting and cleaning-up.	
	16-10-17.		Resting and clea ning-up.	
	17-10-17.		Resting.	
	18-10-17.		Training.	
	19-10-17.		3-Officers and 200- O.R. detailed for carrying ammunition to the front line. Hd.Qrs. CANE TRENCH and HURST PARK. Lieut.A.GODLY in command of party.	
	20-10-17.		Training.	
	21-10-17.		Voluntary Church Services. Working party returned at 10.0 p.m.	
	22-10-17.		Training.	
	23-10-17.		Training. Inspection of Companies in Marching Order by Commanding Officer.	

Army Form C. 2118.

WAR DIARY
or
INTELLIGENCE SUMMARY.
(Erase heading not required.)

Instructions regarding War Diaries and Intelligence Summaries are contained in F.S. Regs., Part II. and the Staff Manual respectively. Title pages will be prepared in manuscript.

Place	Date	Hour	Summary of Events and Information	Remarks and references to Appendices
DIRTY BUCKET CAMP.	24-10-17.		Battalion left DIRTY BUCKET CAMP at 12.0 noon for POPERINGHE. Arrived 1.30 p.m.	App.55.
POPERINGHE.	25-10-17.		Training (under Company arrangements.)	
	26-10-17.		Battalion left POPERINGHE at 2.30 p.m. Marched to PARROY CAMP, arriving 4.30 p.m. Relieved 17th Division at work on roads in vicinity of LANGEMARCK.	App.56.
PARROY CAMP	27-10-17.		Working on roads North of ST.JULIEN. Parties worked in two shifts - 2-Companies commencing work at 6.30 a.m. and 2-Companies at 9.30 a.m.	
	28-10-17.		Work on roads. Hostile aircarft bombed vicinity of camp. No casualties.	
	29-10-17.		Work on roads. Hostile aircraft bombed vicinity of camp. No casualties.	
	30-10-17.		Work on roads.	
	31-10-17.		Work on roads. 2-O.R. wounded.	
			OFFICERS JOINED DURING THE MONTH.	
			2/Lt.W.F.ROBERTS. Joined 2-10-17.	
			Capt. C.F.STALLARD.M.C. Joined 5-10-17.	
			2/Lt.W.U.C.TAYLER Re-joined 22-10-17.	
			2/Lt.E.A.THOMAS. Joined 29-10-17.	
			2/Lt.E.J.CURTIS. Joined 29-10-17.	
			OFFICERS CASUALTIES DURING MONTH.	
			2/Lt.J.A.HORTON. to 55th T.M.B. 5-10-17.	
			2/Lt.F.T.STANLEY. (To England for permanent Commn (Indian Army. 7-10-17.	
			Capt.C.F.STALLARD.M.C. To 12th Bn.E.Surrey Regt. --- 13-10-17.	
			2/Lt.H.BUFFEE. Sick to England. 5-10-17.	
			Capt.F.H.LEWIN.M.C. Killed in Action 12-10-17.	
			2/Lt.A.C.MICHELL. -do- -do-	
			2/Lt.R.W.COLES. -do- -do-	
			2/Lt.J.H.GLADWELL. -do- 14-10-17.	
			Lieut.H.T.GREGORY. Died of Wounds. 12-10-17.	
			2/Lt.G.J.ALLEN. -do- 12-10-17.	
			Capt.I.HEATON. -do- 14-10-17.	
			Capt.P.N.ANSTRUTHER.DSO.MC. Wounded. 12-10-17.	
			Capt.F.H.F.SMITH. -do- -do-	
			Capt.A.R.HOGG. -do- 14-10-17.	
			Lieut.R.D.KENT.M.C. -do- 12-10-17.	
			OFFICERS CASUALTIES DURING MONTH. (Continued)	
			2/Lt.E.GRETHE. Wounded in Action. 12-10-17.	
			2/Lt.H.S.PEGLAR. -do- -do-	
			2/Lt.G.F.JOHNSTONE. -do- -do-	
			2/Lt.A.L.DUPONT. -do- -do-	
			2/Lt.H.T.RAPSON. -do- -do-	
			2/Lt.E.W.DAY. -do- 14-10-17.	

CR Crawford Lieut.Col.
COMDG. 7th BATTN. ROYAL WEST KENT REG.

7th Battalion Royal West Kent Regiment.

ORDER NO. 67.

Ref.Maps.
BELGIUM & FRANCE.
Sheets 27 and 28.

----

1. The 7th Battalion Royal West Kent Regiment, less Details proceeding to Divisional Reinforcement Camp, will move to DIRTY BUCKET CAMP (A.30.a) to-morrow, 9th instant.
    HOUR OF START :- 6.55 a.m.
    STARTING POINT :- On the 3rd Class Road leading from SCHOOL CAMP to the ST JAN TER BIEZEN Road where it runs through the small wood.
    ROUTE:- ST.JAN TER BIEZEN/POPERINGHE Road, - Switch Road North of POPERINGHE, leaving ST.JAN TER BIEZEN/POPERINGHE Road about L.5.central and joining POPERINGHE/ELVERDINGHE Road about G.3.a. - POPERINGHE/ELVERDINGHE Road to A .23.a.20 thence by Sleeper Road(Chemin Militaire) to DIRTY BUCKET CAMP.
    ORDER OF MARCH :-

    "D" Company.
    "C" Company.
    "B" Company and DRUMS.
    "A" Company.
    Headquarters.

    Distances of 200 yds will be maintained between Companies.
    The 1st.Line Transport of units will march in rear of the Brigade. Starting Point :- Entrance to SCHOOL CAMP on ST.JAN TER BIEZEN/POPERINGHE Road; the 1st.Line Transport of this Battalion will march in rear of that of the 8th East Surrey Regt., and in front of that of the 7th Queens Regt; 200 yds distance will be maintained between Transport of units.

2. Advance Party, composed as under, will proceed to DIRTY BUCKET CAMP, mounted, starting at 5.30 a.m.
    Lieut. C.L.MISKIN.
    Lieut. A.A.EASON.
    4-Battalion Runners.
    1- Transport N.C.O.

3. Blankets, on a scale of 1- per man will be rolled in bundels of 10-, securely labelled, and sent to the Q.M.'s Stores by 6.0 a.m.
    Blankets of Details proceeding to Reinforcement Camp will be dumped in one selected hut per Company.
    The Lewis Gun Limbers, Mess Cart, Maltese Cart, and one G.S.Wagon, will be parked in the lines overnight. Nothing that can be loaded overnight will be left unloaded till the morning.
    Officers' Kits to be dumped in front of cookers by 6.0 a.m.
    Officers' Messes to be loaded by 6.30 a.m. Two Lorries will be at Brigade Headquarters at 8.0 a.m. Details proceeding to Divisional Reinforcement Camp will act as Loading Parties; one N.C.O. per Coy from Details will report to the Q.M. at 5.45 a.m., for instructions as to parties required.

4. Lieut.A.GODLY will remain behind until the Camp is clear, and will obtain a party from Details to clear up the lines; he will obtain a Certificate from the Camp Adjutant that the lines have been left in a satisfactory condition.

5. All tables, chairs, benches, and wash bowls will be dumped in Headquarters Hut by the Details by 10.0 a.m.

6. Captain C.F.STALLARD.M.C., will be in charge of the Details. All instructions regarding them have been issued to him separately.

(Signed:-) P.N.ANSTRUTHER. Captain.
Adjutant.

7th Battalion Royal West Kent Regiment.

ORDER NO. 69.

23 October 1917.

Ref. Map Sheet
28. Scale 1/40,000.

1. The Battalion will move from DIRTY BUCKET CAMP to POPERINGHE to-morrow, 24th instant.
   HOUR OF START :- 12.0 Noon.
   STARTING POINT :- Sleeper Road leading from DIRTY BUCKET CAMP, at its junction with CHEMIN MILITAIRE.

   ROUTE :----------- ELVERDINGHE - POPERINGHE ROAD.

   ORDER OF MARCH :- Headquarters.
   Drums.
   "D" Company.
   "C" Company.
   "B" Company.
   "A" Company.
   Stretcher Bearers.
   First Line Transport.

   Distances of 200 yards will be maintained between Companies.

2. An Advanced Party composed as under, will proceed to POPERINGHE by Lorry, starting at 9.0 a.m.
   Lieut. C.L. MISKIN.
   1- Battalion Runner.
   1- Transport N.C.O.

3. Officers' Kits will be taken to Transport Lines by 10.30 a.m.
   Officers' Messes will be dumped at Transport Lines by 10.45 a.m.
   Drummers' Packs and Packs of men certified by Medical Officer will be sent to Q.M. Stores by 8.0 a.m.

4. First Line Transport will leave the Column at the junction of the SWITCH ROAD and ELVERDINGHE - POPERINGHE Road, and proceed to their lines, which will be situated in Rue de BASSIN and on SWITCH ROAD at N. end of Rue de BASSIN.

5. Those men detailed by the Medical Officer as unfit to march, will proceed by Lorry leaving after 11.0 a.m.

(Signed:-) T. T. WADDINGTON. Captain.
A/Adjutant.

SECRET.

F.w.d

WO95/2049/2

55th Infantry Brigade.

Account of operations from 9th to 14th Oct. 1917.

Reference Maps :-
    Sheets 27 and 28 1/40,000
    Sheets ST.JULIEN and POELCAPELLE (Ed.4) 1/10,000.

A. PRELIMINARY MOVEMENTS.

1.   On October 9th the 55th Infantry Brigade moved from SCHOOLS CAMP, ST. JAN TER BIEZEN (Sheet 27 L.3.c.) to DIRTY BUCKET CAMP (Sheet 28. A.30.central).

2.   About midnight on October 9th/10th the G.O.C. 18th Division came to see the G.O.C. 55th Infantry Brigade and gave the following instructions :-

    Owing to the failure of the attack on MEUNIER HOUSE & at the N. end of POELCAPELLE, by the 32nd Infantry Brigade, 11th Division, this attack was to be carried out by the 18th Division. 55th Infantry Brigade would carry out this attack which was to be followed by a further advance on the same day, to be carried out by two battalions of 53rd Infantry Brigade. The line held by 32nd Infantry Brigade was to be taken over on the night of 10th/11th October by 55th Infantry Brigade instead of by 53rd Infantry Brigade as previously ordered.

3.   Owing to the short time available for preparation G.O.C. 55th Infantry Brigade decided provisionally that the attack should be carried out on the same lines as that of 32nd Infantry Brigade, namely, 3 battalions assaulting and one in reserve; that the three assaulting battalions should be, 8th E.Surrey Regt. on the right, 7th Buffs in the centre, 7th R.W.Kent Regt. on the left, and that these battalions should take over their battle fronts from 32nd Infantry Brigade.

4.   The line actually held not being yet definitely established the following frontages were provisionally allotted :-

    8th E.Surrey Regt. from the LEKKERBOTTERBEEK to GLOSTER FARM inclusive.

    7th Buffs from GLOSTER FARM exclusive to the Cross Roads V.19.b.5.1 exclusive.

    7th R.W.Kent Regt. from the Cross Roads V.19.b.5.1. inclusive to about V.19.b.1.8.

5.   It was arranged that all battalions would be conveyed to forward area by busses, 7th Buffs and 7th R.W.Kent Regt. starting at 10. a.m. and 8th E.Surrey Regt. and 7th Queens starting as soon as possible after 1.0 p.m.; that these battalions should proceed as far as KEMPTON PARK where definite orders for relief would be given to them, and that commanding officers of assaulting battalions and advance parties would proceed early to WARWA FARM, the Headquarters of the 32nd Infantry Brigade.

6.   On the morning of the 10th October the Brigade Commander and Commanding officers arrived at Headquarters 32nd Infantry Brigade about 10.0 a.m. After a conference

with G.O.C. 32nd Infantry Brigade instructions were
given to Battalion Commanders for the attack to be
carried out on the lines of the previous attack by the
32nd Infantry Brigade, and objectives and dividing
lines were provisionally decided upon. Each battalion
was to attack on a two company front, these two companies
being detailed for the first objective, while two
companies were detailed to pass through them to the
final objective. Battalion Commanders were able to
give instructions on these points to their Company
Commanders before proceeding to the Headquarters of
the battalions they were to relieve in order to
reconnoitre the ground and arrange details of relief.
Reconnaissance was most difficult owing to the fact that
the enemy had good observation and showed considerable
activity.

7.   7th Buffs and 7th R.W.Kent Regt. arrived in
good time by bus at KEMPTON PARK and the relief by
these battalions of battalions of 32nd Infantry Brigade
was carried out successfully, though great difficulty
was experienced in the matter of guides, and owing to the
state of the ground, the bad weather, and the extreme
darkness of the night. These reliefs were completed
by 3.0 a.m. and 4.0 a.m. respectively.

Owing to traffic restrictions the busses
conveying the 8th E.Surrey Regt. were diverted on the
way up to the rendezvous and were considerably delayed
so that this battalion did not reach the rendezvous until
after dark. The guide supplied to conduct the battalion
as far as the STEENBEEK where platoon guides were to
meet them, lost the way and led the battalion to the
wrong bridge, so that the relief was very much delayed
and the first company of the 8th E.Surrey Regt. did not
arrive at Battalion Headquarters of the battalion to be
relieved until 4.0 a.m. The relief was rushed through, but
could not be properly completed owing to the dawn.

On completion of relief each assaulting battalion
was disposed with 2 companies holding the front line and
2 companies distributed in depth behind.

The 7th Queens were disposed in positions just
E. of the STEENBEEK which had been reconnoitred during
the day by officers of that battalion, and had arrived in
position without mishap.

During the relief of 32nd M.G.Coy. by 35th
M.G.Coy. while guns were being loaded on the tramway at
MINTY FARM, a shell fell in the middle of one section
causing casualties to the whole of the personnel of
four guns.

8.   The line indicated by the frontages given above
was found to be approximately correct, except that the
left flank battalion had advanced their position as far as
the road junction V.20.a.0.8., the line running back thence
to about V.15.d.4.0 where it joined with the 4th Division
on the left.

9.   Brigade orders for the attack were issued to
units at 6.0 a.m. on October 11th; objectives and boundary
lines were as shown on the attached map.

10. In the case of the right battalion the change
in the barrage arrangements and consequent change of the
first objective made considerable alterations necessary
in the instructions already given to Company Commanders.

2.

These instructions could not be given until dusk, as it was not possible to move about during daylight. Company Commanders in their turn had little chance of explaining anything to their subordinates, and in fact had great difficulty in finding their platoons owing to the circumstances of the relief, the darkness and the shell torn ground. One platoon under 2nd Lieut. RIPPETT could not be found at all until it was seen to get up and go forward when our barrage started. In these conditions the men and section commanders had little chance of knowing what their objectives were, and no opportunity of looking at them beforehand in daylight.

11. The centre and left battalions were hardly affected by the alterations in the barrage line and in consequence it was less difficult for Company Commanders to get their instructions down to their subordinates, though in their case also movement by day in and near the front line was greatly restricted by the activity of the enemy.

In these battalions, however, as far as can be ascertained, all platoon and section commanders knew their objectives and what they had to do.

12. An additional change in the instructions originally given to battalion commanders had to be made in the matter of the forming up line, which was ordered to be in advance of the line on which the 32nd Brigade had formed up. At dusk, therefore, on October 11th, discs and tapes were laid by all battalions on lines as follows :-

    8th E.Surrey Regt.   -   V.26.a.6.5 - V.20.c.2.3

    7th Buffs.   -   V.20.c.2.3 - POELCAPELLE Church exclusive V.19.b.7025

    7th R.W.Kent Regt.   -   POELCAPELLE Church inclusive - V.13.d.45.00.

The night of 11th/12th was very dark and very wet, and the men were often knee deep in mud when moving to the forming up positions. In addition, behind our right battalion, the enemy put over some gas shells which considerably hampered the movement of troops coming up from the rear. In spite of this all troops (with the exception of the platoon of the right battalion mentioned above) were in position before zero (5.25 a.m.).

Headquarters of battalions were as follows :-
Right battalion - V.26.b.4.7.
Centre battalion - V.19.d.40.95.
Left battalion - V.19.a.5.1.

B. ACTION OF OCTOBER 12TH.

13. Our artillery barrage appears to have opened erratically and to have been far from heavy.

In the case of the right battalion it is stated that the enemy appeared to be very little inconvenienced by it. Machine Gun fire was opened immediately by guns which, owing either to their closeness to our line or to the thinness of the barrage, were not affected by it. The enemy barrage came down about 4 minutes after zero about 150 yards behind our forming up line.

On the front of the centre battalion the right company commander states that our barrage opened very thinly, but that as his men advanced it thickened on top of his leading troops.

The left company states that the enemy barrage was put down in 2 minutes about 150 yards in front of our forming up position so that it caught our men as they were waiting for our barrage to lift. In both companies it is stated positively that when our barrage lifted it moved back over 100, probably 150, yards.

The left battalion states that our barrage opened correctly, but that some shells fell very short behind the right company and among the left company, causing casualties in the latter. Before our barrage started to move forward the enemy barrage came down just in front of our leading troops. The enemy barrage was light and when our barrage lifted and our troops advanced few casualties were caused by it. Our barrage, however, was very erratic and there appeard to be gaps in it.

14. In spite of our barrage, heavy rifle and machine gun fire was immediately opened by the enemy on the whole front.

The right company commander of the right battalion, who was wounded and returned to battalion headquarters about 3 hours after zero, reported that the men had advanced 500 yards or more from the forming up position. They had gone forward magnificently in face of intense fire, but casualties had been heavy and practically all the leaders were hit. In addition there were many enemy machine guns still holding out between the forming up position and the position reached by the advanced troops.

As regards the left flank, the left company of the left battalion pushed forward, but its right was held up by a post about V.14.c.1.1 and was unable to make further progress; a gap thus occurred between the extreme left platoon and the rest of the left battalion. This platoon pushed forward and reached its objective at V.14.c.25.55, capturing two officers, 50 O.R's. and two machine guns; but never regained touch with the rest of its battalion and became merged with the Household Battalion on its left.

While the troops on the flanks thus made some progress, the centre battalion and the inner companies of the flank battalions were checked almost at once. As regards the centre battalion, this appears, from the statements of the surviving company commander, to have been principally due to the fact that the first lift of the barrage, as stated above, was well over 100 yards and that consequently the troops lost the barrage at once.

15. The companies detailed for the further objectives following up in rear of the leading companies in turn came under the intense fire and lost heavily. Eventually they became merged with the leading companies.

16. The heavy losses which occurred among officers and N.C.Os. were due to efforts to gain ground by fire and movement after the barrage had thus been lost. The mud and water were so bad that to move rapidly from shell hole to shell hole was out of the question. Rifles also got covered with mud and even after they had been cleaned it was difficult to keep them in action for more than a few rounds without cleaning out the breech again, since the men's hands were plastered with mud and each time a fresh clip was put in some mud inevitably went in with it.

17. The situation was for some time very obscure. This was due not only to the fact that nearly all the officers and senior N.C.Os. had become casualties but also that few runners could get back over the open ground owing to rifle and machine gun fire.

By this time, of the 12 company officers per battalion who went into action there were left with the right battalion three, with the centre battalion four and with the left battalion only one.

Eventually it became clear that, except for small parties which may have got further forward on the extreme right and left flanks, little or no progress had been made.

18. About noon there occurred in the centre battalion an incident the explanation of which has not been discovered.

Since the hostile rifle and machine gun fire had somewhat slackened Captain NICHOLSON, commanding the right company of the centre battalion, sent 2nd Lieut. SPENCER to gain touch with 2nd Lieut. KNIGHT who, with elements of the right "leap-frog" Company, was some 400 yards to his left at about V.20.c.15.85.

Shortly before this he had seen a party of the enemy unarmed and carrying a red cross flag approach 2nd Lieut. KNIGHT'S party, apparently with the intention of surrendering. 2/Lt. KNIGHT was seen to converse with the Germans who began to show themselves in increasing numbers but always unarmed.

2/Lt. SPENCER on his way to 2nd Lt. KNIGHT was mortally wounded and Captain NICHOLSON went out to help him. As he was doing so he heard a shout and saw 2nd Lt. KNIGHT and about 30 men being marched off in the direction of MEUNIER HOUSE. He could not get back to his men in time to get them to fire on this party.

19. In the meanwhile the 6th R.Berks Regt. and 8th Suffolk Regt., the battalions of 53rd Infantry Brigade which had been detailed to capture the final objective of 18th Division, had followed close behind the battalions of 55th Brigade.

These battalions had thus become involved in the fight though no information had been given them that the first objectives had been reached.

The assaulting battalions having made little or no progress the 6th R.Berks. Regt. had taken up positions in rear of the right battalion and the right of the centre battalion some 100 yards in rear of the original forming up line, while the 8th Suffolk Regt. had filled the gap between the left flank of the left battalion and the Household Battalion on their left.

20. The 7th Queens (counter attack battalion) remained in their original positions south of the ST.JULIEN - POELCAPELLE Road between DELTA HOUSES and RETOUR CROSS ROADS.

About 2 p.m. the O.C. centre battalion observed from his headquarters a party of the enemy apparently advancing down the main street of the village. Thinking this might possibly be a counter attack he sent to warn a company of 7th Queens to move to the vicinity of his Headquarters where they could instantly counter a counter attack. The enemy were held up by the 7th R.W.Kent Regt. and 8th Suffolk Regt. One Company of the 7th Queens, however, moved forward and took up a position astride the road near the cemetery.

21. About 4.30 p.m. orders were given to the O.C. 7th Queens to move his battalion up in close support of the right and centre battalions. When this had been done the 6th R.Berks Regt. was to be withdrawn.

AAt the same time orders were given to the 8th
Suffolk Regt. to continue to hold the positions on the left
of 7th R.W.Kent Regt. and that the remainder of the battalion
should be disposed in support of these positions and of 7th
R.W.Kent Regt.

The 7th Queens moved into position as ordered but
owing to the darkness and to the heavy losses in officers
only one company of 8th R.Berks.Regt. could be found so
that only one company instead of the whole battalion was
withdrawn.

22. At 8.30 p.m. orders were issued to the three
assaulting battalions that when their position had been
reorganised, posts established on the line held and touch
ensured on both flanks, any surplus men not required for
these posts were to be withdrawn to concentrate in CANE
TRENCH area.

This was duly done in the case of the centre and
left battalions, but the message on the subject to the
right battalion was delayed and did not reach the battalion
until 8.0 a.m. the following morning when it was too late
to withdraw any men from the front line.

23. The work of 55th M.G.Coy. in these operations
was as follows.

Two sections had been detailed for barrage fire.
In consequence, however, of the casualties suffered on the
night of Oct.10th/11th only four guns could be spared for
this purpose. These guns were dug in on their barrage
positions on the 11th. but during the night, owing to the
heavy rain and constant shelling, these positions collapsed
and became useless and the guns were not in a position to
fire at Zero.

Of the remaining two sections two guns had been
detailed to go forward to each of three strong points which
were to have been established in the vicinity of TRACAS
FARM, MEUNIER HOUSE and HULLES HOUSE. While two guns were
held in reserve.

Of these the two guns detailed for TRACAS FARM
eventually came into action near GLOSTER FARM and found
targets on the POELCAPELLE - SPRIET ROAD and also claim to
have hit enemy snipers who were most active during the afternoon. The two guns detailed for MEUNIER HOUSE tried to get
forward but lost heavily from enemy sniping and eventually
dug in in shell holes in positions between GLOSTER FARM and
RETOUR CROSS ROADS. The two guns for HULLES HOUSE did not
move forward from their positions in POELCAPELLE.

C. SUBSEQUENT MOVEMENTS.

24. During the night of 12th/13th positions were
organised and a line of posts established as follows:-

8th E.Surrey Regt.	-	from LEKKERBOTERBEEK about V.22.a.9.9 to GLOSTER FARM inclusive.
7th Buffs.	-	from GLOSTER FARM exclusive to V.20.a.0.0, including a post at V.20.c.3.6 where they had a captured German Machine Gun in action.
7th R.W.Kent Regt.	-	Posts at V.19.b.9.2, V.19.b.88.40 V.20.a.0.6, V.20.a.00.75, V.20.a.0.8 V.20.a.0.9.
8th Suffolk Regt.	-	from V.20.a.09. to the track at V.13.d.95.45

7.

On the front of the centre battalion at about 2 a.m. the enemy attacked our posts at V.20.c.35.60, V.20.c.35.50 and V.20.c.30.45 with bombs. He was driven off by rifle fire and bombs. This appears to have been the only attempt by the enemy to regain the posts he had lost during the day.

During the night also the battalion headquarters of the right battalion, which consisted only of a shell hole with a corrugated iron weatherproof covering, was continually shelled and about 12.30 a.m. sustained a direct hit which caused 7 casualties among the battalion H.Q. personnel.

25. On the morning of October 13th. orders were issued for the relief, at dusk, of the assaulting battalions by 7th Queens and 8th Suffolk Regt. the former taking over the front from the LEKKERBOTERBEEK to about V.19.b.9.2 and the latter taking over the posts held by 7th R.W.Kent Regt. from the latter point to its own right flank.

The relief was accomplished without difficulty and the three assaulting battalions and the remainder of 8th E.Berks.Regt. were withdrawn to CANE TRENCH Area.

26. On the afternoon of October 14th the 7th Buff's, 8th E.Surrey Regt. and 7th R.W.Kent Regt. were conveyed by busses from the CANAL BANK to DIRTY BUCKET CAMP.

During the embussing enemy aeroplanes came over and dropped bombs on the bus column causing casualties to 7th R.W.Kent Regt.

27. On the evening of the same day the 7th Queens and 8th Suffolk Regt. were relieved by 10th Essex Regt. and 9th Norfolk Regt.

This relief also was carried out without difficulty and on its completion the command of the sector was handed over to G.O.C. 53rd Infantry Brigade.

D. CONCLUSION.

28. In estimating the reasons for the failure of the attack the initial difficulties involved must not be lost sight of.

The relief of the units of the 32nd Infantry Brigade, who were disorganised after an unsuccessful attack on the previous day, took a long time to arrange and was far from easy. The Brigade found difficulty in supplying an adequate number of guides and some of these lost their way. In fact the relief alone fully occupied the attention of all concerned until it was completed on the morning of October 11th.

29. Again no one in the Brigade had seen any of the country East of the CANAL until the morning of October 11th. The ground over which it had been intended that the Brigade should attack had been thoroughly studied in the back area by all ranks and objectives had been allotted and were well known. The ground over which the attack was carried out was quite unknown and the attack took place at such short notice that there was little chance of getting information down to platoon commanders much less to the rank and file.

The information and orders which could be given to battalion and company commanders before they took over the line were neither complete nor final, since no orders had then been received by the Brigade. In the case of the right battalion such information as they had could not be communicated to their subordinates by company commanders

8.

owing to the late arrival of their battalion at KEMPTON PARK. After the line had been taken over all communication of orders was most difficult, especially on the front of the right battalion. Movement in daylight forward of all battalion headquarters was under observation by the enemy, who showed much activity with rifle and machine gun fire, while by night it was impossible for company commanders, whose headquarters were in most cases in shell holes without cover of any kind to show lights or to consult and explain from orders and maps.

An attack on the system which had been adopted and in which the battalions had been trained depends for success almost entirely upon the condition that all ranks have a knowledge of the ground and understand exactly what they have to do and where they have to go. This condition, as has been shown above, could not possibly be fulfilled.

30. In addition the weather conditions were exceptionally unfavourable. Rain fell intermittently on the 10th and although the day of the 11th and up till midnight of 11th/12th the weather was fairly fine, at about 12.30 a.m. on 12th a strong S.W. wind rose and heavy rain fell, which continued throughout the rest of the night.

31. As regards the actual operations the chief causes of failure were the faulty nature and inadequacy of the creeping barrage, the lack of standing barrages and the very heavy conditions of weather and ground. Upon these points which have already been brought out in this narrative there is no need to enlarge further.

32. It is necessary to add a few words regarding the signal communications which were maintained forward of Brigade Headquarters.

Owing to the hurry of the relief and the long distance which had to be traversed from DIRTY BUCKET CAMP to VANNA FARM on the day of relief, linesmen and runners had very little time in which to learn their routes. This they had to do largely in the dark and under the instruction of the personnel of the outgoing Brigade who were tired out after the operations of the previous day. It is not surprising therefore that wires forward of Brigade Headquarters, which were very frequently broken by shell fire, were mended with great difficulty, and that messages by runners at night suffered at times considerable delay.

Pigeons, message rockets and extra drums and cable which had been asked for well in advance were received so late as to be of little use, since they did not reach Brigade Headquarters until after midnight of October 11th/12th. Wireless which was established between PHEASANT FARM and Brigade Headquarters worked well, though both stations were several times broken down. Of communication by this means full advantage was taken.

33. The total casualties sustained by the Brigade during the whole period were as follows :-

	Officers.	N.C.Os.	Rank & File.
7th Queens.	6	30	165
7th Buffs.	11	68	317
8th E.Surrey Regt.	10	45	292
7th R.W.Kent Regt.	14	57	340
- do - (Additional from bomb dropped on bus column.)	3	-	35
38th M.G.Coy.	2	16	36
	46	209	1,015

TOTAL CASUALTIES - Officers 46.
Other Ranks. 1222.

---ooOyyy---

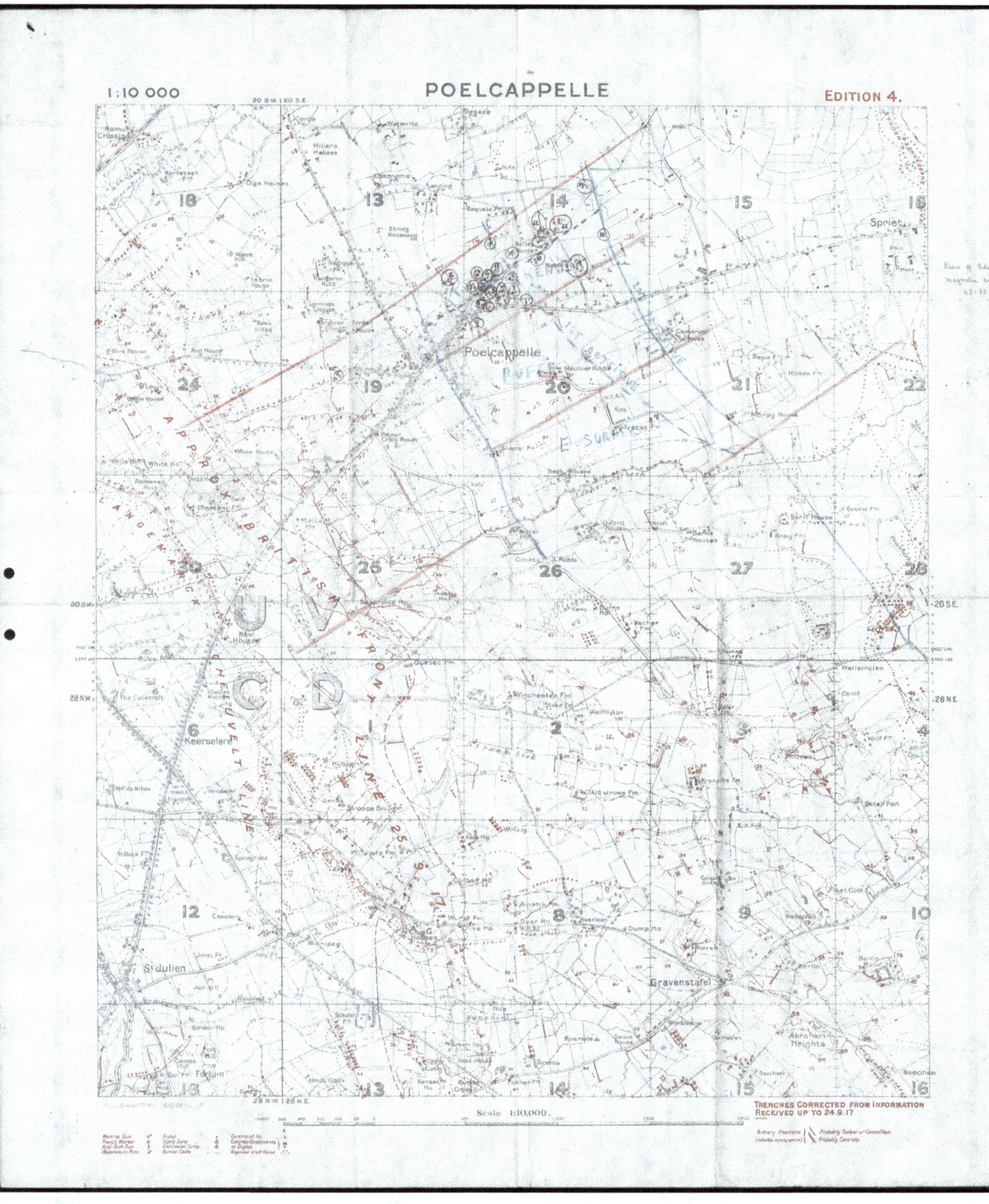

7th Battalion Royal West Kent Regiment.

ORDER NO. 68.

Ref. Map Sheet
POELCAPPELLE.
Ed.4.,1/10,000
and Map K.2.
attached.

11th October 1917

1. To-morrow the 12th instant the XVIII Corps will resume the offensive.
    The attack will be carried out by the 18th Division on the left, and the 9th Division on the right. The 4th Division will be attacking on the left of the 18th Divn.
    The 55th Infantry Brigade will attack on a three Battalion front with the 8th East Surrey Regt., on the right, 7th Buffs in the centre, and the 7th Royal West Kent Regt., on the left. The 7th Queens Regt., will be in reserve.
    The Dividing lines between the three Battalions in the front line, and the boundaries of the 55th Bde. attack are marked in RED on the attached map.

2. Brigade Objectives are as follows :-
    First Objective ------ Dotted BLUE Line.
    Second Objective ----- BLUE LINE.
    NOTE. The coloured lines indicate only the general line of objectives. The actual objectives should be the nearest points to the protective barrage which troops can reach without suffering from its fire.

3. After the capture of the second objective, units of 53rd. Infantry Brigade are to pass through and proceed to the capture of the Divisional final objective.
    These units are to be formed up under the protective barrage for the second objective ready to advance by zero plus 2 hours 30 minutes.

4. The assaulting Battalions will be formed up for attack on the Western blue line shewn on attached map. This line will be marked with tapes and flags.

5. The Battalion will be formed up for attack in two lines by zero minus 1-hour 15 minutes.
    Front line.   "B" Coy., on Right.
                  "C" Coy., on Left.
    Second Line. "D" Coy., on Right.
                  "A" Coy., on Left.
    75 yards between lines.
    The dividing line between Company attacks is shewn by a dotted GREEN Line on the attached map. "B" and "C" Coys., will capture and consolidate on the DOTTED BLUE LINE within the limits of their attack. "D" and "A" Coys., will "leap-frog" "B" and "C" Coys., and will capture and consolidate on the BLUE LINE within the limits of their Company attack.
    Each Company is responsible for capturing and consolidating the various objectives within the rectangle allotted to them, and will form up and carry out the attack on these points in accordance with the attached plan.
    Each Company will watch its flanks carefully, and Company reserves will attack or mask any hostile posts which may be holding out on the flanks and hampering the advance.
    All positions gained must be consolidated and held at all costs.

(2.)

"D" and "A" Coys., will leave small posts in concrete dug-outs in the front line at present held, to prevent their occupation by the enemy, when "D" and "A" Coys., withdraw to form up for the attack. These posts will join their Companies when the latter pass through them to the attack.

6. To form the basis of a definite defensive organisation the following Strong Points will be constructed :-
   A. TRACAS FARM.   V.21.c.0.5.
   B. HELLES HOUSE.   V.14.c.7.5.
   X. MEUNIER HOUSE. V.20.b.1.2.

   A and B will be constructed and garrisoned each by one section 92nd. Field Coy., R.E. with attached infantry.
   The 7th Buffs will be responsible for the construction of X. Two platoons will be detailed for the garrison of this point.

7. The importance of keeping close under the barrage must be impressed on all ranks.
   The compass is to be used to maintain direction.

8. In order to maintain touch special parties of 1- N.C.O. and 4- men will be detailed to meet similar parties of units on flanks as follows :-
   "D" Coy., at V.14.d.25.15.
   "A" Coy., at REQUETE FARM.
   "A" Coy., at hedge at V.14.b.4.4.
   Immediately these parties have met, the fact will be reported by runner to Battn. Hd.Qrs.

9. The 7th Queens Regt., will be in Brigade Reserve with Battn. Hd.Qrs., at PHEASANT FARM.

10. The 55th M.G.Coy., will be disposed as follows :-
    2- dets. will go forward to each of the Strong Points A, B, and X, -One Section in reserve at HAANIXBEER FARM.
    The remainder of the Coy., will be at CANE AVENUE.
    Coy. Hd.Qrs., HAANIXBEER FARM.

11. The attack will be supplemented by an artillery and machine gun barrage.
    (a) The artillery barrage will open at zero on a line 150 yards in front of the forming-up line. It will lift at zero plus 8-minutes, and will move forward by lifts of 100 yards in 8-minutes. The protective barrage on the first objective will lift at zero plus 1-hour 40 minutes, that in front of the second objective at zero plus 3-hours.
    (b) Details of machine gun barrage will be issued later.

12. One section of Tanks (4-machines) has been allotted to the 18th Division. Details of the action of Tanks will be issued later. Each Tank carries 5-boxes of S.A.A. for the use of infantry in the front line. This S.A.A. is carried in a box at the rear (between the horns) of each Tank, and is at the disposal of the infantry when required.

13. (a) Contact aeroplanes will fly over the objectives at :-
        Zero plus 2-hours 30- minutes,
        Zero plus 4-hours 30-minutes
        Zero plus 7-hours.
    Infantry will be ready to light RED flares at these hours, but will not do so unless they are called for by KLAXTON HORN or by the dropping of white lights. Contact aeroplanes will be marked by two black rectangular flags, attached to, and projecting from the lower plane on each side of the fuselage.

(3.)

    (b) An aeroplane will be up continuously during daylight from zero onwards to detect the approach of enemy counter-attacks. Whenever this machine observes hostile parties of 100- or over moving to counter attack, it will drop a smoke bomb on that part of the front to which the enemy is moving. The smoke bomb will burst about 100 feet below the machine into a white parachute flame which descends slowly, leaving a long trail of brown smoke about a foot broad behind it.

14.   In addition to other messages and reports, Company Commanders will forward situation reports every two hours after zero.

15.   At zero hour, the Intelligence Officer will establish a forward command post at V.19.b.6.3. As soon as possible after the first objective is captured, this post will move forward to the vicinity of V.20.a.20.95.

16.   Battalion Hd.Qrs., will remain at V.19.a.55.15.

17.   Zero hour will be notified later.

18.   ACKNOWLEDGE.

    (Signed:-) P. N. ANSTRUTHER. Captain.
    Adjutant.
    7th Battn. Royal West Kent Regiment.

Issued at 4.30 p.m.

Allotment of Sections to objectives and order of formation.

Reference ▬ = Section

1917.

October.   Appendix.

30th.   Work on roads. Hostile
             aircraft bombed vicinity of
             camp. No casualties.

31st.   Work on roads. 2 O.R. wounded.
             OFFICERS JOINED DURING THE MONTH.
             2.Lt.W.F.ROBERTS Joined 2.10.17.
             Capt.C.F.STALLARD M.C.Joined 5.10.17.
             2.Lt. W.U.C.TAYLER Re-joined 22.10.17.
             2.Lt. E.A. THOMAS Joined 29.10.17.
             2.Lt. E.J. CURTIS Joined 29.10.17.

             OFFICERS CASUALTIES DURING MONTH.
             2.Lt.J.A.HORTON. To 35th T.M.B.
                                5.10.17.
             2.Lt.F.T.STANLEY (To England for
                              (permanent Comm.
                              (Indian Army.7.10.17.
             Capt.C.F. STALLARD M.C. To 12th Bn.
                               E.Surrey Regt.13.10.17.
             2.Lt. H. BUFFEE Sick to England 5.10.17.
             Capt.F.H.LEWIN M.C.Killed in Action
                                12.10.17.
             2.Lt.A.C.MITCHELL   do.   do.
             2.Lt.R.W.COLES   do.   do.
             2.Lt.J.H.GLADWELL Killed in Action
                                14.10.17.
             Lieut.H.T.GREGORY Died of Wounds
                                12.10.17.
             2.Lt. G.J. ALLEN Died of Wounds
                                12.10.17.
             Capt.I. HEATON   Died of Wounds
                                14.10.17.
             Capt. F.H.
             ANSTRUTHER D.S.O, M.C. Wounded.
                                12.10.17.
             Capt.F.H.F.SMITH   Wounded 12.10.17.
             Capt. A.R. HOGG   do.   14.10.17.
             Lieut. R.D.KENT M.C. do.   12.10.17.
             2.Lt. E. GRETHE   Wounded in Action
                                12.10.17.
             2.Lt. H.S.BEGLAR   do.   do.
             2.Lt. G.F.JOHNSTONE do.   do.
             2.Lt. A.L.DUPONT   do.   do.
             2.Lt. H.T.RAPSON   do.   do.
             2.Lt. E.W.DAY   do.   14.10.17.

                                         Lieut.Col.

SECRET.

55th Infantry Brigade.

Account of operations from 9th to 14th Oct.1917.

Reference Maps:-
Sheets 27 and 28 1/40,000
Sheets ST.JULIEN and POELCAPELLE (Ed.4) 1/10,000.

A. **PRELIMINARY MOVEMENTS.**

1. On October 9th the 55th Infantry Brigade moved from SCHOOLS CAMP, ST. JAN TER BIEZEN (Sheet 27 L.3.c.) to DIRTY BUCKET CAMP (Sheet 28. A.30 central).

2. About midnight on October 9th/10th the G.O.C. 18th Division came to see the G.O.C. 55th Infantry Brigade and gave the following instructions:-

    Owing to the failure of the attack on MEUNIER HOUSE & the N. end of POELCAPELLE, by the 32nd Infantry Brigade, 11th Division, this attack was to be carried out by the 18th Division. 55th Infantry Brigade would carry out this attack which was to be followed by a further advance on the same day, to be carried out by two battalions of 53rd Infantry Brigade. The line held by 32nd Infantry Brigade was to be taken over on the night of 10th/11th October by 55th Infantry Brigade instead of by 53rd Infantry Brigade as previously ordered.

3. Owing to the short time available for preparation G.O.C. 55th Infantry Brigade decided provisionally that the attack should be carried out on the same lines as that of 32nd Infantry Brigade, namely, 3 battalions assaulting and one in reserve; that the three assaulting battalions should be, 8th E.Surrey Regt. on the right, 7th Buffs in the centre, 7th R.W. Kent Regt. on the left, and that these battalions should take over their battle fronts from 32nd Infantry Brigade.

4. The line actually held not being yet definitely established the following frontages were provisionally allotted:-

    8th E.Surrey Regt. from the LEKKERBOTERBEEK to GLOSTER FARM inclusive.

    7th Buffs from GLOSTER FARM exclusive to the Cross Roads V.19.b.5.1. exclusive.

    7th R.W. Kent Regt. from the Cross Roads V.19.b.5.1. inclusive to about V.19.b.1.8.

5.

5. It was arranged that all battalions would be conveyed to forward area by busses, 7th Buffs and 7th R.W. Kent Regt. starting at 10 a.m. and 8th E.Surrey Regt. and 7th Queens starting as soon as possible after 1.0 p.m. that these battalions should proceed as far as KEMPTON PARK where definite orders for relief would be given to them, and that commanding officers of assaulting battalions and advance parties would proceed early to VARNA FARM, the Headquarters of the 32nd Infantry Brigade.

6. On the morning of the 10th October the Brigade Commander and Commanding Officers arrived at Headquarters 32nd Infantry Brigade about 10.0 a.m. After a conference with G.O.C. 32nd Infantry Brigade instructions were given to Battalion Commanders for the attack to be carried out on the lines of the previous attack by the 32nd Infantry Brigade, and objectives and dividing lines were provisionally decided upon. Each battalion was to attack on a two company front, these two companies being detailed for the first objective, while two companies were detailed to pass through them to the final objective. Battalion Commanders were able to give instructions on these points to their Company Commanders before proceeding to the Headquarters of the battalions they were to relieve in order to reconnoitre the ground and arrange details of relief. Reconnaisance was most difficult owing to the fact that the enemy had good observation and showed considerable activity.

7. 7th Buffs and 7th R.W. Kent Regt. arrived in good time by bus at KEMPTON PARK and the relief by these battalions of battalions of 32nd Infantry Brigade was carried out successfully, though great difficulty was experienced in the matter of guides, and owing to the state of the ground, the bad weather, and the extreme darkness of the night. These reliefs were completed by 3.0 a.m. and 4.0 a.m. respectively.
Owing to traffic restrictions the busses conveying the 8th E.Surrey Regt. were diverted on the way up to the rendezvous and were considerably delayed so that this battalion did not reach the rendezvous until after dark. The guide supplied to conduct the battalion as far as the STEENBEKE where platoon guides were to meet them, lost the way and led the battalion to the wrong bridge, so that the relief was very much delayed and the first company of the 8th E.Surrey Regt. did not arrive at Battalion Headquarters of the battalion to be relieved until 4.0 a.m. The relief was rushed through, but could not be properly completed owing to the dawn.
On completion of relief each assaulting battalion was disposed with 2 companies holding the front line and 2 companies distributed in

depth behind.

The 7th Queens were disposed in positions just E. of the STEENBEEK which had been reconnoitred during the day by Officers of that battalion, and had arrived in position without mishap.

During the relief of 32nd M.G.Coy. by 55th M.G.Coy. while guns were being loaded on the tramway at MINTY FARM, a shell fell in the middle of one section causing casualties to the whole of the personnel of four guns.

8. The line indicated by the frontages given above was found to be approximately correct, except that the left flank battalion had advanced their position as far as the road junction V.20.a.0.8, the line running back thence to about V.15.d.4.0. where it joined with the 4th Division on the left.

9. Brigade orders for the attack were issued to units at 8.0 a.m. on October 11th; objectives and boundary lines were as shewn on the attached map.

10. In the case of the right battalion the change in the barrage arrangements and consequent change of the first objective made considerable alterations necessary in the instructions already given to Company Commanders.
These instructions could not be given until dusk, as it was not possible to move about during daylight. Company Commanders in their turn had little chance of explaining anything to their subordinates, and in fact had great difficulty in finding their platoons owing to the circumstances of the relief, the darkness and the shell torn ground. One platoon under 2nd.Lieut. RIDDETT could not be found at all until it was seen to get up and go forward when our barrage started. In these conditions the men and section commanders had little chance of knowing what their objectives were, and no opportunity of looking at them beforehand in daylight.

11. The centre and left battalions were hardly affected by the alterations in the barrage line and in consequence it was less difficult for Company Commanders to get their instructions down to their subordinates, though in their case also movement by day in and near the front line was greatly restricted by the activity of the enemy.
In these battalions, however, as far as can be ascertained, all platoon and section commanders knew their objectives and what they had to do.

12. An additional change in the instructions originally given to battalion commanders had to be made in the matter of the forming up line, which was ordered to be in advance of the line on which the 32nd Brigade had formed up. At dusk, therefore, on October 11th, discs and tapes were laid by all battalions on lines as follows:-

8th E.Surrey Regt. - V.26.a.6.8. - V.20.c.2.3.

7th Buffs - V.20.c.2.3. - POELCAPELLE
Church exclusive V.19.b.70.25.

7th R.W.Kent Regt. - POELCAPELLE Church inclusive
- V.13.d.45.00.

The night of 11th/12th was very dark and very wet and the men were often knee deep in mud when moving to the forming up positions. In addition, behind our right battalion, the enemy put over some gas shells which considerably hampered the movement of troops coming up from the rear. In spite of this all troops (with the exception of the platoon of the right battalion mentioned above) were in position before zero (5.25 a.m.).

Headquarters of battalions were as follows:-
Right battalion - V.25.b.4.7.
Centre battalion - V.19.d.40.95.
Left battalion - V.19.a.5.1.

13. ACTION OF OCTOBER 12th.

Our Artillery barrage appears to have opened erratically and to have been far from heavy.
In the case of the right battalion it is stated that the enemy appeared to be very little inconvenienced by it. Machine Gun fire was opened immediately by guns which, owing either to their closeness to our line or to the thinness of the barrage, were not affected by it. The enemy barrage came down about 4 minutes after zero about 150 yards behind our forming up line.
On the front of the centre battalion the right company commander states that our barrage opened very thinly, but that as his men advanced it thickened on top of his leading troops.
The left company states that the enemy barrage was put down in 2 minutes about 150 yards in front of our forming up position so that it caught our men as they were waiting for our barrage to lift.
In both companies it is stated positively that when our barrage lifted it moved back over 100, probably 150 yards.
The left battalion states that our barrage opened correctly, but that some shells fell very short behind the right company and among the left company, causing casualties in the latter. Before our barrage started to move forward the enemy barrage came down just in front of our leading troops. The enemy barrage was light and when our barrage lifted and our troops advanced few casualties were caused by it Our barrage, however, was very erratic and there appeared to be large gaps in it.

14. In spite of our barrage, heavy rifle and machine gun fire was immediately opened by the enemy on the whole front.
The right company commander of the right battalion, who was wounded and returned to battalion headquarters about 3 hours after zero, reported that the men had

advanced 500 yards or more from the forming up
position. They had gone forward
magnificently in face of intense fire, but
casualties had been heavy and practically all the
leaders were hit. In addition there were many
enemy machine guns still holding out between the
forming up position and the position reached by the
advanced troops.

As regards the left flank, the left company of the
left battalion pushed forward, but its right was
held up by a post about V.14.c.1.1 and was unable
to make further progress; a gap thus occurred
between the extreme left platoon and the rest of
the left battalion. This platoon pushed forward
and reached its objective at V.14.c.25.55, capturing
two Officers, 50 O.R's and two machine guns; but
never regained touch with the rest of its battalion
and became merged with the Household Battalion on
its left.

While the troops on the flanks thus made some
progress, the centre battalion and the inner companies
of the flank battalions were checked almost at
once. As regards the centre battalion, this
appears, from the statements of the surviving
company commander, to have been principally due to
the fact that the first lift of the barrage, as
stated above, was well over 100 yards and that
consequently the troops lost the barrage at once.

15. The companies detailed for the further objectives
following up in rear of the leading companies in
turn came under the intense fire and lost heavily.
Eventually they became merged with the leading
companies.

16. The heavy losses which occurred among Officers and
N.C.Os were due to efforts to gain ground by fire and
movement after the barrage had thus been lost.
The mud and water were so bad that to move rapidly
from shell hole to shell hole was out of the
question. Rifles also got covered with mud and
even after they had been cleaned it was difficult to
keep them in action for more than a few rounds without
cleaning out the breech again, since the men's
hands were plastered with mud and each time a fresh
clip was put in some mud inevitably went in with it.

17. The situation was for some time very obscure.
This was due not only to the fact that nearly all
the Officers and senior N.C.Os had become casualties
but also that few runners could get back over the
open ground owing to rifle and machine gun fire.
By this time, of the 12 company officers per
battalion who went into action there were left
with the right battalion three, with the centre
battalion four and with the left battalion only one.
Eventually it became clear that, except for small
parties which may have got further forward on the
extreme right and left flanks, little or no progress
had been made.

18. About noon there occurred in the centre battalion an incident the explanation of which has not been discovered.
Since the hostile rifle and machine gun fire had somewhat slackened Captain NICHOLSON, commanding the right company of the centre battalion, sent 2nd.Lieut. SPENCER to gain touch with 2nd.Lieut. KNIGHT who, with elements of the right "leap-frog" Company, was some 400 yards to his left at about V.20.c.15.84.
Shortly before this he had seen a party of the enemy unarmed and carrying a red cross flag approach 2nd.Lieut. KNIGHT'S party, apparently with the intention of surrendering. 2.Lt. KNIGHT was seen to converse with the Germans who began to show themselves in increasing numbers but always unarmed. 2.Lt. SPENCER on his way to 2nd.Lt. KNIGHT was mortally wounded and Captain NICHOLSON went out to help him. As he was doing so he heard a shout and saw 2nd.Lt. KNIGHT and about 30 men being marched off in the direction of MEUNIER HOUSE. He could not get back to his men in time to get them to fire on this party.

19. In the meanwhile the 6th R.Berks Regt. and 8th Suffolk Regt., the battalions of 53rd Infantry Brigade which had been detailed to capture the final objective of 18th Division, had followed close behind the battalions of 55th Brigade.
These battalions had thus become involved in the fight though no information had been given them that the first objectives had been reached.
The assaulting battalions having made little or no progress the 6th R.Berks.Regt. had taken up positions in rear of the right battalion and the right of the centre battalion some 100 yards in rear of the original forming up line, while the 8th Suffolk Regt. had filled the gap between the left flank of the left battalion and the Household Battalion on their left.

20. The 7th Queens (counter attack battalion) remained in their original positions south of the ST.JULIEN - POELCAPELLE Road between DREPA HOUSES and RETOUR CROSS ROADS.
About 2 p.m. the O.C. Centre Battalion observed from his headquarters a party of the enemy apparently advancing down the main street of the village. Thinking this might possibly be a counter attack he sent to warn a company of 7th Queens to move to the vicinity of his Headquarters where they could instantly counter a counter attack. The enemy were held up by the 7th R.W. Kent Regt. and 8th Suffolk Regt. One Company of the 7th Queens, however, moved forward and took up a position astride the road near the cemetery.

21. About 4.30 p.m. orders were given to the O.C. 7th
Queens to move his battalion up in close support
of the right and centre battalions. When this
had been done the 6th R.Berks.Regt. was to be
withdrawn.
At the same time orders were given to the 8th
Suffolk Regt. to continue to hold the positions
on the left of 7th R.W.Kent Regt. and that the
remainder of the battalion should be disposed
in support of these positions and of 7th R.W.
Kent Regt.
The 7th Queens moved into position as ordered
but owing to the darkness and to the heavy
losses in officers only one company of 6th
R.Berks.Regt. could be found so that only one
company instead of the whole battalion was
withdrawn.

22. At 8.50 p.m. orders were issued to the three
assaulting battalions that when their position
had been reorganised, posts established on the
line held and touch ensured on both flanks,
any surplus men not required for these posts
were to be withdrawn to concentrate in CANE
TRENCH Area.
This was duly done in the case of the centre and
left battalions, but the message on the
subject to the right battalion was delayed and
did not reach the battalion until 8.0 a.m. the
following morning when it was too late to
withdraw any men from the front line.

23. The work of 35th M.G.Coy. in these operations
was as follows.
Two sections had been detailed for barrage fire.
In consequence, however, of the casualties
suffered on the night of Oct.10th/11th only
four guns could be spared for this purpose.
These guns were dug in on their barrage
positions on the 11th, but during the night,
owing to the heavy rain and constant shelling,
these positions collapsed and became useless
and the guns were not in a position to fire at
Zero.
Of the remaining two sections two guns had been
detailed to go forward to each of three strong
points which were to have been established in
the vicinity of TRAGAS FARM, MEUNIER HOUSE and
HELLES HOUSE. While two guns were held in reserve.
Of these the two guns detailed for TRAGAS FARM
eventually came into action near GLOSTER FARM and
found targets on the POELCAPELLE - SPRIET ROAD and
also claim to have hit enemy snipers who were most
active during the afternoon. The two guns
detailed for MEUNIER HOUSE tried to get forward
but lost heavily from enemy sniping and eventually
dug in in shell holes in positions between GLOSTER
FARM and RETOUR CROSS ROADS. The two guns for
HELLES HOUSE did not move forward from their
positions in POELCAPELLE.

C. SUBSEQUENT MOVEMENTS.

24. During the night of 12th/13th positions were organised and a line of posts established as follows:-

   8th R.Surrey Regt. — from LEKKERBOTERBEEK about V.26.a.9.6. to GLOSTER FARM inclusive.

   7th Buffs. — from GLOSTER FARM exclusive to V.20.a.0.0. including a post at V.20.c.3.6. where they had a captured German Machine Gun in action.

   7th R.W. Kent Regt — Posts at V.19.b.9.2, V.19.b.85.40 V.20.a.0.6, V.20.a.00.75, V.20.a.0.8, V.20.a.0.9.

   8th Suffolk Regt — from V.20.a.09. to the track at V.13.d.95.45.

   On the front of the centre battalion at about 2 a.m. the enemy attacked our posts at V.20.c.33.60, V.20.c.33.50 and V.20.c.30.45 with bombs. He was driven off by rifle fire and bombs. This appears to have been the only attempt by the enemy to regain the posts he had lost during the day. During the night also the battalion headquarters of the right battalion, which consisted only of a shell hole with a corrugated iron weatherproof covering, was continually shelled and about 2.30 am. sustained a direct hit which caused 7 casualties among the battalion H.Q. personnel.

25. On the morning of October 13th. orders were issued for the relief, at dusk, of the assaulting battalions by 7th Queens and 8th Suffolk Regt. the former taking over the front from the LEKKERBOTERBEEK to about V.19.b.9.3. and the latter taking over the posts held by 7th R.W. Kent Regt. from the latter point to its own right flank.
   The relief was accomplished without difficulty and the three assaulting battalions and the remainder of 6th R.Berks.Regt. were withdrawn to CANE TRENCH Area.

26. On the afternoon of October 14th the 7th Buffs, 8th R.Surrey Regt. and 7th R.W. Kent Regt. were conveyed by busses from the CANAL BANK to DIRTY BUCKET CAMP.
   During the embussing enemy aeroplanes came over and dropped bombs on the bus column causing casualties to 7th R.W. Kent Regt.

27. On the evening of the same day the 7th Queens and 8th Suffolk Regt. were relieved by 10th Essex Regt.

12.

and 8th Norfolk Regt.
This relief also was carried out without difficulty and on its completion the command of the sector was handed over to G.O.C. 53rd Infantry Brigade.

D. CONCLUSION.

28. In estimating the reasons for the failure of the attack the initial difficulties involved must not be lost sight of.
The relief of the units of the 32nd Infantry Brigade, who were disorganised after an unsuccessful attack on the previous day, took a long time to arrange and was far from easy. The Brigade found difficulty in supplying an adequate number of guides and some of these lost their way. In fact the relief alone fully occupied the attention of all concerned until it was completed on the morning of October 11th.

29. Again no one in the Brigade had seen any of the country East of the CANAL until the morning of October 11th. The ground over which it had been intended that the Brigade should attack had been thoroughly studied in the back area by all ranks and objectives had been allotted and were well known. The ground over which the attack was carried out was quite unknown and the attack took place at such short notice that there was little chance of getting information down to platoon commanders much less to the rank and file.
The information and orders which could be given to battalion and company commanders before they took over the line were neither complete nor final, since no orders had then been received by the Brigade. In the case of the right battalion such information as they had could not be communicated to their subordinates by company commanders owing to the late arrival of their battalion at KEMPTON PARK. After the line had been taken over all communication of orders was most difficult, especially on the front of the right battalion. Movement in daylight forward of all battalion headquarters was under observation by the enemy, who showed much activity with rifle and machine gun fire, while by night it was impossible for company commanders, whose headquarters were in most cases in shell holes without cover of any kind to show lights or to consult and explain from orders and maps.
An attack on the system which had been adopted and in which the battalions had been trained depends for success almost entirely upon the condition that all ranks have a knowledge of the ground and understand exactly what they have to do and where they have to go. This condition, as has been shown above, could not possibly be fulfilled.

30. In addition the weather conditions were exceptionally unfavourable. Rain fell intermittently on the 10th and although on the day of the 11th and up till midnight of 11th/12th the weather was fairly

fine, at about 12.30 a.m. on 12th a strong S.W. wind rose and heavy rain fell, which continued throughout the rest of the night.

31. As regards the actual operations the chief causes of failure were the faulty nature and inadequacy of the creeping barrage, the lack of standing barrages and the very heavy conditions of weather and ground. Upon these points which have already been brought out in this narrative there is no need to enlarge further.

32. It is necessary to add a few words regarding the signal communications which were maintained forward of Brigade Headquarters.
Owing to the hurry of the relief and the long distance which had to be traversed from DIRTY BUCKET CAMP to VARNA FARM on the day of relief, linesmen and runners had very little time in which to learn their routes. This they had to do largely in the dark and under the instruction of the personnel of the outgoing Brigade who were tired out after the operations of the previous day. It is not surprising therefore that wires forward of Brigade Headquarters, which were very frequently broken by shell fire, were mended with great difficulty, and that messages by runners at night suffered at times considerable delay.
Pigeons, message rockets and extra drums and cable which had been asked for well in advance were received so late as to be of little use, since they did not reach Brigade Headquarters until after midnight of October 11th/12th. Wireless which was established between PHEASANT FARM and Brigade Headquarters worked well, though both stations were several times broken down. Of communication by this means full advantage was taken.

33. The total casualties sustained by the Brigade during the whole period were as follows:-

	Officers.	N.C.Os.	Rank & File.
7th Queens	6	30	163
7th Buffs	11	62	317
8th E.Surrey Regt.	10	45	242
7th R.W.Kent Regt.	14	57	240
- do - (Additional from bomb dropped on bus column)	3	-	38
35th M.G. Coy.	2	15	36
	46	209	1,013

TOTAL CASUALTIES   - Officers   46
                          Other Ranks 1,222.

APPENDIX 54.

7th Battalion Royal West Kent Regiment.
REPORT ON OPERATIONS NEAR POELCAPELLE.
10th - 13th October 1917.

Ref.Map
POELCAPPELLE.
Ed.4. 1/10,000.

On the night of the 10th/11th October 1917, the Battalion relieved the 6th Battn. Yorkshire Regt. in the front line.   Relief complete at 4.0 a.m. on the 11th October.
The dispositions of the Battalion then were:-
"D" Coy.   From V.20.a.12.48 to V.20.a.00.80.
"A" Coy.   From V.20.a.00.80 to V.19.b.75.95.
"C" Coy.   From V.19.c.95.70 to V.19.c.55.95.
"B" Coy.   From U.30.b.60.65 to U.30.b.25.80.

On the night of the 11th/12th October, tapes were laid by Capt. P.B. ANSTRUTHER D.S.O, M.C., and Capt. I. HEATON, on which the Battalion formed up for an attack.   The front line extended from the CHURCH in POELCAPPELLE to V.13.d.40.05, the second line about 70 yards in rear. The night was very dark and wet, and the Companies were knee-deep in mud when moving to the forming-up place. When withdrawing to the forming up line, "D" Coy. left 3 - posts (1 N.C.O. and 3 men each) and "A" Coy. 2 posts (1 N.C.O. and 3 men each) in concrete "pill-boxes" to prevent their occupation by the enemy. "A" Coy. had 14 casualties from shell fire when moving to the forming-up position as far as known the other Companies had none.

Forming up was successfully carried out, and the lines were in position ready to advance by half an hour before zero.
Front Line   -   "B" Coy on right, "C" Coy on left.
Second line   -   "D" Coy on right, "A" Coy on left.
Touch was established with the 7th Battn. Buffs on the right and the Household Battn., on the left.

At 5.25 a.m. on the 12th October the barrage opened. Some of the "heavies" were dropping short and fell behind "B" Coy on the right of the line, and amongst "A" Coy. on the left, causing casualties in the latter Company. Before our barrage started to move forward, the enemy barrage came down in front of the line on which the leading Companies were formed up.   The enemy barrage was slight, and when our barrage lifted and the Battalion advanced, few casualties were caused by it. The Battalion had many casualties from machine gun and rifle fire when advancing up to the line originally held.

"B" Coy. found their first objective was not held, and occupied it.   On advancing beyond it to attack the next, the Company came under very heavy machine gun and rifle fire from the BREWERY and the right flank, and all the Officers became casualties.   Sergeant TEBBITT then assumed command of the Company, but was unable to gain any ground to the front. "D" Coy. advancing behind pushed into, and became merged with "B" Coy at about 6.30 a.m, but owing to the intense machine gun and rifle fire, were unable to get forward. All the Officers except Lieut. C.A.W. DUFFIELD were now casualties, and the remnants of both Companies eventually "dug-in" on a line approximately the same as the original front line.

On the left "C" Coy. pushed forward and captured the enemy post at V.13.d.30.15 at about 5.45 a.m, taking 2 prisoners. The barrage on the centre and left was very erratic, and there appeared to be great gaps in it. At this point, owing to casualties, a gap occurred in the line, the right of "C" Coy. closing in on the Village of POELCAPPELLE where they were held up by a post at V.14.c.10.10, and were unable to make further progress. They eventually dug-in on a line approximately V.19.b.90.80 to V.19.b.80.95. All the Officers had now become casualties.

Meanwhile the left platoon of "C" Coy pushed forward at about 7.0 a.m. and gained their final objective, capturing 2 Officers, 50 O.R, and 2 machine guns at V.14.c.25.55. This platoon subsequently lost touch with the remainder of "C" Coy. and became merged with the Household Battalion on their left.

When advancing, the left of "A" Coy. lost direction and closed in towards the right. On reaching the line where "C" Coy. had been checked they became merged with that Coy, and, owing to heavy machine gun and rifle fire from "pill-boxes" at V.14.c.10.10, and V.14.c.12.20 and the right flank, they were unable to advance. It was now about 5.45 a.m. and all the Officers were casualties. The Coy. eventually dug in on the same line as "C" Coy.

At about 11.30 a.m. Lieut. C.A.W. DUFFIELD Commanding "D" Coy, being at that time the only Officer with the Companies, seeing that further advance was impossible, undertook the re-organisation of the Companies in his vicinity, and established a line of posts approximately on the line V.19.b.85.20 - V.19.b.75.40 - V.19.b.90.60 V.19.b.95.80 - V.19.b.90.90. - V.19.b.90.95, obtaining touch with the 7th Battalion Buffs on the right, and the 8th Battalion Suffolk Regt. on the left.

The Battalion was relieved on the night of the 13th/14th October by the 8th Battn. Suffolk Regt. at 11.0 p.m. The Battalion withdrew and concentrated at GOURNIER FARM, where they bivouacked for the remainder of the night.

Strength of Battalion going into action:-
      16 Officers
      605 Other Ranks.

Casualties:-

      14 Officers.
      312 Other Ranks.

Field.
17.10.17.

C.H.L. CINNAMOND, Lt.Col.
Commanding 7th Battalion Royal West Kent R.

7th Battalion Royal West Kent Regiment.

REPORT ON OPERATIONS NEAR POELCAPPELLE

10th -- 13th October 1917.

Ref.Map.
POELCAPPELLE.
Ed.4. 1/10,000.

    On the night of the 10th/11th October 1917, the Battalion relieved the 6th Battn. Yorkshire Regt. in the front line. Relief complete at 4.0 a.m. on the 11th October. The dispositions of the Battalion then were :-

    "D" Coy.   From V.20.a.12.48 to V.20.a.00.80
    "A" Coy.   From V.20.a. 00.80 to V.19.b.75.95.
    "C" Coy.   From V.19.c.95.70 to V.19.c.55.95.
    "B" Coy.   From U.30.b.60.65. to U.30.b.25.80.

    On the night of the 11th/12th October, tapes were laid by Capt.P.B.ANSTRUTHER.D.S.O.,M.C., and Capt.I.HEATON, on which the Battalion formed up for an attack. The front line extended from the CHURCH in POELCAPPELLE to V.13.d.40.05, the second line about 70 yards in rear. The night was very dark and wet, and the Companies were knee-deep in mud when moving to the forming-up place. When withdrawing to the forming up line, "D" Coy., left 3- posts (1-N.C.O. and 3- men each) and "A" Coy 2-posts (1-N.C.O. and 3- men each) in concrete "pill-boxes" to prevent their occupation by the enemy. "A" Coy., had 14- casualties from shell fire when moving to the forming-up position as far as known the other Companies had none.

    Forming-up was successfully carried out, and the lines were in position ready to advance by half an hour before zero.
    Front line :-   "B" Coy on right, "C" Coy on left.
    Second line :- "D" Coy on right, "A" Coy on left.
    Touch was established with the 7th Battn. Buffs on the right and the Household Battn., on the left.

    At 5.25 a.m. on the 12th October the barrage opened. Some of the "heavies" were dropping short and fell behind "B" Coy on the right of the line, and amongst "A" Coy on the left, causing casualties in the latter Company. Before our barrage started to move forward, the enemy barrage came down in front of the line on which the leading Companies were formed up. The enemy barrage was light, and when our barrage lifted and the Battalion advanced, few casualties were caused by it. The Battalion had many casualties from machine gun and rifle fire when advancing up to the line originally held.

    "B" Coy found their first objective was not held, and occupied it. On advancing beyond it to attack the next, the Company came under very heavy machine gun and rifle fire from the BREWERY and the right flank, and all the Officers became casualties. Sergeant TEBBITT then assumed command of the Company, but was unable to gain any ground to the front. "D" Coy advancing behind pushed into, and became merged with "B" Coy at about 6.30 a.m., but owing to the intense machine gun and rifle fire, were unable to get forward. All the Officers except Lieut.C.A.W.DUFFIELD were now casualties, and the remanants of both Companies eventually "dug-in" on a line approximately the same as the original front line

    On the left "C" Coy pushed forward and captured the enemy post at V.13.d.30.15 at about 5.45 a.m., taking 2- prisoners. The barrage on the centre and left was very erratic, and there appeared to be great gaps in it. At this point, owing to casualties, a gap occurred in the line, the right of "C" Coy closing in on the Village of POELCAPPELLE where they were held up by a post at V.14.c.10.10, and were unable to make

(2).

further progress. They eventually dug-in on a line approximately V.19.b.90.80 to V.19.b.80.95. All the Officers haa d now become casualties.

Meanwhile the left platoon of "C" Coy pushed forward at about 7.0 a m. and gained their final objective, capturing 2-Officers, 50- O.R., a nd 2- machine guns at V.14.c.25.55. This platoon subsequently lost touch with the remainder of "C" Coy and became merged with the Household Battalion on their left.

When advancing, the left of "A" Coy lost direction and closed in towards the right. On reaching the line where "C" Coy had been checked they became merged with that Coy., and, owing to heavy machine gun and rifle fire from "pill-boxes" at V.14.c.10.10., and V.14.c.12.20 and the right flank, they were unable to advance. It was now about 5.45 a.m. and all the Officers were casualties. The Coy eventually dug-in on the same line as "C" Coy.

At about 11.30 a.m. Lieut.C.A.W.DUFFIELD Commanding "D" Coy., being at that time the only Officer with the Companies, seeing that further advance was impossible, undertook the re-organisation of the Companies in his vicinity, and established a line of posts approximately on the line V.19.b.85.20 - V.19.b.75.40 - V.19½.b.90.60 V.19.b.95.80 - V.19½.b.90.90. - V.19.b.90.95, obtaining touch with the 7th Battalion Buffs on the right, and the 8th Battalion Suffolk Regt., on the left.

The Battalion was relieved on the night of the 13th/14th October by the 8th Battn. Suffolk Regt.,at 11.0 p.m. The Battalion withdrew and concentrated at GOURNIER FARM, where they bivouacked for the remainder of the night.

    Strength of Battalion going into action :-
        16-Officers.
        605. Other Ranks.

    Casualties :-
        14- Officers.
        312- Other Ranks.

            (Signed:-) C.H.L.CINNAMOND. Lieut.Col.
      Commanding 7th Battalion Royal West Kent Regt.

Field.
17-10-17.

7th Battalion Royal West Kent Regiment.
REPORT ON OPERATIONS NEAR POELCAPPELLE.

Ref.Map.
POELCAPPELLE. Ed.4
1/10,000

10th -- 13th October 1917.

On the night of the 10th/11th October 1917, the Battalion relieved the 6th Battalion Yorkshire Regiment in the front line. Relief complete at 4.0 a.m. on the 11th October. The dispositions of the Battalion then were :-
"D" Coy. from V.20.a.12.48 to V.20.a.00.80
"A" Coy. from V.20.a.00.80 to V.19.b.75.95
"C" Coy. from V.19.c.95.70 to V.19.c.55.95
"B" Coy. from U.30.b.60.65 to U.30.b.25.80

On the night of the 11th/12th October, tapes were laid by Captain P.N.ANSTRUTHER.D.S.O.,M.C., and Captain I.HEATON, on which the Battalion formed up for attack. The front line extended from the CHURCH in POELCAPPELLE to V.13.d.40.05, the second line about 70 yards in rear. The night was very dark and wet, and the Companies were knee-deep in mud when moving to the forming-up place. When withdrawing to the forming-up line, "D" Coy. left 3-posts (1-N.C.O. and 3-men each), and "A" Coy. 2-posts (1-N.C.O. and 3-men each) in concrete "pill-boxes" to prevent their occupation by the enemy. "A" Coy. had 14- casualties from shell fire when moving to the forming-up position; as far as known the other Companies had none.

Forming-up was successfully carried out, and the lines were in position ready to advance by half an hour before zero.
Front Line :- "B" Coy. on right, "C" Coy. on left.
Second Line:- "D" Coy. on right, "A" Coy. on left.
Touch was established with the 7th Battalion Buffs on the right and the Household Battalion on the left.

At 5.25 a.m. on the 12th October the Barrage opened. Some of the "heavies" were dropping short and fell behind "B" Coy. on the right of the line, and amongst "A" Coy. on the left, causing casualties in the latter Company. Before our barrage started to move forward, the enemy barrage came down just in front of the line on which the leading Companies were formed up. The enemy barrage was light, and when our barrage lifted and the Battalion advanced, few casualties were caused by it. The Battalion had many casualties from machine gun and rifle fire when advancing up to the line originally held.

"B" Coy. found their first objective was not held, and occupied it. On advancing beyond it to attack the next, the Company came under very heavy machine gun and rifle fire from the BREWERY and the right flank, and all the Officers became casualties. Sergeant TEBBITT then assumed command of the Company, but was unable to gain any ground to the front. "D" Coy. advancing behind, pushed into, and became merged with "B" Coy. at about 6.30 a.m., but owing to the intense machine gun and rifle fire, were unable to get forward. All the Officers except Lieut. C.A.W.DUFFIELD were now casualties, and the remnants of both Companies eventually "dug-in" on a line approximately the same as the original front line.

On the left "C" Coy. pushed forward and captured the enemy post at V.13.d.30.15 at about 5.45 a.m., taking two prisoners. The barrage on the centre and left was very erratic, and there appeared to be great gaps in it. At this point, owing to casualties, a gap occurred in the line, the right of "C" Coy. closing in on the Village of POELCAPPELLE where they were held up by a post at V.14.c.10.10 and were unable to make further progress. They eventually dug in on a line approximately V.19.b.90.80 to V.19.b.80.95. All the Officers had now become casualties.

Meanwhile the left Platoon of "C" Coy. pushed forward at about 7.0 a.m. and gained their final objective, capturing two Officers 50- O.R. and 2- machine guns at V.14.c.25.55. This platoon subsequently lost touch with the remainder of "C" Coy, and became merged with the Household Battalion on their left.

When advancing, the left of "A" Coy. lost direction and closed in towards the right. On reaching the line where "C" Coy. had been checked, they became merged with that Company, and, owing to heavy machine gun and rifle fire from "pill-boxes" at V.14.c.10.10 and V.14.c.12.20 and the right flank, they were unable to advance. It was now about 5.45 a.m. and all the Officers were casualties. The Company eventually dug in on the same line as "C" Coy.

At about 11.30 a.m. Lieut.C.A.W.DUFFIELD, Commanding "D" Coy, being at that time the only Officer with the Companies, seeing that further advance was impossible, undertook the re-organisation of the Companies in his vicinity, and established a line of posts approximately on the line V.19.b.85.20 - V.19.b.75.40 - V.19.b.90.60 V.19.b.95.80 - V.19.b.90.90 - V.19.b.90.95., obtaining touch with the 7th Battn. Buffs on the right, and the 8th Battn. Suffolk Regt., on the left.

The Battalion was relieved on the night of the 13th/14th October by the 8th Battn. Suffolk Regt., at 11.0 p.m. The Battalion withdrew and concentrated at GOURNIER FARM, where they bivouacked for the remainder of the night.

Strength of Battalion going into Action :-
16-OFFICERS---------------605-O.R.

Casualties :-
14-OFFICERS---------------312-O.R.

CR Curramond
Lieut.Col.
Commanding 7th Battalion Royal West Kent Regt.

Field.
17-10-17.

7th BATTALION THE ROYAL WEST KENT REGIMENT.

1917.

October.	SCHOOL CAMP near ST.JAN-TER-BIEZEN.	Appendix.
1st.	Training.	
2nd.	Training.	
3rd.	Training.	
4th.	Training. Battalion Attack Scheme.	
5th.	Training.	
6th.	Training.	
7th.	Divine Services.	
8th.	Training.	
9th.	Battalion left SCHOOL CAMP 6.55 am, and marched to DIRTY BUCKET CAMP. Arrived 10.0 a.m.	App.52.
	DIRTY BUCKET CAMP.	
10th.	Battalion moved at 10.5 a.m, for KEMPTON PARK, by 'busses. At 8.0 p.m. moved to relieve 6th Batt. Yorkshire Regt., in the front line. Relief complete at 4.0 a.m. 11th Oct.	
	LINE.	
11th.	Battalion holding front line. Disposition of Coys:- "B" and "C" Coys...Front Line. "A" and "D" Coys...In Support. Enemy artillery active.	
12th.	Battalion attacked. Zero 5.25 a.m. Enemy shelling exceptionally heavy.	App.53. " 54.
	GOURNIER FARM.	
13th.	Battalion relieved by 8th Battalion Suffolk Regiment. Relief complete 11.0 p.m. Battalion bivouacked for remainder of night at GOURNIER FARM.	
14th.	Battalion moved by Lorries to DIRTY BUCKET CAMP. Move complete 4.0 p.m. As Battalion were entering Lorries at CANAL BANK	

7th BATTALION THE ROYAL WEST KENT REGIMENT.

1917.

October.   SCHOOL CAMP near ST.JAN-TER-   Appendix.
                BIEZEN.

1st.   Training.

2nd.   Training.

3rd.   Training.

4th.   Training. Battalion Attack
                Scheme.

5th.   Training.

6th.   Training.

7th.   Divine Services.

8th.   Training.

9th.   Battalion left SCHOOL CAMP 6.55 a.m.
                and marched to DIRTY BUCKET CAMP.
                Arrived 10.0 a.m.   App.52.

                DIRTY BUCKET CAMP.

10th.   Battalion moved at 10.5 a.m.
                for KEMPTON PARK, by 'busses.
                At 8.0 p.m. moved to relieve
                6th Batt. Yorkshire Regt., in
                the front line. Relief
                complete at 4.0 a.m. 11th Oct.

                LINE.

11th.   Battalion holding front line.
                Disposition of Coys:-
                "B" and "C" Coys...Front Line.
                "A" and "D" Coys...In Support.
                Enemy artillery active.

12th.   Battalion attacked. Zero 5.25 a.m.
                Enemy shelling exceptionally heavy.   App.53.
                                                       " 54.

                GOURNIER FARM.

13th.   Battalion relieved by 8th Battalion
                Suffolk Regiment. Relief complete
                11.0 p.m. Battalion bivouacked
                for remainder of night at GOURNIER
                FARM.

14th.   Battalion moved by Lorries to
                DIRTY BUCKET CAMP. Move complete
                4.0 p.m. As Battalion were
                entering Lorries at CANAL BANK

1917.

October.   Appendix

14th.   several casualties were caused
(Ctd).   by hostile aircraft.

           DIRTY BUCKET CAMP.

15th.   Resting and cleaning up.

16th.   Resting and cleaning up.

17th.   Resting.

18th.   Training.

19th.   3 Officers and 200 O.R. detailed
           for carrying ammunition to the
           front line. Hd.Qrs. CANE TRENCH
           and HURST PARK. Lieut. A. GODLY
           in command of party.

20th.   Training.

21st.   Voluntary Church Services.
           Fatigue party returned at 10.0 pm.

22nd.   Training.

23rd.   Training. Inspection of Companies
           in Marching Order by Commanding
           Officer.

24th.   Battalion left DIRTY BUCKET CAMP
           at 12.0 noon for POPERINGHE.
           Arrived 1.30 p.m.   App.55

           POPERINGHE.

25th.   Training (under Company
           arrangements).

26th.   Battalion left POPERINGHE at
           2.30 p.m. Marched to PARROY
           CAMP, arriving 4.30 p.m.   App.56
           Relieved 17th Division at work
           on roads in vicinity of LANGEMARCK.

           PARROY CAMP.

27th.   Working on roads North of ST.JULIEN.
           Parties worked in two shifts –
           2 Companies commencing work at
           6.30 a.m. and 2 Companies at
           9.30 a.m.

28th.   Work on roads.

29th.   Work on roads. Hostile aircraft
           bombed vicinity of camp. No
           casualties.

1917.

October.   Appendix

14th.   several casualties were caused
(Ctd).   by hostile aircraft.

             DIRTY BUCKET CAMP.

15th.   Resting and cleaning up.

16th.   Resting and cleaning up.

17th.   Resting.

18th.   Training.

19th.   3 Officers and 200 O.R. detailed
             for carrying ammunition to the
             front line. Hd.Qrs. CANE TRENCH
             and HURST PARK. Lieut. A. GODLY
             in command of party.

20th.   Training.

21st.   Voluntary Church Services.
             Fatigue party returned at 10.0 pm.

22nd.   Training.

23rd.   Training. Inspection of Companies
             in Marching Order by Commanding
             Officer.

24th.   Battalion left DIRTY BUCKET CAMP
             at 12.0 noon for POPERINGHE.
             Arrived 1.30 p.m.   App.55

             POPERINGHE.

25th.   Training (under Company
             arrangements).

26th.   Battalion left POPERINGHE at
             2.50 p.m. Marched to PARNOY
             CAMP, arriving 4.30 p.m.   App.56
             Relieved 17th Division at work
             on roads in vicinity of LANGEMARCK.

             PARNOY CAMP.

27th.   Working on roads North of ST.JULIEN.
             Parties worked in two shifts -
             2 Companies commencing work at
             6.30 a.m. and 2 Companies at
             9.30 a.m.

28th.   Work on roads.

29th.   Work on roads. Hostile aircraft
             bombed vicinity of camp. No
             casualties.

1917.

October.   Appendix.

30th.   Work on roads. Hostile aircraft bombed vicinity of camp. No casualties.

31st.   Work on roads. 2 O.R. wounded.

OFFICERS JOINED DURING THE MONTH.

2.Lt.W.F.ROBERTS Joined 2.10.17.
Capt.C.F.STALLARD M.C. Joined 5.10.17.
2.Lt. W.U.C.TAYLER Re-joined 22.10.17.
2.Lt. E.A. THOMAS Joined 29.10.17.
2.Lt. E.J. CURTIS Joined 29.10.17.

OFFICERS CASUALTIES DURING MONTH.

2.Lt.J.A.HORTON. To 55th T.M.B. 5.10.17.
2.Lt.P.T.STANLEY (To England for (permanent Commn. (Indian Army. 7.10.17.
Capt.C.F. STALLARD M.C. To 12th Bn. E.Surrey Regt. 13.10.17.
2.Lt. H. BUFFEE Sick to England 5.10.17.
Capt.F.H.LEWIN M.C. Killed in Action 12.10.17.
2.Lt.A.C.MITCHELL   do.   do.
2.Lt.R.W.COLES   do.   do.
2.Lt.J.H.GLADWELL Killed in Action 14.10.17.
Lieut.H.T.GREGORY Died of Wounds 12.10.17.
2.Lt. G.J. ALLEN Died of Wounds 12.10.17.
Capt.I. HEATON Died of Wounds 14.10.17.
Capt. P.N. ANSTRUTHER D.S.O, M.C. Wounded. 12.10.17.
Capt.F.H.F.SMITH Wounded 12.10.17.
Capt. A.R. HOGG   do. 14.10.17.
Lieut. R.D.KENT M.C. do. 12.10.17.
2.Lt. E. GRETHE Wounded in Action 12.10.17.
2.Lt. H.S.PEGLAR   do.   do.
2.Lt.G.F.JOHNSTONE do.   do.
2.Lt.A.L.DUPONT   do.   do.
2.Lt.H.T.RAPSON   do.   do.
2.Lt.E.W.DAY   do. 14.10.17.

                                                                                 Lieut.Col.

SECRET.

55th Infantry Brigade.

Account of operations from 9th to 14th Oct. 1917.

Reference Maps:-
    Sheets 27 and 28 1/40,000
    Sheets ST.JULIEN and POELCAPELLE (Ed.4) 1/10,000.

A. PRELIMINARY MOVEMENTS.

1. On October 9th the 55th Infantry Brigade moved from SCHOOLS CAMP, ST. JAN TER BIEZEN (Sheet 27 L.3.c.) to DIRTY BUCKET CAMP (Sheet 28. A.30 central).

2. About midnight on October 9th/10th the G.O.C. 18th Division came to see the G.O.C. 55th Infantry Brigade and gave the following instructions:-

    Owing to the failure of the attack on MEUNIER HOUSE & the N. end of POELCAPELLE, by the 32nd Infantry Brigade, 11th Division, this attack was to be carried out by the 18th Division. 55th Infantry Brigade would carry out this attack which was to be followed by a further advance on the same day, to be carried out by two battalions of 53rd Infantry Brigade. The line held by 32nd Infantry Brigade was to be taken over on the night of 10th/11th October by 55th Infantry Brigade instead of by 53rd Infantry Brigade as previously ordered.

3. Owing to the short time available for preparation G.O.C. 55th Infantry Brigade decided provisionally that the attack should be carried out on the same lines as that of 32nd Infantry Brigade, namely, 3 battalions assaulting and one in reserve; that the three assaulting battalions should be, 8th E.Surrey Regt. on the right, 7th Buffs in the centre, 7th R.W. Kent Regt. on the left, and that these battalions should take over their battle fronts from 32nd Infantry Brigade.

4. The line actually held not being yet definitely established the following frontages were provisionally allotted:-

    8th E.Surrey Regt. from the LEKKERBOTEERBEEK to GLOSTER FARM inclusive.

    7th Buffs from GLOSTER FARM exclusive to the Cross Roads V.19.b.5.1. exclusive.

    7th R.W. Kent Regt. from the Cross Roads V.19.b.5.1. inclusive to about V.19.b.1.8.

5. It was arranged that all battalions would be conveyed to forward area by busses, 7th Buffs and 7th R.W. Kent Regt. starting at 10 a.m. and 8th E.Surrey Regt. and 7th Queens starting as soon as possible after 1.0 p.m. that these battalions should proceed as far as KEMPTON PARK where definite orders for relief would be given to them, and that commanding officers of assaulting battalions and advance parties would proceed early to VARNA FARM, the Headquarters of the 32nd Infantry Brigade.

6. On the morning of the 10th October the Brigade Commander and Commanding Officers arrived at Headquarters 32nd Infantry Brigade about 10.0 a.m. After a conference with G.O.C. 32nd Infantry Brigade instructions were given to Battalion Commanders for the attack to be carried out on the lines of the previous attack by the 32nd Infantry Brigade, and objectives and dividing lines were provisionally decided upon. Each battalion was to attack on a two company front, these two companies being detailed for the first objective, while two companies were detailed to pass through them to the final objective. Battalion Commanders were able to give instructions on these points to their Company Commanders before proceeding to the Headquarters of the battalions they were to relieve in order to reconnoitre the ground and arrange details of relief. Reconnaisance was most difficult owing to the fact that the enemy had good observation and showed considerable activity.

7. 7th Buffs and 7th R.W. Kent Regt. arrived in good time by bus at KEMPTON PARK and the relief by these battalions of battalions of 32nd Infantry Brigade was carried out successfully, though great difficulty was experienced in the matter of guides, and owing to the state of the ground, the bad weather, and the extreme darkness of the night. These reliefs were completed by 3.0 a.m. and 4.0 a.m. respectively.
Owing to traffic restrictions the busses conveying the 8th E.Surrey Regt. were diverted on the way up to the rendezvous and were considerably delayed so that this battalion did not reach the rendezvous until after dark. The guide supplied to conduct the battalion as far as the STEENBEKE where platoon guides were to meet them, lost the way and led the battalion to the wrong bridge, so that the relief was **very** much delayed and the first company of the 8th E.Surrey Regt. did not arrive at Battalion Headquarters of the battalion to be relieved until 4.0 a.m. The relief was rushed through, but could not be properly completed owing to the dawn.
On completion of relief each assaulting battalion was disposed with 2 companies holding the front line and 2 companies distributed in

depth behind.

The 7th Queens were disposed in positions just E. of the STEENBEEK which had been reconnoitred during the day by Officers of that battalion, and had arrived in position without mishap.

During the relief of 32nd M.G.Coy. by 55th M.G.Coy. while guns were being loaded on the tramway at MINTY FARM, a shell fell in the middle of one section causing casualties to the whole of the personnel of four guns.

8. The line indicated by the frontages given above was found to be approximately correct, except that the left flank battalion had advanced their position as far as the road junction V.20.a.0.8, the line running back thence to about V.15.d.4.0. where it joined with the 4th Division on the left.

9. Brigade orders for the attack were issued to units at 8.0 a.m. on October 11th; objectives and boundary lines were as shewn on the attached map.

10. In the case of the right battalion the change in the barrage arrangements and consequent change of the first objective made considerable alterations necessary in the instructions already given to Company Commanders.
These instructions could not be given until dusk, as it was not possible to move about during daylight. Company Commanders in their turn had little chance of explaining anything to their subordinates, and in fact had great difficulty in finding their platoons owing to the circumstances of the relief, the darkness and the shell torn ground. One platoon under 2nd.Lieut. RIDDETT could not be found at all until it was seen to get up and go forward when our barrage started. In these conditions the men and section commanders had little chance of knowing what their objectives were, and no opportunity of looking at them beforehand in daylight.

11. The centre and left battalions were hardly affected by the alterations in the barrage line and in consequence it was less difficult for Company Commanders to get their instructions down to their subordinates, though in their case also movement by day in and near the front line was greatly restricted by the activity of the enemy.
In these battalions, however, as far as can be ascertained, all platoon and section commanders knew their objectives and what they had to do.

12. An additional change in the instructions originally given to battalion commanders had to be made in the matter of the forming up line, which was ordered to be in advance of the line on which the 32nd Brigade had formed up. At dusk, therefore, on October 11th, discs and tapes were laid by all battalions on lines as follows:-

7.

```
8th E.Surrey Regt. - V.26.a.6.5. - V.20.c.2.3.
7th Buffs          - V.20.c.2.3. - POELCAPELLE
                     Church exclusive V.19.b.7025.
7th R.W.Kent Regt. - POELCAPELLE Church inclusive
                     - V.13.d.45.00.
```

The night of 11th/12th was very dark and very wet and the men were often knee deep in mud when moving to the forming up positions. In addition, behind our right battalion, the enemy put over some gas shells which considerably hampered the movement of troops coming up from the rear. In spite of this all troops (with the exception of the platoon of the right battalion mentioned above) were in position before zero (5.25 a.m.).

Headquarters of battalions were as follows:-
Right battalion - V.25.b.4.7.
Centre battalion - V.19.d.40.95.
Left battalion - V.19.a.5.1.

13. ACTION OF OCTOBER 12th.

Our Artillery barrage appears to have opened erratically and to have been far from heavy.
In the case of the right battalion it is stated that the enemy appeared to be very little inconvenienced by it. Machine Gun fire was opened immediately by guns which, owing either to their closeness to our line or to the thinness of the barrage, were not affected by it. The enemy barrage came down about 4 minutes after zero about 150 yards behind our forming up line.
On the front of the centre battalion the right company commander states that our barrage opened very thinly, but that as his men advanced it thickened on top of his leading troops.
The left company states that the enemy barrage was put down in 2 minutes about 150 yards in front of our forming up position so that it caught our men as they were waiting for our barrage to lift.
In both companies it is stated positively that when our barrage lifted it moved back over 100, probably 150 yards.
The left battalion states that our barrage opened correctly, but that some shells fell very short behind the right company and among the left company, causing casualties in the latter. Before our barrage started to move forward the enemy barrage came down just in front of our leading troops. The enemy barrage was light and when our barrage lifted and our troops advanced few casualties were caused by it. Our barrage, however, was very erratic and there appeared to be large gaps in it.

14. In spite of our barrage, heavy rifle and machine gun fire was immediately opened by the enemy on the whole front.
The right company commander of the right battalion, who was wounded and returned to battalion headquarters about 3 hours after zero, reported that the men had

advanced 500 yards or more from the forming up
position.   They had gone forward
magnificently in face of intense fire, but
casualties had been heavy and practically all the
leaders were hit.   In addition there were many
enemy machine guns still holding out between the
forming up position and the position reached by the
advanced troops.

As regards the left flank, the left company of the
left battalion pushed forward, but its right was
held up by a post about V.14.c.1.1 and was unable
to make further progress: a gap thus occurred
between the extreme left platoon and the rest of
the left battalion.   This platoon pushed forward
and reached its objective at V.14.c.25.55, capturing
two Officers, 50 O.R's and two machine guns; but
never regained touch with the rest of its battalion
and became merged with the Household Battalion on
its left.

While the troops on the flanks thus made some
progress, the centre battalion and the inner companies
of the flank battalions were checked almost at
once.   As regards the centre battalion, this
appears, from the statements of the surviving
company commander, to have been principally due to
the fact that the first lift of the barrage, as
stated above, was well over 100 yards and that
consequently the troops lost the barrage at once.

15. The companies detailed for the further objectives
following up in rear of the leading companies in
turn came under the intense fire and lost heavily.
Eventually they became merged with the leading
companies.

16. The heavy losses which occurred among Officers and
N.C.Os were due to efforts to gain ground by fire and
movement after the barrage had thus been lost.
The mud and water were so bad that to move rapidly
from shell hole to shell hole was out of the
question.   Rifles also got covered with mud and
even after they had been cleaned it was difficult to
keep them in action for more than a few rounds without
cleaning out the breech again, since the men's
hands were plastered with mud and each time a fresh
clip was put in some mud inevitably went in with it.

17. The situation was for some time very obscure.
This was due not only to the fact that nearly all
the Officers and senior N.C.Os had become casualties
but also that few runners could get back over the
open ground owing to rifle and machine gun fire.
By this time, of the 12 company officers per
battalion who went into action there were left
with the right battalion three, with the centre
battalion four and with the left battalion only one.
Eventually it became clear that, except for small
parties which may have got further forward on the
extreme right and left flanks, little or no progress
had been made.

18. About noon there occurred in the centre battalion an incident the explanation of which has not been discovered.
Since the hostile rifle and machine gun fire had somewhat slackened Captain NICHOLSON, commanding the right company of the centre battalion, sent 2nd.Lieut. SPENCER to gain touch with 2nd.Lieut. KNIGHT who, with elements of the right "leap-frog" Company, was some 400 yards to his left at about V.20.c.15.84.
Shortly before this he had seen a party of the enemy unarmed and carrying a red cross flag approach 2nd.Lieut. KNIGHT'S party, apparently with the intention of surrendering. 2.Lt. KNIGHT was seen to converse with the Germans who began to show themselves in increasing numbers but always unarmed. 2.Lt. SPENCER on his way to 2nd.Lt. KNIGHT was mortally wounded and Captain NICHOLSON went out to help him. As he was doing so he heard a shout and saw 2nd.Lt. KNIGHT and about 30 men being marched off in the direction of MEUNIER HOUSE. He could not get back to his men in time to get them to fire on this party.

19. In the meanwhile the 6th R.Berks Regt. and 8th Suffolk Regt., the battalions of 53rd Infantry Brigade which had been detailed to capture the final objective of 18th Division, had followed close behind the battalions of 55th Brigade.
These battalions had thus become involved in the fight though no information had been given them that the first objectives had been reached.
The assaulting battalions having made little or no progress the 6th R.Berks.Regt. had taken up positions in rear of the right battalion and the right of the centre battalion some 100 yards in rear of the original forming up line, while the 8th Suffolk Regt. had filled the gap between the left flank of the left battalion and the Household Battalion on their left.

20. The 7th Queens (counter attack battalion) remained in their original positions south of the ST.JULIEN - POELCAPELLE Road between DELTA HOUSES and RETOUR CROSS ROADS.
About 2 p.m. the O.C. Centre Battalion observed from his headquarters a party of the enemy apparently advancing down the main street of the village. Thinking this might possibly be a counter attack he sent to warn a company of 7th Queens to move to the vicinity of his Headquarters where they could instantly counter a counter attack. The enemy were held up by the 7th R.W. Kent Regt. and 8th Suffolk Regt. One Company of the 7th Queens, however, moved forward and took up a position astride the road near the cemetery.

21. About 4.30 p.m. orders were given to the O.C. 7th Queens to move his battalion up in close support of the right and centre battalions. When this had been done the 6th R.Berks.Regt. was to be withdrawn.
At the same time orders were given to the 8th Suffolk Regt. to continue to hold the positions on the left of 7th R.W.Kent Regt. and that the remainder of the battalion should be disposed in support of these positions and of 7th R.W. Kent Regt.
The 7th Queens moved into position as ordered but owing to the darkness and to the heavy losses in officers only one company of 6th R.Berks.Regt. could be found so that only one company instead of the whole battalion was withdrawn.

22. At 8.50 p.m. orders were issued to the three assaulting battalions that when their position had been reorganised, posts established on the line held and touch ensured on both flanks, any surplus men not required for these posts were to be withdrawn to concentrate in CANE TRENCH Area.
This was duly done in the case of the centre and left battalions, but the message on the subject to the right battalion was delayed and did not reach the battalion until 8.0 a.m. the following morning when it was too late to withdraw any men from the front line.

23. The work of 55th M.G.Coy. in these operations was as follows.
Two sections had been detailed for barrage fire. In consequence, however, of the casualties suffered on the night of Oct.10th/11th only four guns could be spared for this purpose. These guns were dug in on their barrage positions on the 11th, but during the night, owing to the heavy rain and constant shelling, these positions collapsed and became useless and the guns were not in a position to fire at Zero.
Of the remaining two sections two guns had been detailed to go forward to each of three strong points which were to have been established in the vicinity of TRACAS FARM, MEUNIER HOUSE and HELLES HOUSE. While two guns were held in reserve. Of these the two guns detailed for TRACAS FARM eventually came into action near GLOSTER FARM and found targets on the POELCAPELLE - SPRIET ROAD and also claim to have hit enemy snipers who were most active during the afternoon. The two guns detailed for MEUNIER HOUSE tried to get forward but lost heavily from enemy sniping and eventually dug in in shell holes in positions between GLOSTER FARM and RETOUR CROSS ROADS. The two guns for HELLES HOUSE did not move forward from their positions in POELCAPELLE.

C. SUBSEQUENT MOVEMENTS.

24. During the night of 12th/13th positions were organised and a line of posts established as follows:-

    8th E.Surrey Regt. - from LEKKERBOTERBEEK about V.26.a.9.6. to GLOSTER FARM inclusive.

    7th Buffs. - from GLOSTER FARM exclusive to V.20.a.0.0, including a post at V.20.c.3.6, where they had a captured German Machine Gun in action.

    7th R.W. Kent Regt - Posts at V.19.b.9.2, V.19.b.85.40 V.20.a.0.6, V.20.a.00.75, V.20.a.0.8, V.20.a.0.9.

    8th Suffolk Regt - from V.20.a.09. to the track at V.13.d.95.45.

    On the front of the centre battalion at about 2 a.m. the enemy attacked our posts at V.20.c.33.60, V.20.c.33.50 and V.20.c.30.45 with bombs. He was driven off by rifle fire and bombs. This appears to have been the only attempt by the enemy to regain the posts he had lost during the day. During the night also the battalion headquarters of the right battalion, which consisted only of a shell hole with a corrugated iron weatherproof covering, was continually shelled and about 2.30 am. sustained a direct hit which caused 7 casualties among the battalion H.Q. personnel.

25. On the morning of October 13th. orders were issued for the relief, at dusk, of the assaulting battalions by 7th Queens and 8th Suffolk Regt. the former taking over the front from the LEKKERBOTERBEEK to about V.19.b.9.3. and the latter taking over the posts held by 7th R.W. Kent Regt. from the latter point to its own right flank.
    The relief was accomplished without difficulty and the three assaulting battalions and the remainder of 6th R.Berks.Regt. were withdrawn to CANE TRENCH Area.

26. On the afternoon of October 14th the 7th Buffs, 8th E.Surrey Regt. and 7th R.W. Kent Regt. were conveyed by busses from the CANAL BANK to DIRTY BUCKET CAMP.
    During the embussing enemy aeroplanes came over and dropped bombs on the bus column causing casualties to 7th R.W. Kent Regt.

27. On the evening of the same day the 7th Queens and 8th Suffolk Regt. were relieved by 10th Essex Regt.

and 8th Norfolk Regt.
This relief also was carried out without difficulty and on its completion the command of the sector was handed over to G.O.C. 53rd Infantry Brigade.

D. **CONCLUSION.**

28. In estimating the reasons for the failure of the attack the initial difficulties involved must not be lost sight of.
The relief of the units of the 32nd Infantry Brigade, who were disorganised after an unsuccessful attack on the previous day, took a long time to arrange and was far from easy. The Brigade found difficulty in supplying an adequate number of guides and some of these lost their way. In fact the relief alone fully occupied the attention of all concerned until it was completed on the morning of October 11th.

29. Again no one in the Brigade had seen any of the country East of the CANAL until the morning of October 11th. The ground over which it had been intended that the Brigade should attack had been thoroughly studied in the back area by all ranks and objectives had been allotted and were well known. The ground over which the attack was carried out was quite unknown and the attack took place at such short notice that there was little chance of getting information down to platoon commanders much less to the rank and file.
The information and orders which could be given to battalion and company commanders before they took over the line were neither complete nor final, since no orders had then been received by the Brigade. In the case of the right battalion such information as they had could not be communicated to their subordinates by company commanders owing to the late arrival of their battalion at KEMPTON PARK. After the line had been taken over all communication of orders was most difficult, especially on the front of the right battalion. Movement in daylight forward of all battalion headquarters was under observation by the enemy, who showed much activity with rifle and machine gun fire, while by night it was impossible for company commanders, whose headquarters were in most cases in shell holes without cover of any kind to show lights or to consult and explain from orders and maps.
An attack on the system which had been adopted and in which the battalions had been trained depends for **success** almost entirely upon the condition that all ranks have a knowledge of the ground and understand exactly what they have to do and where they have to go. This condition, as has been shown above, could not possibly be fulfilled.

30. In addition the weather conditions were exceptionally unfavourable. Rain fell intermittently on the 10th and although on the day of the 11th and up till midnight of 11th/12th the weather was fairly

13.

fine, at about 12.30 a.m. on 12th a strong S.W. wind rose and heavy rain fell, which continued throughout the rest of the night.

31. As regards the actual operations the chief causes of failure were the faulty nature and inadequacy of the creeping barrage, the lack of standing barrages and the very heavy conditions of weather and ground. Upon these points which have already been brought out in this narrative there is no need to enlarge further.

32. It is necessary to add a few words regarding the signal communications which were maintained forward of Brigade Headquarters.
Owing to the hurry of the relief and the long distance which had to be traversed from DIRTY BUCKET CAMP to VARNA FARM on the day of relief, linesmen and runners had very little time in which to learn their routes. This they had to do largely in the dark and under the instruction of the personnel of the outgoing Brigade who were tired out after the operations of the previous day. It is not surprising therefore that wires forward of Brigade Headquarters, which were very frequently broken by shell fire, were mended with great difficulty, and that messages by runners at night suffered at times considerable delay.
Pigeons, message rockets and extra drums and cable which had been asked for well in advance were received so late as to be of little use, since they did not reach Brigade Headquarters until after midnight of October 11th/12th. Wireless which was established between PHEASANT FARM and Brigade Headquarters worked well, though both stations were several times broken down. Of communication by this means full advantage was taken.

33. The total casualties sustained by the Brigade during the whole period were as follows:-

	Officers.	N.C.Os.	Rank & File.
7th Queens	6	30	163
7th Buffs	11	62	317
8th E.Surrey Regt.	10	45	222
7th R.W.Kent Regt.	14	57	240
- do - (Additional from bomb dropped on bus column)	3	-	35
55th M.G. Coy.	2	15	36
	46	209	1,013

TOTAL CASUALTIES - Officers 46
Other Ranks 1,222.

APPENDIX 54.

7th Battalion Royal West Kent Regiment.
REPORT ON OPERATIONS NEAR POELCAPELLE.
10th - 13th October 1917.

Ref.Map
POELCAPPELLE.
Ed.4. 1/10,000.

On the night of the 10th/11th October 1917, the Battalion relieved the 6th Battn. Yorkshire Regt. in the front line.   Relief complete at 4.0 a.m. on the 11th October.
The dispositions of the Battalion then were:-
"D" Coy.   From V.20.a.12.48 to V.20.a.00.80.
"A" Coy.   From V.20.a.00.60 to V.19.b.75.95.
"C" Coy.   From V.19.c.95.70 to V.19.c.55.95.
"B" Coy.   From U.30.b.60.65 to U.30.b.25.80.

On the night of the 11th/12th October, tapes were laid by Capt. F.B. ANSTRUTHER D.S.O. M.C., and Capt. I. HEATON, on which the Battalion formed up for an attack. The front line extended from the CHURCH in POELCAPPELLE to V.13.d.40.05, the second line about 75 yards in rear. The night was very dark and wet, and the Companies were knee-deep in mud when moving to the forming up place. When withdrawing to the forming up line, "D" Coy. left 3 - posts (1 N.C.O. and 3 men each) and "A" Coy. 2 posts (1 N.C.O. and 3 men each) in concrete "pill-boxes" to prevent their occupation by the enemy. "A" Coy. had 14 casualties from shell fire when moving to the forming-up position as far as known the other Companies had none.

Forming up was successfully carried out, and the lines were in position ready to advance by half an hour before zero.
Front Line   -   "B" Coy on right, "C" Coy on left.
Second line   -   "D" Coy on right, "A" Coy on left.
Touch was established with the 7th Battn. Buffs on the right and the Household Battn., on the left.

At 5.25 a.m. on the 12th October the barrage opened. Some of the "heavies" were dropping short and fell behind "B" Coy on the right of the line, and amongst "A" Coy. on the left, causing casualties in the latter Company. Before our barrage started to move forward, the enemy barrage came down in front of the line on which the leading Companies were formed up.   The enemy barrage was slight, and when our barrage lifted and the Battalion advanced, few casualties were caused by it. The Battalion had many casualties from machine gun and rifle fire when advancing up to the line originally held.

"B" Coy. found their first objective was not held, and occupied it.   On advancing beyond it to attack the next, the Company came under very heavy machine gun and rifle fire from the BREWERY and the right flank, and all the Officers became casualties.   Sergeant TEBBITT then assumed command of the Company, but was unable to gain any ground to the front. "D" Coy. advancing behind pushed into, and became merged with "B" Coy at about 6.30 a.m, but owing to the intense machine gun and rifle fire, were unable to get forward. All the Officers except Lieut. C.A.W. DUFFIELD were now casualties, and the remnants of both Companies eventually "dug-in" on a line approximately the same as the original front line.

On the left "C" Coy. pushed forward and captured the enemy post at V.13.d.30.15 at about 5.45 a.m, taking 2 prisoners. The barrage on the centre and left was very erratic, and there appeared to be great gaps in it. At this point, owing to casualties, a gap occurred in the line, the right of "C" Coy. closing in on the Village of POELCAPPELLE where they were held up by a post at V.14.c.10.10, and were unable to make further progress. They eventually dug-in on a line approximately V.19.b.90.80 to V.19.b.80.95. All the Officers had now become casualties.

Meanwhile the left platoon of "C" Coy pushed forward at about 7.0 a.m. and gained their final objective, capturing 2 Officers, 50 O.R, and 2 machine guns at V.14.c.25.55. This platoon subsequently lost touch with the remainder of "C" Coy. and became merged with the Household Battalion on their left.

When advancing, the left of "A" Coy. lost direction and closed in towards the right. On reaching the line where "C" Coy. had been checked they became merged with that Coy. and, owing to heavy machine gun and rifle fire from "pill-boxes" at V.14.c.10.10, and V.14.c.12.20 and the right flank, they were unable to advance. It was now about 5.45 a.m. and all the Officers were casualties. The Coy. eventually dug in on the same line as "C" Coy.

At about 11.30 a.m. Lieut. C.A.W. DUFFIELD Commanding "D" Coy, being at that time the only Officer with the Companies, seeing that further advance was impossible, undertook the re-organisation of the Companies in his vicinity, and established a line of posts approximately on the line V.19.b.85.20 - V.19.b.75.40 - V.19.b.90.60 V.19.b.95.80 - V.19.b.90.90. - V.19.b.90.95, obtaining touch with the 7th Battalion Buffs on the right, and the 8th Battalion Suffolk Regt. on the left.

The Battalion was relieved on the night of the 13th/14th October by the 8th Battn. Suffolk Regt. at 11.0 p.m. The Battalion withdrew and concentrated at GOURNIER FARM, where they bivouacked for the remainder of the night.

Strength of Battalion going into action:-
        16 Officers
        605 Other Ranks.

Casualties:-
        14 Officers.
        312 Other Ranks.

Field.   C.H.L.GIBBAMOND, Lt.Col.
17.10.17.   Commanding 7th Battalion Royal West Kent R.

4th Bn.
R W Kent Regt
October &
November
1917

Casualties:-
        14 Officers.
        312 Other Ranks.

Field.
17.10.17.

C.H.L. CINNAMOND, Lt.Col.
Commanding 7th Battalion Royal West Kent R.

APP. 56

7th Battalion Royal West Kent Regiment.

ORDER No.70.

Ref.Map Sheet.
28 Scale 1/40,000.

26th October 1917.

    The Battalion will move from POPERINGHE to PARROY CAMP.
B.16.c.&.d. to-day 26th October 1917.
    HOUR OF START :- 1.0.p.m.
    Starting Point :- Cross Roads.G.3.c.20.95.
    ROUTE :- ELVERDINGHE-Road Junction B.10.c.5.0.

    ORDER OF MARCH :- Headquarters.
                    Drums.
                    "C" Company.
                    "B" Company.
                    "A" Company.
                    "D" Company.
                    Stretcher Bearers.
                    First Line Transport.
Distances of 200 yards will be maintained between Companies.

    Officers' Kits will be stacked in the yard by the Orderly Room by 12.noon.
    Officers' Messes will be packed by 12.noon.
    Blankets and Drummers Packs will be sent to Q.M.Stores by 10.30.a.m.

                                    (Signed). T.T.WADDINGTON. Captain
                                          a/Adjutant.

7th Battalion Royal West Kent Regiment.

ORDER No. 71.

Ref. Map
Sheet 27.
1/40,000.

2nd. November 1917.

1. The Battalion will march to PROVEN Railway Station to-morrow, proceeding from thence to ELVERDINGHE by train.
    Dress :-   Full Marching Order.
    Hour of Start :- 9.25 a.m.
    Starting Point :- CROSS ROADS at X.25.b.31 (Sheet 19.)
        (N.B. Cross Roads are 450 yds down the
         road leading from Brigade Hd.Qrs over
         the Railway through the Camp)
    Order of March:-
        "Headquarters".
        "A" Company.
        Drums.
        "B" Company.
        "C" Company.
        "D" Company.

    200 yds interval will be maintained between Companies.

2. 2/Lt.H.N.EDWARDS and the five C.Q.M.S's will meet the Staff Captain at Road Junction where road past Brigade Headquarters meets PROVEN - ROUSBRUGGE Road at 7.50 a.m., parading at the Orderly Room at 7.30 a.m.

3. 2/Lt.H.G.J.HINES and 1- Battalion Runner will report to a representative of Staff Captain at CROSS ROADS at F.1.c.3.1., at 9.30 a.m.

4. First Line Transport will move by road.
    Hour of March :- 8.0 a.m.
    Starting Point :- ROAD JUNCTION at X.25.b.5.4.
    Order of March :-
        8th East Surrey Regt.
        7th Royal West Kent Regt.
        55th M.G.Coy.
    A distance of 200 Yds will be maintained between units.

    Route :- ROAD JUNCTION X.27.a.4.3. - ROAD JUNCTION
             X.28.c.9.1. - thence by CHEMIN MILITAIRE Bra.
             via A.2.b.9.4. - S.28.d.8.7. to DEWIPPE CABARET -
             WOESTAN.

5. Officers' Kits and messes will be stacked near the JUNCTION of RAILWAY and ROAD past Brigade Headquarters by 7.0 a.m.
    Blankets will be rolled in bundles of 10- and stacked at the same place by 7.30 a.m.
    The Q.M. will send a guide to F.1.c.3.1. at 8.0 a.m. to take over two lorries from a representative of 55th Brigade.

(Signed:-) T.T.WADDINGTON. Captain.
A/Adjutant.

WAR DIARY or INTELLIGENCE SUMMARY.

(Erase heading not required.)

Army Form C. 2118.

7 R.W. Kent Regt. Nov 17

Place	Date	Hour	Summary of Events and Information	Remarks and references to Appendices
PARROY CAMP	1-11-17		Battn. moved to PRIVET Camp by lorries. Hour of start:- 6.pm. Arrived:- 7.30 pm.	
PRIVET CAMP	2-11-17		Parades under Company arrangements. Baths.	
	3-11-17		Battn. moved to LARRY Camp (Nr. ELVERDINGHE), in support. Entrained at PROVEN 10.30 am. Arrived in huts:- 12.30 pm.	App.57
LARRY CAMP	4-11-17		Voluntary Church Services.	
	5-11-17		1st line Transport and Q.M. Stores moved to Camps:- A.5.c. and A.11.A. Composite Platoon rejoined 92nd Field Coy. R.E. Working on light Railways in Forward Area.	
	6-11-17		Parades under Coy. arrangements and protective sandbagging of huts.	
	7-11-17		Working parties. 1 Coy working under 92nd Field Coy. R.E. on Forward Tramways 3 Coys under Corps Tramways.	
	8-11-17		Working parties for 7th inst.	
	9-11-17		1 Coy.(D) detailed for work under 92nd Field Coy R.E. remaining 3 Coys. Training. Football Match 7th R. W. Kent Regt v 8th E. Surrey Regt. Result Nil- Nil.	
	10-11-17		"Training."	
	11-11-17		Voluntary Church Services.	
	12-11-17		Training.	
	13-11-17		Small Working Parties detailed for work in vicinity of Camp and BOESINGHE Camp.	
	14-11-17		Working Parties.	
	15-11-17		Working Parties:- 1 Coy on Tramways by night under 92nd Field Coy R. E. 3 Officers 100 O.R. for laying cable Forward from WOOD HOUSE to LES CINQ CHEMINS. 1 Coy at 8.30 am. and 1 Coy (less 1 platoon) at 9.a.m. to work under 92nd Field Coy R.E.	
	16-11-17 - 22-11-17		Working parties as for 15th inst.	
	23-11-17		Working Parties:- Camp Drainage.	
	24-11-17 - 29-11-17		Working Parties.	
	30-11-17		Working parties and training under Coy. arrangements.	

OFFICERS JOINED DURING THE MONTH.

2/Lt. W. J. GODDARD. 2-11-17   2/Lt. W. F. DRAIN.   10-11-17
" Lieut. R. K. YOUNG. 10-11-17   " A. J. GIBSON.   "
" B. VAUGHAN.   "   " S. A. FRENCH.   13-11-17
2/Lt. H. LYNCH-WATSON. "   Capt. E. G. SAVAGE.   23-11-17
" E. C. ROBERTSON.   "   1st Lieut. R. B. LEITH (American Army) 30-11-17

CASUALTIES IN ACTION.   2/Lt. W. F. ROBERTS.   Wounded 14-11-17

Army Form C. 2118.

WAR DIARY
or
INTELLIGENCE SUMMARY.
(Erase heading not required.)

Instructions regarding War Diaries and Intelligence Summaries are contained in F. S. Regs., Part II. and the Staff Manual respectively. Title pages will be prepared in manuscript.

Place	Date	Hour	Summary of Events and Information	Remarks and references to Appendices
			HONOURS AND AWARDS.	
			The undermentioned awarded decorations for gallantry and devotion to duty in action:-	
			THE MILITARY CROSS.	
			Capt REYNOLDS W.L.B.,R.A.M.C.	
			Capt The Revd. COOKE. G.C.R.,A.C.D.	
			Lieut. Duffield. C.A.W.	
			BAR TO THE DISTINGUISHED CONDUCT MEDAL.	
			1201 Sgt. Coleman. A.	
			THE DISTINGUISHED CONDUCT MEDAL.	
			3489 Sgt Hamblin. C.	
			12076 Pte. Ives. L.	
			BAR TO THE MILITARY MEDAL.	
			1616 L/C. MacCullum. J. H.	
			6552 Pte. Fairbrother E.	
			THE MILITARY MEDAL.	
			1435 Sgt. Saddington. G.	
			9334 " Tebbitt. F.	
			2074 L/C. Wells. B. H.	
			18617 Pte. Savage. A.	
			11137 " Wallard. A.	
			25615 " Perry. J.	
			THE MILITARY MEDAL (Cont.)	
			21077 Pte Fever. F.	
			2672 " Meen A.	
			18148 " Tyrrell. E. T.	
			18140 " Little. T.	

CR Cummoney
Lieut. Colonel.
Commanding 7th Battalion Royal West Kent Regiment.

Army Form C. 2118.

WAR DIARY
or
INTELLIGENCE SUMMARY.
(Erase heading not required.)

Instructions regarding War Diaries and Intelligence Summaries are contained in F. S. Regs., Part II. and the Staff Manual respectively. Title pages will be prepared in manuscript.

Place	Date	Hour	Summary of Events and Information	Remarks and references to Appendices
PARROY CAMP	1-11-17		Bntn. moved to THIVET Camp by lorries. Hour of Start:- 6 p.m. Arrived:- 7.30 p.m.	
THIVET CAMP	2-11-17		Troops under Company arrangements.	
	3-11-17		Bath. moved to LARRY CAMP (Nr. FRESNOY EN WOEVRE), in support. Details at PROUVEN 10.30 a.m.	(App. 5)
LARRY CAMP	4-11-17		Arrived in Hutsi. 12.30 P.M.	
	5-11-17		Voluntary Church Services.	
	6-11-17		1st Rfct Transport and M.T. Stores moved to Camper- M.5.b. sht. ll... Remount Platoon rejoined 52nd Field Coy. R.E. working on light Railways in Forward Area.	
	7-11-17		Baths and armoury arrangements as Previous day. Smoke Helmets of Bath. Working parties, 1 Coy working under 59th Field Coy. On Tower Tramway 3 Coys under Corps surveys.	
	8-11-17		Working parties for 7th inst.	
	9-11-17		1 Coy (Less 1 pl) on work with 52nd Field Coy R.E. Tramways & Board Walks.	
	10-11-17		Tactical Match 7th R. E. Kent Regt v 5th Q. Surrey Regt. Result Nil- Nil.	
	11-11-17		Voluntary Church Services.	
	12-11-17		Training.	
	13-11-17		Small working parties detailed for work in vicinity of Camp and FRESNOIS Camp.	
	14-11-17		Working Parties:- 1 Coy on Tramway by THIGHA lumer Wood, 1 pl A.D., 3 Officers 100 O.R. for Light Cable Repair from DESCHOEN to BRAY DUNES. 1 Coy 2 Bn.s. and 1 pl (Less 1 platoon) at 6.am 20 work on Ref No.4 shti ll. 65 Coy K.R.	
	15-11-17		1-11-17 working parties as for 15th inst.	
	26-11-17		Working Parties:- Camp Fatiques.	
	29-11-17		Working Parties.	
	30-11-17		Working parties and fatigues as per day.	

OFFICERS JOINED DURING THE MONTH:
2/Lt. R. J. HOGGARD. 8-11-17
" G. W. LYNG 20-11-17
" G. SHEPHERD "
" D. G. ROBERTSON "

2/Lt. TRAIN 10-1-17
A. L. GIBSON "
S. A. FRENCH 25-11-17
M. G. BAXTER 23-11-17

CASUALTIES
by T.J. Nicholls Major 0-11-17

A.D.S.S./Forms/C.2118.

Army Form C. 2118.

WAR DIARY
or
INTELLIGENCE SUMMARY.
(Erase heading not required.)

Summary of Events and Information

HONOURS AND AWARDS.

The undermentioned awarded decorations for gallantry and devotion to duty in action:—

THE MILITARY CROSS.

Capt REYNOLDS. W.L.E.,R.A.M.C.
Capt. The Revd. COOKE. O.C.R.,A.C.D.
Lieut. Duffield. W
BAR TO THE DISTINGUISHED CONDUCT MEDAL.

1201 Sgt. Coleman. A.

THE DISTINGUISHED CONDUCT MEDAL.

3489 Sgt Hamblin. G.
12076 Pte. Ives. L.

BAR TO THE MILITARY MEDAL.

1616 L/C. MacCullum. J. H.
6552 Pte. Fairbrother E.

THE MILITARY MEDAL.

1435 Sgt. Saddington. G.
9334 " Tebbitt. F.
2074 L/C. Wells. E. H.
18617 Pte. Savage. A.
11137 " Kallond. A.
25615 " Perry. W.

THE MILITARY MEDAL (Cont.)

21077 Pte Fever. F.
2672 " Meen A.
18148 " Tyrrell. H. T.
18140 " Little. T.

CR Cunnington
Lieut. Colonel.
Commanding 7th Battalion Royal West Kent Regiment.

7th BATTALION THE ROYAL WEST KENT REGIMENT.

1917.

November.	PARROY CAMP.	Appendix.
1st.	Battn moved to PRIVET Camp by lorries. Hour of start:- 6 p.m. Arrived:- 7.30 p.m.	
	PRIVET CAMP.	
2nd.	Parades under Company arrangements. Baths.	
3rd.	Battn. moved to LARMY Camp (nr. ELVERDINGHE), in support. Entrained at PROVEN 10.30 a.m. Arrived in huts:- 12.30 pm.	App.5.
	LARMY CAMP.	
4th.	Voluntary Church Services.	
5th.	1st Line Transport and Q.M.Stores moved to Camps:- A.5.c. and A.11.a. Composite Platoon rejoined 92nd Field Coy. R.E. working on light Railways in Forward Area.	
6th.	Parades under Coy. arrangements and protective sandbagging of huts.	
7th.	Working parties. 1 Coy working under 92nd Field Coy. R.E. on Forward Tramways 3 Coys under Corps Tramways.	
8th.	Working parties for 7th inst.	
9th.	1 Coy. (D) detailed for work under 92nd Field Coy. R.E. remaining 3 Coys. Training. Football Match 7th R.W. Kent Regt. v 8th E.Surrey Regt. Result Nil - Nil.	
10th.	Training.	
11th.	Voluntary Church services.	
12th.	Training.	
13th.	Small Working Parties detailed for work in vicinity of Camp and BOESINGHE Camp.	
14th.	Working parties.	
15th.	Working parties:- 1 Coy. on Tramways by night under 92nd Field Coy. R.E. 3 Officers 100 O.R. for laying cable Forward from WOODHOUSE to LES CINQ	

1917.

November.   Appendix.

15th.   CHEMINS.   1 Coy at 8.30 am. and
(Ctd).   1 Coy. (less 1 platoon) at 9 am
            to work under 92nd Field Coy.R.E.

16th. -   Working parties as for 16th inst.
22nd.

23rd.   Working parties.   Camp Drainage.

24th.-   Working Parties.
29th.

30th.   Working parties and Training
            under Coy. arrangements.

OFFICERS JOINED DURING THE MONTH.

2.Lt.W.J.GODDARD   2.11.17.
Lieut. R.K. YOUNG   10.11.17.
    " B. VAUGHAN   "
2.Lt.H.LYNCH-WATSON   "
    " E.C.ROBERTSON   "

OFFICERS CASUALTIES.

2.Lt.   W.F. Roberts   Wdd. in Action
                            17.11.17.
2.Lt.   W.F. DRAIN   10.11.17.
    "   A.J. GIBSON   "
    "   S.A. FRENCH   13.11.17.
Capt.   E.G. SAVAGE   23.11.17.
1st Lieut.R.B.LEITH (American Army)
                            30.11.17.

HONOURS AND AWARDS.

The undermentioned awarded decorations
for gallantry and devotion to duty
in action:-

THE MILITARY CROSS.

Capt.REYNOLDS W.L.E. R.A.M.C.
Capt.The Revd.COOKE, G.C.R. A.C.D.
Lieut. DUFFIELD C.A.W.

BAR TO THE DISTINGUISHED CONDUCT MEDAL.

1301. Sgt. Coleman. A.

THE DISTINGUISHED CONDUCT MEDAL.

3489 Sgt. Hamblin C.
12076 Pte. Ives L.

BAR TO THE MILITARY MEDAL.

1616. L/C. MacCullum, J.H.
6552. Pte. Fairbrother E.

THE MILITARY MEDAL.

1435 Sgt. Saddington G.
9334 "   Tebbitt F.
2074 L/C. Wells E.H.
18617 Pte. Savage A.
11137 " Wallond A.
26515 " Perry J.
21077 " Fever F.
2672   " Meen A.
18148 " Tyrrell H.T.
18140 " Little T.

C.H.L. CINNAMOND, Lieut-Colonel,
Commanding 7th Battalion Royal West Kent Regt

7th BATTALION THE ROYAL WEST KENT REGIMENT.

1917.

November.	PARROY CAMP.	Appendix.
1st.	Battn moved to PRIVET Camp by lorries. Hour of start:- 6 p.m. Arrived:- 7.30 p.m.	
	PRIVET CAMP.	
2nd.	Parades under Company arrangements. Baths.	
3rd.	Battn. moved to LARRY Camp (nr. ELVERDINGHE), in support. Entrained at PROVEN 10.30 a.m. Arrived in huts:- 12.30 pm.	App.5.
	LARRY CAMP.	
4th.	Voluntary Church Services.	
5th.	1st Line Transport and Q.M.Stores moved to Camps:- A.5.c. and A.11.a. Composite Platoon rejoined 92nd Field Coy, R.E. working on light Railways in Forward Area.	
6th.	Parades under Coy. arrangements and protective sandbagging of huts.	
7th.	Working parties, 1 Coy working under 92nd Field Coy. R.E. on Forward Tramways 3 Coys under Corps Tramways.	
8th.	Working parties for 7th inst.	
9th.	1 Coy. (D) detailed for work under 92nd Field Coy. R.E. remaining 3 Coys. Training. Football Match 7th R.W. Kent Regt. v 8th E.Surrey Regt. Result Nil - Nil.	
10th.	Training.	
11th.	Voluntary Church services.	
12th.	Training.	
13th.	Small Working Parties detailed for work in vicinity of Camp and BOESINGHE Camp.	
14th.	Working parties.	
15th.	Working parties:- 1 Coy. on Tramways by night under 92nd Field Coy. R.E. 3 Officers 100 O.R. for laying cable Forward from WOODHOUSE to LES CINQ	

1917.

November.   Appendix.

15th. (Ctd).   CHEMINS. 1 Coy at 8.30 am. and
               1 Coy. (less 1 platoon) at 9 am
               to work under 92nd Field Coy.R.E.

16th. - 22nd. Working parties as for 16th inst.

23rd.   Working parties. Camp Drainage.

24th.- 29th.   Working Parties.

30th.   Working parties and Training
               under Coy. arrangements.

OFFICERS JOINED DURING THE MONTH.

2.Lt.W.J.GODDARD   2.11.17.
Lieut. R.K. YOUNG   10.11.17.
"   B.VAUGHAN   "
2.Lt.H.LYNCH-WATSON   "
"   E.C.ROBERTSON   "

OFFICERS CASUALTIES.

2.Lt. W.F.Roberts   Wdd.in Action
                           17.11.17.
2.Lt. W.F. DRAIN   10.11.17.
"   A.J. GIBSON   "
"   S.A. FRENCH   13.11.17.
Capt. E.G. SAVAGE   23.11.17.
1st Lieut.R.B.LEITH (American Army)
                           30.11.17.

HONOURS AND AWARDS.

The undermentioned awarded decorations
for gallantry and devotion to duty
in action:-

THE MILITARY CROSS.

Capt.REYNOLDS W.L.E, R.A.M.C.
Capt.The Revd.COOKE, G.C.R, A.C.D.
Lieut. DUFFIELD C.A.W.

BAR TO THE DISTINGUISHED CONDUCT MEDAL.

1201. Sgt. Coleman, A.

THE DISTINGUISHED CONDUCT MEDAL.

3489 Sgt. Hamblin C.
12076 Pte.Ives L.

BAR TO THE MILITARY MEDAL.

1616. L/C. MacCullum, J.H.
6552. Pte. Fairbrother E.

THE MILITARY MEDAL.

1435 Sgt. Baddington G.
9834 "   Tebbitt F.
2074 L/C. Wells R.H.
10617 Pte. Savage A.
11137 " Wallond A.
26515 " Perry J.
21077 " Fever F.
2675   " Meen A.
10148 " Tyrrell H.T.
16140 " Little T.

        C.H.L. CINNAMOND, Lieut-Colonel,
    Commanding 7th Battalion Royal West Kent Regt.

BAR TO THE MILITARY MEDAL.

1616. L/C. MacCullum, J.H.
6552. Pte. Fairbrother E.

THE MILITARY MEDAL.

1435 Sgt. Saddington G.
9334 "   Tebbitt F.
2074 L/C. Wells E.H.
18617 Pte. Savage A.
11137 "   Wallond A.
26515 "   Perry J.
21077 "   Fever F.
2672   "   Meen A.
18148 "   Tyrrell H.T.
18140 "   Little T.

                                    C.H.L. CINNAMOND, Lieut-Colonel,
                        Commanding 7th Battalion Royal West Kent Regt.

7th BATTALION THE ROYAL WEST KENT REGIMENT.

1917.

November.	PARROY CAMP.	Appendix.
1st.	Battn moved to PRIVET Camp by lorries. Hour of start:- 6 p.m. Arrived:- 7.30 p.m.	

PRIVET CAMP.

2nd.	Parades under Company arrangements. Baths.	
3rd.	Battn. moved to LARRY Camp (nr. ELVERDINGHE), in support. Entrained at PROVEN 10.30 a.m. Arrived in huts:- 12.30 pm.	App.5.

LARRY CAMP.

4th.	Voluntary Church Services.
5th.	1st Line Transport and Q.M.Stores moved to Camps:- A.5.c. and A.11.a. Composite Platoon rejoined 92nd Field Coy, R.E, working on light Railways in Forward Area.
6th.	Parades under Coy. arrangements and protective sandbagging of huts.
7th.	Working parties, 1 Coy working under 92nd Field Coy. R.E. on Forward Tramways 3 Coys under Corps Tramways.
8th.	Working parties for 7th inst.
9th.	1 Coy. (D) detailed for work under 92nd Field Coy. R.E. remaining 3 Coys. Training. Football Match 7th R.W. Kent Regt. v 8th E.Surrey Regt. Result Nil - Nil.
10th.	Training.
11th.	Voluntary Church services.
12th.	Training.
13th.	Small Working Parties detailed for work in vicinity of Camp and BOESINGHE Camp.
14th.	Working parties.
15th.	Working parties:- 1 Coy. on Tramways by night under 92nd Field Coy. R.E. 3 Officers 100 O.R. for laying cable Forward from WOODHOUSE to LES CINQ

1917.

November.   Appendix.

15th. (Ctd). CHEMINS. 1 Coy at 8.30 am. and 1 Coy. (less 1 platoon) at 9 am to work under 92nd Field Coy.R.E.

16th. - 22nd. Working parties as for 16th inst.

23rd. Working parties. Camp Drainage.

24th.-29th. Working Parties.

30th. Working parties and Training under Coy. arrangements.

OFFICERS JOINED DURING THE MONTH.

2.Lt.W.J.GODDARD   2.11.17.
Lieut. R.K. YOUNG   10.11.17.
"   B. VAUGHAN   "
2.Lt.H.LYNCH-WATSON   "
"   E.C.ROBERTSON   "

OFFICERS CASUALTIES.

2.Lt. W.F.Roberts   Wdd.in Action
                    17.11.17.
2.Lt. W.F. DRAIN   10.11.17.
"   A.J. GIBSON   "
"   S.A. FRENCH   13.11.17.
Capt. E.G. SAVAGE   23.11.17.
1st Lieut.R.B.LEITH (American Army)
                    30.11.17.

HONOURS AND AWARDS.

The undermentioned awarded decorations for gallantry and devotion to duty in action:-

THE MILITARY CROSS.

Capt.REYNOLDS W.L.E, R.A.M.C.
Capt.The Revd.COOKE, G.C.R, A.C.D.
Lieut. DUFFIELD C.A.W.

BAR TO THE DISTINGUISHED CONDUCT MEDAL.

1201. Sgt. Coleman, A.

THE DISTINGUISHED CONDUCT MEDAL.

3489 Sgt. Hamblin C.
12076 Pte.Ives L.

Army Form C. 2118.

WAR DIARY
or
INTELLIGENCE SUMMARY.
(Erase heading not required.)

Instructions regarding War Diaries and Intelligence Summaries are contained in F.S. Regs., Part II. and the Staff Manual respectively. Title pages will be prepared in manuscript.

Section "D" 7 R W Kent Vol 28

Place	Date	Hour	Summary of Events and Information	Remarks and references to Appendices
LARRY CAMP.	1-12-17.		3- Coys., burying cable at WOOD HOUSE under Divisional Signal Coy.	
	2-12-17.		Voluntary Church Services.	
	3-12-17.		Working Parties.	
	4-12-17.		-do-	
	5-12-17.		-do-	
	6-12-17.		-do- Football Match v.7th Buffs. 7th R.W.Kent. 2-goals; 7th Buffs. nil.	App. 58
	7-12-17.		Battalion left Camp at 10.30 p.m.; marched to BABOON CAMP (B.6.b - Belgium 28.N.W.), via ELVERDINGHE - BOESINGHE RDAD, relieving 7th Batt. Bedfordshire Regt., in Support.	" 59.
BABOON CAMP.	8/10-12-17.		Working Parties.	
	10-12-17.		Battalion relieved 7th Bedford Regt in left sector. "A" and "C" Coys., Front Line ; "B" Coy in support; "D" Coy in reserve. Hour of start 3.30 p.m.	
LINE.	11-12-17.		Battalion holding Line.	
	12-12-17.		-do-. Night of 12th/13th. Inter-Company relief, "B" and "D" Coys taking over front line, "A" and "C" Coys the support and reserve.	
	13-12-17.		Battalion holding Line.	
	14-12-17.		Battalion relieved by 7th Buffs; proceeded to Support Position at BABOON CAMP.	
BABOON CAMP.	15-12-17.		Battalion relieved by 2/6 Battn Kings Liverpool Regt. Entrained at BOESINGHE at 10.0 a.m., arriving at WATTEN at 2.0 p.m., marching thence to NORTLEULINGHEM.	" 60
NORTLEULINGHEM.	17-12-17.		In Billets. Cleaning-up and inspection under Company arrangements.	
	18-12-17.		Training. Firing practice on "B" range, 2nd Army School of Musketry.	
	19-12-17.		-do-. -do- -do- -do-	
	20-12-17.		-do-. -do- -do- -do-	
	21-12-17.		-do-. -do- -do- -do-	
	22-12-17.		-do-. -do- -do- -do-	
	23-12-17.		Voluntary Church Services.	
	24-12-17.		Training. Battalion Dinner at 1.0 p.m.	
	25-12-17.		Christmas Day.	
	26/27-12-17.		Training.	
	28-12-17.		Battalion marched to AUDRUICQ. Entrained 10.3 0 a.m.; detrained at PROVEN at 3.0 p.m. Marched to PORTSMOUTH CAMP, arriving 5.30 p.m.	" 61

T2134. Wt. W708–776. 500000. 4/15. Sir J.C. & S.

Army Form C. 2118.

WAR DIARY
or
INTELLIGENCE SUMMARY.
(Erase heading not required.)

Instructions regarding War Diaries and Intelligence Summaries are contained in F.S. Regs., Part II. and the Staff Manual respectively. Title pages will be prepared in manuscript.

Place	Date	Hour	Summary of Events and Information	Remarks and references to Appendices
PORTSMOUTH CAMP.	29-12-17.		Parades.	
	30-12-17.		Voluntary Church Services. Testing of Box Respirators.	
	31-12-17.		Battalion marched to BOESINGHE III Area; hour of start 9.0 a.m. Arrived at "J" Camp at 12.0 noon. (A.8.b. Belgium 28.N.W.)	App. 62
			OFFICERS JOINED DURING THE MONTH.	
			2/Lt. H.T. RAPSON. rejoined 2-12-17.	
			Lt. P.B. WHITROW. joined 7-12-17.	
			2/Lt. W.A. SHEARING. " 7-12-17.	
			2/Lt. R. RICHARDSON. " 7-12-17.	
			2/Lt. D. SIMPSON. " 17-12-17.	
			OFFICERS' CASUALTIES DURING THE MONTH.	
			Lieut. R.K. YOUNG. Sick, to England from 27-11-17.	
			2/Lt. A.J. GIBSON. To 6th Battn. R.W.Kent Regt. 27-12-17.	
			2/Lt. R. RICHARDSON. -do- -do-	
			2/Lt. S. ALLCHIN. Killed in Action. 13-12-17.	
			Capt. E.G. SAVAGE. Wounded -do- -do-	

Alf Trupp? Major
for Lieut.Col.
Commanding 7th Battalion Royal West Kent Regiment.

7th Battalion Royal West Kent Regiment.

ORDER NO. 72.

7th December 1917.

Ref. Map.
BELGIUM.
Sheet 28.N.W.
1/20,000.

1. The Battalion will move to BABOON CAMP to-day.
   Dress :- Full Marching Order with 1- blanket per man rolled round the pack.
   Hour of start :- 10.45 p.m.
   Starting point :- GASOMETER, ELVERDINGHE - BOESINGHE ROAD.
   (B.15.a.4.8.)
   Order of March :- Drums.
   "Hd.Qrs."
   "A" Coy.
   "B" Coy.
   "D" Coy.
   "C" Coy.
   100x interval will be maintained between platoons.

2. Lieut. C.A.W. DUFFIELD. M.C., C.Q.M.S., and 1- runner per Coy., and 2- runners from Hd.Qrs will parade at Orderly Room at 8.0 p.m. to proceed ahead of Battalion to BABOON CAMP.

3. First Line Transport will remain in its present location.
   1- Lewis Gun Limber for "A" and "B" Coys, and
   1- Lewis Gun Limber for "C" and "D" Coys will report at "A" and "C" Coys Hd.Qrs. at 9.0 p.m.
   1- limber for Coy messes will report at Coy HdQrs, beginning at "C" Coy at 9.0 p.m.
   Mess Cart will report at Battn Hd.Qrs at 9.30 p.m.
   1- limber for Pioneers and spare H.Q. Stores at Hd.Qrs at 9.0 p.m.
   1- limber for medical stores will report to Sgt. Dickman at 9.0 p.m.
   1- limber for Signallers Stores and Orderly Room will report to Orderly Room at 8.0 p.m.
   Coy Cookers will be ready to move at 7.30 p.m.
   Officers' Kits will be stacked at respective Hd.Qrs. at 3.30 p.m.
   1- servant per Coy will go with Officers' Kits.
   1- blanket per man will be rolled in bundles of 10- and stacked at respective Coy. Hd.Qrs. at 3.30 p.m.

(Signed:-) T.T. WADDINGTON. Captain.
            Adjutant.

7th Battalion Royal West Kent Regiment.

APP 59

Order No. 73.   9th December 1917.

1. The Battalion will releive the 7th Bedford Regt in the left sector tomorrow.
   Hour of Start :- 3.30.p.m.
   Order of March :- "A" Coy Front line Coy left Sector.
                     "C" Coy Front line Right Sector.
                     "B" Coy Support Coy.
                     "D" Coy.Reserve Coy.
                     "H.Q" Coy.

   Coys will move in parties of not more than 25. Company Commanders ensuring that groups specified are not split up.
   DRESS :- Full Marching Order without greatcoats and haversacks Jerkins and 1 waterbottle will be carried in p/ pack.

   The spare waterbottle will be slung also Gum boots.
   Lewis Gun sections will carry 16 full drums per gun the remainder will be dumped with platoon kit.

2. Spare Kit will be put in haversacks and dumped by platoons in COLDSTREAM CAMP in a hut to be specified later. Great coats will be tied up by sections labelled and dumped in the same hut.

   Kits of officers going up the line will be dumped in a hut in COLDSTREAM CAMP.
   All kit to be ready by 11.a.m.
   A guard of 1.N.C.O and 2 men from Regimental Police will remain with this kit until Battln comes out of the line.

3. Gum Boots. 1 pair per man.
   Waterbottles. 1 extra per man
   4 Gas rattles per Coy and 1 for Battln H.Q. will be drawn from drying shed at 10.30.a.m. tomorrow.

4. Coy Commanders will ensure that every man has a muzzle cover. If orthodox covers are not available an improvised one of rag will be made.

5. O.C. Support Coy will detail 1 N.C.O and 2 Lewis Gunners to report to Bn.H.Q. on arrival to man an A.A. Gun.

6. Guides. 2 for Bn.H.Q., 1 per Coy H.Q. and 1 per platoon will report tomorrow morning from the 7th Bedford Regt.

7. Coys will report releif complete by the word BABOON only.

8. Details not going up the line will parade outside "C" Coy H.Q. at 1.30.a.m. to proceed to "H" CAMP.
   1 limber for kit of the 6 officers will report at 11.a.m.

                              (Signed). T.T.WADDINGTON.   Captain,
                                            Adjutant.

APP. 60

7th Battalion Royal West Kent Regiment.

ORDER No. 74.   15th December 1917.

1. The Battalion will move by train from BOESINGHE Station to WATTEN, and thence by march to NORTLEULINGHEM to-morrow.

2. Companies will move off at 200 yards interval.
   Order of March :-

       Headquarters.
       "A" Company.
       "B" Company.
       "C" Company.
       "D" Company.

   Hour of start :- 8.30 a.m.

   Starting Point :- Road at Headquarters "C" Company.

   Dress :- Full marching order; one day's rations; one blanket rolled round the pack.

3. Lewis Guns and accessories will be carried to the train, and dumped at WATTEN Station on arrival.

4. One blanket per man, rolled tightly in tens will be dumped at B.5.d.7.1. by 7.45 a.m. (50 yds North East of BOESINGHE Cross Roads).

   The undermentioned stores will be dumped outside "C" Company Headquarters :-

   By 6.30 a.m.
    (Officers' Kits.
    (4 Camp Kettle per Company, and two steamers
    ("H.Q." Coy.
    (Canteen Stores.
    (Orderly Room Boxes.

   By 7.30 a.m. Officers' Mess Boxes.

5. Sergt. Clothier will report the Camp clean, to M.O. at 8.0 a.m.

        (Signed :-) T.T.WADDINGTON. Captain.
                 Adjutant.

7th Battalion Royal West Kent Regiment.

ORDER NO. 74.

27th December 1917.

Ref. Map.
Sheet 27A/N.E.

1. The Battalion will march to AUDRUICQ to-morrow, and thence by train to the PROOSDY Area, detraining at PROVEN.
   Hour of Start :- 6.15 a.m.
   Starting Point :- Fork Roads at J.34.d.8.4.
   Order of March :- Headquarters.
   Drums.
   "D" Company.
   "B" Company.
   "C" Company.
   "A" Company.
   Stretcher Bearers.
   Dress :- Full Marching Order, with one blanket rolled neatly round the Pack.

2. Lieut.A.A.EASON will proceed to the Station as Entraining Officer, starting ½hour before the Battalion. He will report to the Orderly Room to-night for entraining particulars.

3. Officers' Valises will be dumped at Q.M.Stores by 5.30 a.m.
   Officers' Mess Boxes will be sent to Hd.Qr.Mess by 5.45 a.m.
   The Mess Cart will report at Orderly Room at 5.30 a.m., and thence to Hd.Qr.Mess.
   Drummers' Packs and Rifles, and those of Sick men, will be taken to Q.M. Stores by 5.30 a.m.
   Blankets will be rolled tightly in bundles of 10 and taken to the Q.M. Stores by 5.0 a.m.
   Lewis Gun Limbers will be loaded overnight in the Transport Lines.
   NOTHING THAT IT IS POSSIBLE TO LOAD OVERNIGHT WILL BE LEFT UNTIL THE MORNING.

4. The Q.M. will detail 4- O.R's for loading purposes. They will proceed to the STATION by Lorry.
   An unloading party consisting of 10- O.R's will be found by the Company on Duty, on arrival at the places of entrainment and detrainment.

5. Men excused carrying a pack (names to be notified later), will report to 2/Lt.E.A.THOMAS at "D" Coy. Hd.Qrs. at 5.0 a.m., and will be marched to the STATION, arriving there not later than 9.0 a.m.
   Sick men, unable to march, (names to be notified later) will parade at Q.M. Stores by 8.0 a.m., and proceed thence by Lorry.

6. On arrival in the new Area the following distances will be maintained :-
   Between Battalions-----------500 yds.
   Between Companies-----------100 yds.

7. O.C.Coys., will ensure that Billets are left in a thoroughly clean condition.
   A portion of the First Line Transport, as under, will proceed by train. The Transport Officer will arrange the hour of start so as to arrive at AUDRUICQ STATION at 11.0 a.m. :-
   MALTESE CART; MESS CART; COOKERS; WATER CARTS; PACK ANIMALS; RIDING HORSES.
   The remainder of the 1st Line Transport will report to the Transport Officer of the 8th East Surrey Regt. at the Cross Roads LA BALANCE on the CALAIS-ST.OMER ROAD,(Ref.Map.27.a/S.E.), at 9.0 a.m. This column will stage at LEDERZEELE on the night 28th/29th inst. The Transport Officer will send forward a representative to take over billets from the Area Commandant, LEDERZEELE.

(Signed:-) C.L.MISKIN. Lieut.
A/Adjutant.

7th Battalion Royal West Kent Regiment.   APP 62

ORDER NO. 76

30th December 1917.

1. The Battalion will proceed to the MORSINGRE III area to-morrow and march to "J" Camp.
   Hour of Start   :- 9.0 a.m.
   Starting Point   :- Where Railway crosses PORTSMOUTH CAMP & PRIVETT CAMP ROAD, just East of PRIVETT CAMP.
   Order of March   :-
                         Headquarters "A" Echelon.
                         Drums.
                         "A" Company.
                         "B" Company.
                         "C" Company.
                         "D" Company.
                         Headquarters "B" Echelon.
                         Stretcher Bearers.
                         First Line Transport.
   Dress :- Full Marching Order with One Blanket.

   The following distances will be maintained on the march :-
         Between Battalions---------------------------------500 yds.
            "   Companies---------------------------------100 yds.
            "   sections of 6- vehicles----------------- 25 yds.

2. One Battalion Runner will report to a representative of the Staff Captain at CROSS ROADS immediately N.W. of PROVEN at 8.0 a.m. to-morrow, and will guide lorries to this Camp.
   Men excused carrying packs (names to be notified later), will march independently under the Orderly Officer, reporting to him outside the Guard Tent at 8.30 a.m.

3. 2/Lt. F.D.GAUSDEN will remain behind and will hand over to the incoming Unit.
   The Q.M. will detail 4- O.R. for loading. In addition, the Coy on Duty will supply a loading party of 1- N.C.O. and 10- O.R.
   The latter party will report to 2/Lt. F.D.GAUSDEN on completion of their task, and will be marched to "J" Camp.
   On arrival in "J" Camp, the Company on Duty will supply a further party of 1- N.C.O. and 10- men for unloading.

4. Blankets will be rolled tightly in bundles of 10- and taken to the Q.M. Stores by 7.30 a.m.
   Officers' Kits will be dumped outside the Q.M. Stores by 8.0 a.m.
   Officers' Mess Boxes will be sent to the Transport Lines by 7.45 a.m.
   Lewis Gun limbers will be loaded overnight.
   The Mess Cart will report to Hd.Qrs.Mess at 8.15 a.m.
   Orderly Room Boxes will be sent to Q.M. Stores by 8.0 a.m.
   Canteen Stores will be loaded in one limber overnight.
   Pioneers' Tools and Signalling Gear will be loaded in one limber overnight.
   Drummers' Packs and rifles, and those of men excused carrying them will be taken to the Q.M. Stores by 7.30 a.m.

5. Officers Commanding Coys will ensure that billets are left in a thoroughly clean condition.

                              (Signed:-)   C. L. WICKIE. Lieut.
                                             A/Adjutant.

Army Form C. 2118.

WAR DIARY
or
INTELLIGENCE SUMMARY.
(Erase heading not required.)

Instructions regarding War Diaries and Intelligence Summaries are contained in F.S. Regs., Part II. and the Staff Manual respectively. Title pages will be prepared in manuscript.

7th R. Kent Regt.

Vol. 29

Place	Date	Hour	Summary of Events and Information	Remarks and references to Appendices
"J" CAMP.	1-1-18.		Parades under Company arrangements.	
	2-1-18.		Battalion relieved the 2/5th Battn., KING'S LIVERPOOL REGT., in Reserve at BABOON CAMP. Hour of Start :- 9.30 a.m. Arrival 12.30 p.m. Starting Point :- DE WIPPE CROSS ROADS. Route :- WOESTAN - ELVERDINGHE - BOESINGHE. Composite Platoon rejoined 92nd Fld.Co.R.E.	App. 63.
BABOON CAMP.	3-1-18 to 5-1-18.		Parades under Company arrangements. Baths at ELVERDINGHE. Pedicure treatment at Camp.	
	6-1-18.		Voluntary Church Services. Battalion relieved 7th Battn THE BUFFS in the Left Battalion Sector. Hour of Start :- 3.0 p.m. Relief complete 8.0 p.m.	App. 64.
IN THE LINE.	7-1-18.		Battalion holding Line.	
	8-1-18.		-do- * Under cover of a heavy barrage, Bosche attacked our front line posts, one * of which was captured, with three of the garrison.	
	9-1-18.		Inter-Company Relief.	App. 65.
	10-1-18.		Battalion holding Line.	
			-do- . Battalion relieved by 11th Battn ROYAL FUSILIERS. Entrained at BOESINGHE Siding, and detrained at INTERNATIONAL CORNER. Thence to "J" Camp, arriving at 12.30 a.m. 11th Jan.	
"J" CAMP.	11-1-18.		Battalion resting and cleaning-up. 36 O.R. Reinforcements arrived.	
	12-1-18.		Parades under Company arrangements. Baths at "H" Camp.	
	13-1-18.		Voluntary Church Services. Inspection of rifles by Armourer Sergt.	
	14-1-18.		Training.	
	15-1-18.		-do- . Inspection of Box Respirators by Brigade Gas Officer.	
	16/17-1-18.		-do-	
	18-1-18.		Battalion moved to BABOON CAMP, entraining from INTERNATIONAL CORNER at 11.30 a.m., and detraining at BOESINGHE. Move complete 3.0 p.m. Details moved to DUBLIN CAMP.	App. 66.
BABOON CAMP.	19-1-18.		Inspections etc., under Company arrangements.	
	20-1-18.		Voluntary Divine Service. Wiring parties at night.	
	21-1-18.		Battalion relieved 7th Battn THE BUFFS in Left Sector of 18th Divl. Front. Hour of start:- 4.0 p.m. Route :- CLARGES STREET. Relief complete 7.45 a.m. 22nd.	App. 67.
IN THE LINE.	22-1-18.		Battalion holding Line.	68.
	23-1-18.		-do-	
	24-1-18.		Battalion relieved by 11th Battn ROYAL FUSILIERS. Commencement of relief 7.45 p.m. Entrained at BOESINGHE Siding and detrained at INTERNATIONAL CORNER - thence to "J" Camp, arriving 10.30 p.m. Details moved from DUBLIN CAMP to "J" CAMP.	App. 69. 70.

Army Form C. 2118.

WAR DIARY
or
INTELLIGENCE SUMMARY.
(Erase heading not required.)

Instructions regarding War Diaries and Intelligence Summaries are contained in F. S. Regs., Part II. and the Staff Manual respectively. Title pages will be prepared in manuscript.

Place	Date	Hour	Summary of Events and Information	Remarks and references to Appendices
"J" CAMP.	25-1-18.		Battalion resting and cleaning-up. Baths.	
	26-1-18.		-do-	
	27-1-18.		Divine Services.	
	28-1-18.		Inspection of all Coys by the C.O.	
	29-1-18.		Parades under Company arrangements.	
	30-1-18.		-do-	
	31-1-18.		Battalion moved to HERZEELE Area, entraining at INTERNATIONAL CORNER at 10.0 a.m., detraining at PROVEN. Thence, by metre gauge line to HERZEELE, arriving in Billets at 12.30 p.m. Transport moved by road, arriving at 4.0 p.m.	App.71.
			OFFICERS JOINED DURING THE MONTH.	
			2/Lt.R.H.MARSH. Joined 7-1-18.	
			2/Lt.L.P.SOLOMONS. " 7-1-18.	
			2/Lt.E.V.SAWYER. " 7-1-18.	
			2/Lt.R.SINGLETON-GATES. Joined 17-1-18.	
			OFFICERS' CASUALTIES DURING THE MONTH.	
			2/Lt.E.J.CURTIS. Died of Wounds. 22-1-18.	
			HONOURS & AWARDS.	
			D.C.M. -------- 2340. C.S.M. Wicken.J.	
			M.M. ---------- 18380. Pte. Goldie.W.	
			9277. Cpl. Hall.E.T.	
			1421. Cpl. Buttwell.J.	
			1148. Pte. Arnold.R.J.	
			HONOURS & AWARDS.	
			Meritorious Service Medal.	
			1505. Sgt.(A/Q.M.S.) Wells.A. (Attd.55thI.B.)	
			Divisional Commander's Parchment Letter.	
			18380. Pte. Goldie.W.	
			9277. Cpl. Hall.E.T.	
			1421. Cpl. Buttwell.J.	
			1148. Pte. Arnold.R.J.	
			12076. Pte. Ives.L.	

Field. 6-2-18.

A. Murray, Major.
Commanding 7th Battalion Royal West Kent Regiment.

Ref.Map.
Belgium
28.N.E.

7th Battalion Royal West Kent Regiment.

ORDER NO. ~~96~~ 97

APP. 63

1st January 1918.

1. The Battalion will march to BABOON CAMP to-morrow.

   Hour of Start :- 8.40 a.m.
   Starting Point :- INTERNATIONAL CORNER (A.9.a.12.35)
   Order of March :-

       Hq.Qrs. "A" Echelon.
       "B" Company.
       Drums.
       "C" Company.
       "D" Company.
       "A" Company.
       Hd.Qrs. "B" Echelon.
       Stretcher Bearers.------1st Line Transport.

   Dress :- Full marching order, with one blanket.
   Drummers will carry steel helmets slung on shoulder.
   Men excused carrying packs will carry one blanket neatly rolled and slung across, bandolier fashion.
   The following distances will be maintained :-
       Between Battalions---------------------500 yds.
          "   Companies----------------------100 yds.
          "   sections of 6- vehicles------ 25 yds.

   2/Lt.W.A.SHEARING and the undermentioned N.C.O's will proceed ahead as an Advance Party to take over the Camp. The party will report to this Officer at Hq.Qrs.Mess at 7.30 a.m. Dress :- Full marching order.

       "A" Co------C.Q.M.S.   "C" Co--------1- N.C.O.
       "B" Co------1- N.C.O   "D" Co--------C.Q.M.S.

   Sick men will be taken to BABOON CAMP by 2/Lieut.C.D.TIRBUTT. They will start ½ hour after the Battalion is clear of the Camp, reporting to this Officer at the Guard Room at 9.0 a.m.
   Men excused carrying packs will march independently under 2/Lt. H.G.CHANDLEY, reporting to him at the GUARD ROOM at 9.0 a.m.
   The ORDERLY OFFICER will report to the Orderly Room at 7.45 a.m. for instructions as to handing over the Camp to incoming Unit.

2. The Q.M. will detail 4- O.R. for loading, and the Coy on Duty will detail 6- O.R. as a loading party. Both parties will proceed with the Orderly Officer to BABOON CAMP on completion of their task.
   On arrival at BABOON CAMP the Coy on Duty will detail 1- N.C.O and 10- men for unloading.

3. Blankets will be rolled tightly in bundles of 10- and taken to Q.M. Stores by 7.0 a.m.
   Officers' Kits will be dumped at Q.M. Stores by 7.30 a.m.
   Officers' Mess Boxes will be sent to Q.M. Stores by 7.45 a.m., and will be loaded on L.G.Limbers.
   The Mess Cart will report to H.Q.Mess at 8.0 a.m.
   Drummers' Packs and rifles, and those of men excused carrying them will be sent to Q.M. Stores by 7.0 a.m. The Q.M. will arrange to have them loaded on the French Cart.
   Medical Stores will be sent to Q.M. Stores by 7.0 a.m.
   Orderly Room Boxes will be sent to Q.M. Stores by 7.45 a.m., and will be loaded on one limber.
   Canteen Stores and Signal Gear will be taken to Q.M.Stores by 7.0 a.m.

4. Officers Commanding Coys., will ensure that billets are left in a thoroughly clean condition.

        (Signed:-)   C.L.MISKIN. Lieut.
                             A/Adjutant.

Appendix "B".

Artillery Arrangements before and during the attack.

1. During the preparatory stages before "Z" day our Artillery will be engaged in:-

   (a) Obtaining mastery of the enemy's Artillery i.e. Counter Battery work.

   (b) Bombarding with a view to destroying the enemy's defences. The bombardment will be intensified for several days prior to the day of attack.

   (c) Cutting all wire which can impede the progress of our troops.

   (d) Isolating the whole enemy garrison in the whole area to be attacked.

2. The Barrage arrangements on "Z" day will be as follows:-

   (a) The barrage will open on the enemy front line and remain stationary there from zero to zero plus 5-minutes.

   (b) The general rate of advance will be 100 yards in four minutes.

   (c) There will be halts on the various objectives as follows:-

   On the BLUE LINE - approx 30-minutes.
   On the BLACK LINE - approx 4-hours.
   On the GREEN LINE - approx 1 to 1½-hours.
   (before patrols can go out)

3. (a) A protective barrage will rest in the case of the BLUE LINE and BLACK LINE about 500-yards beyond those lines; in the case of the GREEN LINE about 500-yards beyond it.

   (b) The timings of the protective barrages beyond the successive will be:-

   Beyond the BLUE line - 0 plus 45-minutes.
                           to 0 plus 1-hr. 25-minutes.
   Beyond the BLACK line - 0 plus 1-hr. 55-minutes.
                           to 0 plus 6-hrs. 25-minutes.
   Beyond the GREEN line - 0 plus 7-hrs. 45-minutes
                           to 0 plus 9-hrs. 40-minutes.

   (c) The protective Barrages beyond the BLUE and BLACK lines will be intensified for 5-minutes before lifting in order to show the troops that the moment for continuing the advance has arrived; i.e. that beyond the BLUE line will be intensified from 0 plus 1-hr. 15-minutes to 0 plus 1-hr. 25-minutes; that beyond the BLACK line from 0 plus 6-hrs. 20-minutes to 0 plus 6-hrs. 25-minutes.

4. Artillery Support to the Advance from the GREEN line will be as follows:-

   (a) From 7-hrs. 25-minutes to 9-hrs. 40-minutes all guns that can bear - less counter battery guns and such as are required to mark the limit of the protective barrage - will search the area contained between the limit of the protective barrage and the general line J.4. b.15.- fork roads at J.4. b.16. - line of the road Running to the road junction at D.27. c. 26.

   (Continued over).

(b) From 8-hrs. 40-minutes to 9-hrs. 5-minutes every available gun except those required for counter battery work and the 34th Divisional Artillery Group will search the area between J.4.d.13 - fork roads at J.4.b.16. - line of the road running to the road junction at D.27.b.86. and the BROODSEINDE - NOORDEMHOEK road at intense rate, with the proviso that from 9-hrs. no fire is to be put within 400-yds of the Western Boundary of this area.

(c) At 9-hrs. 5-minutes every gun that can bear - except those used for counter battery work - will lift to a protective line 500-yards East of the BROODSEINDE - NOORDEMHOEK Road.

(d) There will be a protective barrage on the right flank from 8-hrs. 40-minutes onwards.

5. During the operations, with the G.O.C. each attacking Infantry Brigade, there will be an R.F.A. Battery Commander whose battery will when required be at the direct disposal of the Brigadier General.
Similarly the G.O.C. Division will have a direct call on one 6" Howitzer Battery.

Appendix "B".

Artillery Arrangements before and during the attack.

1. During the preparatory stages before "Z" day our Artillery will be engaged in:-

   (a) Obtaining mastery of the enemy's Artillery i.e. Counter Battery work.

   (b) Bombarding with a view to destroying the enemy's defences. The bombardment will be intensified for several days prior to the day of attack.

   (c) Cutting all wire which can impede the progress of our troops.

   (d) Isolating the whole enemy garrison in the whole area to be attacked.

2. The Barrage arrangements on "Z" day will be as follows:-

   (a) The barrage will open on the enemy front line and remain stationary there from zero to zero plus 5-minutes.

   (b) The general rate of advance will be 100 yards in four minutes.

   (c) There will be halts on the various objectives as follows:-

   On the BLUE LINE - approx 30-minutes.
   On the BLACK LINE - approx 4-hours.
   On the GREEN LINE - approx 1 to 1½-hours.
   (before patrols can go out)

3. (a) A protective barrage will rest in the case of the BLUE/BLACK LINE and BLACK LINE about 300-yards beyond these lines; in the case of the GREEN LINE about 500-yards beyond it.

   (b) The timings of the protective barrages beyond the successive will be:-

   Beyond the BLUE line - 0 plus 46-minutes.
   to 0 plus 1-hr.23-minutes.
   Beyond the BLACK line - 0 plus 1-hr. 35-minutes.
   to 0 plus 6-hrs. 20-minutes.
   Beyond the GREEN line - 0 plus 7-hrs. 48-minutes
   to 0 plus 9-hrs. 40-minutes.

   (c) The protective Barrages beyond the BLUE and BLACK lines will be intensified for 8-minutes before lifting in order to show the troops that the moment for continuing the advance has arrived, i.e. that beyond the BLUE line will be intensified from 0 plus 1-hr. 15-minutes to 0 plus 1-hr. 23-minutes; that beyond the BLACK line from 0 plus 6-hrs. 20-minutes to 0 plus 6-hrs. 28-minutes.

4. Artillery Support to the Advance from the GREEN line will be as follows:-

   (a) From 7-hrs. 28-minutes to 8-hrs. 40-minutes all guns that can bear - less counter battery guns and such as are required to mark the limit of the protective barrage - will search the area contained between the limit of the protective barrage and the general line J.4. b.15.- fork roads at J.4. b.16. - line of the road running to the road junction at D.27. b. 86.

(Continued over).

(b) From 8-hrs. 40-minutes to 9-hrs. 5-minutes every available gun except those required for counter battery work and the 24th Divisional Artillery Group will search the area between J.4.d.15 - fork roads at J.4.b.10. - line of the road running to the road junction at D.27.b.86. and the BROODSEINDE - NOORDEMHOEK road at intense rate, with the proviso that from 9-hrs. no fire is to be put within 400-yds of the Western Boundary of this area.

(c) At 9-hrs. 5-minutes every gun that can bear - except those used for counter battery work - will lift to a protective line 800-yards East of the BROODSEINDE - NOORDEMHOEK Road.

(d) There will be a protective barrage on the right flank from 8-hrs. 40-minutes onwards.

5. During the operations, with the G.O.C. each attacking Infantry Brigade, there will be an R.F.A. Battery Commander whose battery will when required be at the direct disposal of the Brigadier General.
Similarly the G.O.C. Division will have a direct call on one 6" Howitzer Battery.

SECRET.

APP. 64.

7th Battalion Royal West Kent Regiment.

ORDER No. 77a.

5th January 1918.

Ref. special
Map to be issued

1. The Battalion will relieve the 7th Battn The Buffs in the LEFT BATTALION SECTOR on the night of the 6th/7th January 1918

2. "B" Coy and "D" Coy will be in the Front Line; "B" Coy on the RIGHT; "D" Coy on the LEFT; "C" Coy in SUPPORT; "A" Coy in RESERVE at VEE BEND.

3. Guides for the Coys in the front line and support Coys will be provided on the scale of 1- for each post and Coy H.Q., except that 1- guide only will be provided for Post No.8B and the Lewis Gun posts on either side of it.
   One guide will be provided for the Coy in reserve.
   These guides will report at BABOON CAMP on the morning of the 6th January, and will be accommodated by the Company whom they have come to guide.

4. Maps shewing Posts etc., will be issued to each Company.

5. Companies will move off in the following order ; 25 yards interval will be maintained between each 5 posts or platoons, 50 yards between Companies.
           Battalion H.Q.
           "D" Coy.
           "B" Coy.
           "C" Coy.
           "A" Coy.

   Starting Point :- Junction of SCOUT LANE and CLARGES STREET.
   Hour of Start :- 3.0 p.m.
   Route   :- CLARGES STREET.

6. Each Lewis Gun Post will take over 8 magazines from the 7th Battn The Buffs. 8 Magazines will be carried up.

7. "A" Coy will find a Lewis Gun, 1 N.C.O., and 3 men for anti-aircraft work at Battn H.Q.; this team will parade with and march to the trenches with Battn H.Q.

8. The Pack will be carried by supporting straps, and will contain Iron Rations; two days' rations; two "Tommies' Cookers"; leather jerkin; waterproof sheet; 3 pairs of socks. Gum boots will be carried slung, 1 sandbag and some hay in each. Haversacks will not be worn, but all small kit not required will be packed inside and sent to the Transport Lines. Orders as to greatcoats will be issued later.

OVER.

2.

9. Coys will obtain a supply of foot powder for use in the trenches from the Medical Officer.

10. The following reports are required daily from Coys,, to reach Battn. H.Q. at the hours stated :-
Situation Report at 3.0 a.m. and 3.0 p.m.)
Intelligence Report (6.0 a.m. to 6.0 p.m.))
Patrol Report.)
Work Report. (6.0 a.m. to 6.0 p.m.))   4.0 a.m.
Material required for Work.)
Disposal map.)

Details regarding these reports have been issued by the Intelligence Officer to Coys.

11. Lists of trench stores taken over will be sent to Battn. H.Q. before 4.0 a.m. on the 7th instant.

12. Companies will report relief complete by the code-word "THAW".

13. ACKNOWLEDGE.

(Signed:-) W.A.SHEARING. 2/Lt.
A/Adjutant.

ISSUED TO :-

Copy No.1. C.O.
2. 2nd in Commd.
3. Adjutant.
4. O.C. "H.Q"
5. O.C. "A" Coy.
6. O.C. "B" Coy.
7. O.C. "C" Coy.
8. O.C. "D" Coy.
9. FILE.
10. Spare copy.

APP. A

INSTRUCTIONS TO BE READ IN CONJUNCTION WITH

PRELIMINARY ORDER No. ~~63~~ 64.

7th. Battalion Royal West Kent Regiment.

1. **MOPPING-UP PARTIES.**

Mopping-up parties will billet with the Battn., to which they are attached on "Y"/"Z" night.

"A" Company will join the 6th. Northamptonshire Regt., at CANAL RESERVE CAMP (H.27.a.84).

"B" Company will join the 7th. Bedfordshire Regt., at CANAL RESERVE CAMP (H.27.a.84).

"D" Company less ½ Company will join the 11th Royal Fusiliers at CHATEAU SEGARDM (H.30.a.88)

(margin note: This is now cancelled)

The mopping-up Companies of the 7th Royal West Kent Regt., will not be used unless the 54th Brigade is used to make an attack on the RED LINE.

In the event of the 53rd. Infantry Brigade taking the RED LINE, the mopping-up parties will be detached from Battalions of the 54th Brigade at RITZ AREA prior to taking over the line. Mopping-up parties of the 7th Royal West Kent Regiment will, therefore, not go into support in J.4.c., as previously arranged.

"A" and "B" Companies will each take 2 Lewis Guns, and 20 magazines per gun with them.

"D" Company will take 1 Lewis Gun and 20 magazines.

The following ammunition, bombs, etc., will be carried by these parties, viz:-

    Lewis Gunners---------------------------50 rounds S.A.A.
    Remainder of mopping-up parties-------50%, - 170 rounds S.A.A., and 2 Mills Bombs;
                                      50%, - 50 rounds S.A.A., and 10 Mills Bombs.

Each man will in addition carry two sandbags, and 50 Lethal Bombs will also be distributed amongst the parties.

The distribution of S.A.A. should be arranged before joining the Battalion to which attached, and the necessary buckets for Bombs carried.

Bombs and Sandbags will be drawn from the Dumps of the Units to which the moppers-up are attached.

2. **CARRYING PARTY.**

Carrying parties will take all Lewis Guns with them.

"C" Company, 4 Guns and 20 magazines per Gun.

Half "D" Company, 2 Guns and 20 magazines per Gun.

Ammunition, Bombs etc., to be carried :-

    Lewis Gunners-------------------50 rounds S.A.A.
    Rifle Grenadiers----------------170 rounds S.A.A., 6 Rifle Grenades.
    Bombers-------------------------170 rounds S.A.A. 5 Mills Bombs.
    Riflemen------------------------170 rounds S.A.A. 2 Mills Bombs.

Each man will carry two Sandbags.

In addition, the following stores will be drawn by Battalion Headquarters :- 42. S.O.S. Signals ,--120. 1" Very Lights.

These munitions etc., will be drawn from the Dump at CHATEAU SEGARD (H.23.c.91).

(2).

2. CARRYING PARTIES.
   (Contd.)
   The Officer Commanding Carrying Party will report to 54th Brigade Hd.Qrs., CANAL RESERVE CAMP at Zero hour on "Z" day, where he will receive full instructions.
   Lewis Guns, Bombs etc., should be left in a cellar or other convenient place whilst actual carrying is in progress. A suitable guard should be left in charge. When the task of carrying is finished, the Lewis Guns etc., will be collected again by the Carrying Party.

3. INTELLIGENCE.
   The following INTELLIGENCE OFFICES are being established on "Z" day. Battalion Commanders, or Company and Platoon Commanders when the latter are moving forward independently, will send to these Offices to ascertain if any messages have been received for them, and to give or obtain all information available. Any difficulties encountered, or casualties sustained, since passing last Office should also be reported.
   Individuals should also report in passing, when they desire to obtain information or have any information to give.

OFFICE.	MAP REF.	OFFR. IN CHARGE.	TIME OF OPENING.
(a) Div.H.Q.	H.27.b.65.70	G.S.O.,3.	Zero.
(b) CHATEAU SEGARD.	H.30.b.20	Lt.Col.le FLEMING. Attd.18th Divn.	Zero plus 1 hour 30 mins.
(c) Bde.H.Q. (RITZ TRENCHES)	I.17.d.10	An Officer 54th. Bde.	Zero plus 5 hours; to take the place of Adv.Bde.H.Q., 53rd.Bde when it moves forward.
(d) GERMAN Front Trenches.	J.13.a.20.15.	Capt.G.WELCH, 6th Royal Berks Regt.	Zero plus 5 hours.
(e) Adv.Bde H.Q.	J.14.a.50	An Officer of 53rd.Bde.Staff	Zero plus 6 hours.

4. INFORMATION TO ENEMY.
   Officers and men are not to carry anything which might assist the enemy in future operations, such as Orders, Plans and Maps (except the special operation maps issued for the actual attack). If captured by the enemy, they must refuse to answer all questions, and must give no information whatsoever except their names and Regiments.

5. FIRST LINE TRANSPORT.
   Will remain in present location.
   Regimental Baggage Wagons will be loaded ready for moving by midnight on "X"/"Y" night.

6. SURPLUS KIT AND PACKS.
   All packs and surplus kit will be stored at First Line Transport Lines under Brigade arrangements.

7. RATIONS.
   Every man will carry Rations for "Z" day and "Z" plus 1 day, in addition to his Iron Ration. These rations will be drawn by

(3.)

7. **RATIONS.** (Contd.) Companies from the Battalion on "Y" day. During operations, mopping-up parties and carrying parties will continue to be rationed by the Battalion.

   All ranks are to have Breakfast before leaving Camp on "Z" day.

   Cookers will be sent to cook for "A" and "B" Companies on the morning of "Z" day. Camp kettles for "D" Company less ½ Coy.

8. **WATER.** All Water Bottles must be full at Zero plus 6 hours. Water for use on "Z" day must be carried forward by the troops in petrol tins, which will be dumped in the Camps occupied by Units on "Y"/"Z" night.

9. **DRESS.** Fighting Order, Haversack on back, Box Respirator at the "Alert".

   Officers will be dressed the same as the men. Sticks will not be carried.

10. **MEDICAL ARRANGEMENTS.**

    These will be communicated by the Medical Officer to Officers Commanding Companies.

11. **LOOTING.**

    All ranks are to be wqarned that any man found looting the dead or wounded will be shot on the spot.

12. **LOCATION OF BATTALION HD.QRS.**

    On "Y"/"Z" night---------CHATEAU SEGARD. Area No.5.(H.24.c.35.)
    On morning of
    "Z" day.----------------   -do-   -do-

    ---------------oOo---------------

SECRET.

APP. 65

7th Battalion Royal West Kent Regiment.

ORDER No. 78.   7th January 1918.

Ref. Special
Map issued to
Coys.

1. "A" and "C" Coys will relieve "D" and "B" Coys in the front line on night of the 8th/9th January.
    "A" Coy will relieve "D" Coy in the Left Company Sector.

    "C" Coy will relieve "B" Coy in the Right Company Sector.

    "B" Coy will go into support and "D" Coy into reserve at VEE BEND.

    Posts will be taken over as at present held.

2. Guides will be provided by the Coys in the front line on the scale of 1 per post and Coy H.Q.
    Details of relief will be arranged between O's C. Coys concerned, but the relief should not begin before 1.0 p.m. on the 8th Jan., to ensure that rations have arrived and have been distributed before the relief begins.

3. Two days' rations for "A" and "D" Coys will be dumped at VEE BEND on the evening of the 8th Jan.
    "A" Coys will carry forward ttheir rations with them when proceeding to relieve "D" Coy. The rations for "D" Coy will be left at VEE BEND.
    Two days' rations for "B" and "C" Coys will be dumped at Battn H.Q. on the evening of the 8th Jan. The O.C. "C" Coy., will be informed when they arrive, and will send a carrying party to take them to "C" Coy H.Q. "C" Coy will carry forward their rations with them when relieving "B" Coy. The rations for "B" Coy will be left at "C" Coy H.Q.

4. Completion of relief will be reported by Coys by the Code Word "BON".

5. Acknowledge.

                                    (Signed:-) W.A. SHEARING. 2/Lt.
                                                         A/Adjutant.
                            7th Battalion Royal West Kent Regiment.

ISSUED TO:-
    Copy No.1. O.C. "A" Coy.
         2.   O.C. "B" "
         3.   O.C. "C" "
         4.   O.C. "D" "
         5.   File.

Copy No 2
APP. 66

7th Battalion Royal West Kent Regiment.
Order No.80.

Ref.Map Sheet 28 N.E.1/20,000.   17th January 1918.

1. The Battalion will move tomorrow the 18th January to BABOON CAMP proceeding from INTERNATIONAL CORNER STN to BOESINGHE by rail, thence by march to BABOON CAMP.
   Transport will move by road.

2. Companies will move off in the following order at 100 yds interval.
   H.Q. Company.
   "A" Company.
   "B" Company.
   "C" Company.
   "D" Company.

   Starting Point. Where Light Railway crosses road at N.E. corner of Camp.
   Hour of start. 11.30.a.m.

3. Dress :- Marching Order with one blanket folded round the pack.

4. An advance party consisting of 2/Lt.G.SIMPSON.,Coy Qr Ms Sgts and 1 O.R. per Coy (including H.Q.Coy) will parade at the Guard Room at 8.30.a.m. and proceed by road to take over BABOON CAMP from the 11th Bn. Royal Fusiliers.

5. Details not proceeding to BABOON CAMP (i.e. sick men unfit for duty in the line) will be accommodated in DUMLE CAMP., 2/Lt.F.B. BERTRAM and Sgt A.BARKER.,H.Q.Coy will remain with the details. Orders regarding details will be issued later.

6. Blankets tightly rolled in bundles of 10, Officers valises.,Coy Mess stores,Canteen stores.,Orderly Room boxes and Shops., Signalling gear will be dumped beside the Guard room by 10.a.m.

7. Two cookers and 1 water cart only will proceed to BABOON CAMP., the others will remain at the Transport lines.
   H.Q.Coy cooking utensils will be loaded on the cookers.

8. The Transport Officer will detail the following transport to report at "J" CAMP at 10.a.m.
   2 G.S.Wagons (these have been ordered to report to him at transport lines at 8.30.a.m.).
   Maltese Cart.
   Mess Cart.
   6 Limbers.
   French Cart.

9. Transport is detailed as under :-
   1.G.S.Wagon.   Blankets.
   -do-   Officers valises.
   1 Limber.   Orderly Room.,Shops & Signalling Gear.
   1 Limber.   Canteen.
   1 Limber.   Coy Messes.
   2 Limbers.   Lewis Guns and magazines.
   1 Limber.   Details.
   1 French Cart.   Details.

10. Each Company will bring to BABOON CAMP 4 Lewis Guns and 17 magazines in carriers per gun. The 8 Lewis Guns at present with S.A.D.O.S. will be picked up ~~with these~~ by the Transport Officer on the way to BABOON CAMP.

11. ACKNOWLEDGE.

                                           W.A.Heain
                                        2/Lt., a/Adjutant.
                                   7th Battln Royal West Kent Regt.

Issue at 6.45 p.m.

Copy No. 1.   O.C.
     2.   O.C. H.Q.Coy.
     3.   O.C. A.Coy.
     4.   O.C. B.Coy.
     5.   O.C. C.Coy.
     6.   O.C. D.Coy.
     7.   T.O.
     8.   Q.M.
     9.   War Diary.
    10.   Spare.

War Diary

SECRET.   COPY No.

7th Battalion Royal East Kent Regiment.   ORDER No.81.

                                                             20th January 1918.

1. The Battalion will relieve the 7th Bn.The Buffs in the left sector of the 18th Divisional Front on the night of the 21st/22nd January.

2. "A" and "C" Companies will be in the front line, "A" on the right "C" on the left "B" Coy in support., "D" Coy in reserve.

3. Guides for the Companies in the front line, and support Coy will be provided on the scale of 1 for each post., Platoon and Company H.Q. One guide will be provided for the Company in reserve. These guides will meet the Battln on the switch track just N of ONTUSE BEND.

4. Maps showing posts etc., will be issued to each Company.

5. Companies will move off in the following order; 50 yards distance will be maintained between each 2 posts or platoons., 200 yards between Companies. Care must be taken that Companies do not bunch up at the place where the guides are waiting.
   Battln.H.Q.
   "C" Coy.
   "A" Coy.
   "B" Coy.
   "D" Coy.

   Starting Point :- Junction of SCOUT AVENUE and CLARGES STREET.
   Hour of Start :- 4.0.p.m.
   Route :- CLARGES STREET.

6. Each Lewis Gun post will take over 8 magazines from the 7th Bn.The Buffs except at 6 CHAINS post where 16 magazines will be handed over, 8 of these will be sent to Bn.H.Q., when the relief is complete 8 Magazines per gun will be carried up.

7. The Reserve Coy will find a Lewis Gun, (1 N.C.O and 3 men) for Anti-Aircraft work at Bn.H.Q. this team will parade with and march up to the front line with Battln H.Q.

8. The Pack will be carried by supporting straps and will contain IRON RATIONS, two days rations; two "Tommies Cookers"; leather jerkins, 3 pairs of socks, waterproof sheet.   Gum boots will be carried slung. Haversacks will not be worn, but all small kit not required will be placed inside and in the pockets of the Great-coats and sent to the Transport Lines.

9. Coys will obtain a supply of foot powder for use in the trenches from the Medical Officer.

10. The following Reports are required daily from Coys to reach Battln H.Q. at the hours stated :-
    SITUATION REPORT at 3.0.a.m. and 3.0.p.m.
    INTELLIGENCE REPORT (6.0.a.m. to 6.0.p.m.)
    PATROL REPORT.   )
    WORK REPORT.(6.0.a.m. to 6.0.p.m).   ) 4.0.a.m.
    Material required for work.   )
    Dispositions and Map.   )

    Details regarding these reports will be given by the Intelligence Officer to Companies.

11. Lists of trench stores., maps etc taken over will be sent to Battln H.Q. before 4.0.a.m. on the 23rd instant.

12. Companies will report relief complete by the code word "CORK".

                                                                    F.L.O.

13. Companies in the front line will be relieved nightly.
   "D" Coy will relieve "C" Coy.
   "B" Coy will relieve "A" Coy.
   and vice versa.
   Details of relief will be arranged between O.C.Coys concerned, but the posts in the front line will not be withdrawn until relieved by the companies in rear.
   O.C. Coys will report to Batsln H.Q. by 4.0.a.m. daily the hour at which their reliefs will begin and completion of relief will be reported each night by companies by the code word "BUG"

14. Acknowledge.

W.A. Shearing

2/Lt. a/Adjutant.
7th Bn. Royal West Kent Regiment.

Copies to :-
   1. C.O.
   2. 2nd in Command.
   3. Adjutant.
   4. O.C. H.Q.Coy.
   5. O.C. "A" Coy.
   6. O.C. "B" Coy.
   7. O.C. "C" Coy.
   8. O.C. "D" Coy.
   9. J/O. War Diary.
  10. Spare.

SECRET.

APP 68

AMENDMENTS TO BATTALION ORDER NO.81. d/ 20-1-1918.

21st January 1918.

Ref. paragraph. 3.
Guides will be provided as under and not as therein stated.
Each guide will have a number and will guide posts as hereunder stated.

LEFT COMPANY.

Guide No.1.	Left Coy. H.Q.
" 2.	No.12 Post.
" 3.	No.11 Post.
" 4.	No.10 Post.
" 5.	No.9. Post.
" 6.	G, F, E, D. posts.
" 12.	7, and 8 posts.

RIGHT COMPANY.

Guide No.7.	Right Coy. H.Q.
" 8.	Posts 1 & 2.
" 9.	" 3 & 3a
" 10.	" 4, 4a & 5.
" 11.	Post 6.
" 13.	Posts A, and B.
" 14.	Post. C.

SUPPORT COMPANY.

Guide No.15.	Support Coy H.Q.
" 16.	EGYPT WEST POST.
" 17.	5 CHEMINS POST.
" 18.	UCKFIELD POST.
" 19.	SUEZ FARM POST.

RESERVE COMPANY.

Guide will be on KOEKUIT ROAD where path runs off to VEE BEND.

....

Coys will march off with posts in the above sequence (i.e. Left Coy H.Q. No.12 post, No.11, No.10, No.9, G, F, E, D, and so on), and should know the number of their guide as well as their post.

....

Reference paragraph 6, Lewis Gun Magazines will be handed over at Coy., H.Q.(i.e. 32 drums in 8 baskets at each Coy H.Q.) and not as therein stated.

(Signed:-) W.A. SHEARING. 2/Lt.
A/Adjutant.
7th Battalion Royal West Kent Regiment.

COPIES to all recipients of
BATTALION ORDER No.81.

7th Battalion Royal West Kent Regiment.

Order No. X.   23rd January 1918.

APP 69

1. Details will move from DUBLIN CAMP to "J" CAMP tomorrow.

2. Hour of Start :- 12.15.p.m.

3. Billeting Party :- 2/Lt.C.D.TIRBUTT., and CQMS's will proceed to "J" Camp at 11.0.a.m. to take over.

4. CSM Sheen and 8 Other Ranks will proceed at 9.30.a.m. and will be responsible for the unloading and stacking under cover all Kits etc that arrive.

5. Dinners will be served at "J" Camp on arrival.

6. The following transport will report at DUBLIN CAMP at the times stated :-
   2 G.S.Wagons at 9.0.a.m. to convey Officer's Kits., Blankets., Mens Kits and overcoats.

   2 G.S.Wagons and the French Cart will report at DUBLIN CAMP at 11.30.a.m. to convey wood., Officers Messes and Shops etc.
   1 Limber will convey 2 Hd Qr Lewis Guns and 16 Lewis Gun drums of Hd Qrs and 32 Lewis Gun drums per Company.
   1 Limber for Orderly Room and Canteen.
   The Maltese Cart for Medical Stores.

7. Men who cannot march will ride in a G.S.Wagon at 12.0.Noon., mens packs to be carried will be sent by the same wagon.
   A list of the above will be given to Sgt.Drummer Lock.

8. 2 Cookers will proceed to "J" CAMP at 11.30.a.m.

Major,
7th Battln Royal West Kent Regiment.

SECRET.

APP 70

8th Battalion Royal West Kent Regiment.

ORDER No. 82.

24th January 1918.

Ref. Map
BIXSCHOOTE.
1/10,000.

1. The Battalion will be relieved on the Left Sector of the 18th Divnl. front by the 11th Battn. Royal Fusiliers on the night of 24th/25th January.

2. On completion of relief the Battalion will move via CLARGES ST. to BOESINGHE STATION and entrain there for INTERNATIONAL CORNER, thence to "J" Camp.

3. "B" and "D" Coys., will supply guides as under :-
"B" Coy guides for Posts 1, 2, 3, 4, 5, 6, 3a, 4a, A, B, C, Right Coy. H.Q., SUEZ FARM, UCKFIELD POST, LES 5 CHEMINS, EGYPT WEST; total 16 guides.
"D" Coy guides for Posts 7, 8, 9, 10, 11, 12, D, E, F, G, Left Coy H.Q., and two guides for Battn. H.Q; total 13 guides.
All guides must know the number, letter or name of the post to which they are guides, and will be in possession of a paper giving this information.

4. The O.C. "B" Coy will detail an Officer to take charge of the guides. This Officer will remain with the guides until all Posts of the Relieving Unit have moved off with their guides.
Guides will meet the incoming Unit on CLARGES STREET SWITCH near LOUVOIS FARM. where guides will rendezvous where the duckboards cross the KOEKUIT Road at 5.0 p.m., and will be marched from there by the Officer in charge. Guides will return with the garrisons of the posts relieved, rejoining their Coys at BOESINGHE.

5. All Trench Stores, maps etc., will be handed over to the incoming Unit and receipts obtained.

6. Eight L.G. Magazines in buckets or carriers will be handed over at each L.G. Post and receipts obtained. The receipts will be separate from those obtained for Trench Stores.
Eight Magazines per gun will be brought out by Companies.

7. Gum Boots will not be handed over in the Line, but will be brought out and sent to Divnl. Gum Boot Drying Room LYONS CAMP by 2.0 p.m. 25th inst. On the morning of 25th inst., Coys will have boots tied together in pairs ready to hand in when called for.

8. Companies will wire completion of relief by Code word "BON"

9. The Divnl. Motor Kitchen will be in position at BOESINGHE STATION

P.T.O.

10.   Acknowledge.

(Signed:-) W.A. SHEARING. 2/Lt.
A/Adjutant.
7th Battn. Royal West Kent Regt.

COPIES TO :-
  1. O.C. "A" Coy.
  2. O.C. "B" Coy.
  3. O.C. "C" Coy.
  4. O.C. "D" Coy.
  5. DIARY.

C O P Y.

To O.C. "D" Coy.

Ref. Batt. Order No.82 dated 24-1-18, - para 4, for second paragraph read :-
"Guides will meet the incoming unit on CKARGES STREET SWITCH near LOUVOIS FARM. The guides will rendezvous where the duckboards cross the KOEKUIT ROAD at 5.0 p.m., and will be marched from there by the officer in charge. Guides will return with the garrisons of the Posts relieved, rejoining their Coys at BOESINGHE.

(Signed:-) W.A. SHEARING. 2/Lt.
A/Adjutant.
7th Battn. R.W. Kent Regt.

24-1-18.

7th Battn. Royal West Kent Regiment.

Order No.1.

6th January 1916.

1. The Battalion will move from "J" Camp on January 31st to the ISMAILIA area proceeding from ISMAILIA to MOASCAR CAMP by rail.
Transport will move by road.

2. Companies will parade in the following order and will move off at intervals of 50 yards between Coys.
    H.Q. Company.
    "A" Company.
    "B" Company.
    "C" Company.
    "D" Company.
Starting point where Light Railway crosses the road at N.W. corner of the Camp. Hour of Start :- 9.30.a.m.

3. Dress. Full marching Order with one Blanket folded round the pack. The Gunners will parade with packs slung. These will be dumped on arrival there and a party will be detailed from U/s sick to guard them.

4. Blankets to be tightly rolled in bundles of 10 and tied at each end and in the centre, and to be dumped outside the Guard Room at 7.0.a.m. Officers Valises to be dumped at 8.0.a.m.
Signalling Gear & Orderly Room Boxes to be loaded by 8.0.a.m.
Lewis Gun Limber will be loaded by 8.45.a.m. and Officers Mess Boxes will be loaded on Coy Lewis Gun limber by 8.45.a.m.
Shops, Canteen and R.C. cooking utensils to be dumped beside Guard Room at 8.0.a.m.

5. Transport has been allotted as follows :-
    4 Limbers for Lewis Guns and Officers Mess Boxes.
    1 Limber for Signalling Gear.
    1 Limber for Orderly Room Boxes.
    Maltese Cart for Medical Stores.
    Mess Cart for H.Q. Mess Boxes.
    1 Lorry for Officers Kits, Shops, Canteen and R.C.Cooking utensils
    1 Lorry for Blankets.

6. 2/Lieut DABBNER will report to the Staff Captain at GEBEL WMT at 8.30.a.m. and will be responsible for the entrainment of the Battn.

7. On arrival at MOASCAR the Battn will detrain and then proceed from there at 11.45.a.m. by the metre gauge railway to ISMAILIA.

8. The Transport will move under the Command of the 55th Brigade S.O. as per Order "S" issued separately to the Battn T.O.

9. All the Transport mentioned in paragraph 5 will report to "J" Camp at 7.30.a.m. and when loaded will parade on the road running along side of the camp, joining the Brigade Transport Column as it passes "J" Camp at about 10.0.a.m.

10. 2 Cookers will proceed to ISMAILIA in advance of Transport column for the purpose of preparing dinners for the Battn on arrival at ISMAILIA. Hour of start :- 8.0.a.m.

ACKNOWLEDGE.

(signed) W.A.Kearns
Issued at 3.30 p.m.   a/Adjt., 7th Bn. R.W. Kent Regiment.

Copy No.1. C.O.
    No.2.   O.C. "H.Q." Coy.
    No.3.   O.C. "A" Coy.
    No.4.   O.C. "B" Coy.
    No.5.   O.C. "C" Coy.
    No.6.   O.C. "D" Coy.
    No.7.   T.O.
    No.8.   M.O.

1915 July –
1917 Dec

ROYAL WEST KENT
(QUEEN'S OWN)

A/740/82.

Casualties of 7th R.W. Kent Regt.

On the night of 26th/27th April 1916 South East of MAMICOURT, after successfully bombing an enemy saphead, L/Cpl. T. STEWART heard of some men of a similar party being wounded. He immediately returned and brought in a wounded man. Private F.W. MANNING who, though of small size, also succeeded in bringing in a wounded man, under heavy bombing and shelling by the enemy.

On the 1st July 1916 during some heavy hand to hand fighting for more than two hours, the crater area near CARNOY, Sergeant P.G. UPTON displayed great gallantry and resource. He personally led an attack on a concrete machine gun emplacement which was causing many casualties and killed all the detachment. (D.C.M.)

Near TRONES WOOD on the 13th July 1916 Sgt. C.J. CRAME led his section in the attack on a German strong point. In the first attack he was wounded in the foot. He had his wound dressed and returned to his section which he again led to the attack. He was again wounded, but after having the wound dressed again went to his command. This happened a third time. Though three times wounded he remained with his section until it was relieved and even then refused to leave it until ordered to do so by his platoon officer. (D.C.M. and Russian Order of St. George, 3rd Class).

The operations in the SCHWABEN REDOUBT for September were carried out in trenches a foot deep in slippery mud, persistent rain, almost continual shelling and generally under most nerve trying conditions. Owing to its commanding position the redoubt was continually being attacked by the enemy. In these circumstances 2/Lieut. A.S. HAYFIELD displayed conspicuous gallantry during frequent bombing attacks. In one of these the enemy by a heavy bombardment and use of flamenwerfer succeeded in taking 200 yards of trench in the N.E. face of the Redoubt. This officer personally led a bombing party and with the aid of Stokes Mortars and Lewis Guns succeeded in regaining the lost trench and in addition captured 100 yards more. He also led a party that pushed forward in the trench on the Western face. Under heavy shell fire he moved about in the coolest manner possible encouraging his men and displayed the utmost energy until wounded on the 4th. Owing to conditions he was unable to be moved till next day. The enemy again attacked on the 5th. Though suffering intense pain his only thoughts were for his brother who was in the action at the time.

On the 24th February 1917 Cpl. C. ROWLAND took a patrol from EAST MIRAUMONT ROAD to examine COULEE TRENCH, which was reported by the Division on our right to be occupied. He penetrated about 1000 yards and found the trench full of dead Germans and brought back other important information. About 11 a.m. on the 25th Feby this N.C.O. led a patrol into the village of IRLES reaching the main street at southern end of village but could not proceed further owing to heavy hostile shelling.

Throughout the operations of 3rd and 4th May 1917 Ptes. J.W. THIRKETTLE and W. REYNOLDS carried on their task as stretcher bearers. For nearly 30 hours they were engaged in bringing in wounded men from in front of our line under heavy shell and machine gun fire and without the protection of the RED CROSS FLAG.

On the night of the 11th/12th July 1917 Sergt. L. MOON was in charge of a ration carrying party near ZILLEBEKE. His party came under intense shell fire in a congested communication trench and in spite of the fact that his arm was practically blown off, he continued to command and encourage his men until his party had been extricated from a very difficult situation. Though suffering great pain he refused all attention until he had satisfied himself that all was safe and correct.

During the operations near POELCAPPELLE on the 12th and 13th October 1917 Private W. BOARER, whilst acting as Company runner, made six journeys in daylight from the advanced posts to Battalion Headquarters. This was done in spite of heavy machine gun fire and sniping.

When not employed as a runner he went several times to the Aid Post at GLOSTER FARM to get stretchers and succeeded in getting back four seriously wounded men. He maintained wonderful cheerfulness in spite of the very bad conditions.

On the 21st March 1918 near VENDEUIL, Private A.C. COLEMAN and 3 other signallers went out to repair the telephone lines between Battalion Headquarters and FORT VENDEUIL as their maintenance of communication was extremely important. In spite of heavy gas shelling he succeeded in doing this. Three minutes later the line was cut and he again went out and repaired it. He then proceeded to a test box to lay a new line to the reserve Company. He only returned to Battalion Headquarters because he was ordered to do so by the Signal Officer. At that time he was fully aware that the enemy had penetrated between our posts in that vicinity and had machine guns active. He was out altogether 4 hours continuously exposed to gas shelling. His work necessitated frequent removal of his box respirator. The wires were broken in over 40 places. Later he exposed himself so as to fire on parties of the enemy attempting to capture 2 field guns.

The sector taken over by the Battalion near MORLANCOURT had been held immediately before by the Australians who had done a minor attack. It was thus still in an active state. On the 3rd August a stretcher bearer named Private T. DODDINGTON went out in front of the line to search for and bring in an officer and man who had been wounded on patrol the previous night. Although it became daylight before his work was completed he accomplished it and later brought in another stretcher bearer who had been wounded. Later in the day Pte. DODDINGTON stood up on the parapet of the front line with a Red Cross Flag and remained standing there to test the enemy, who had previously fired on stretcher bearers. He afterwards continued carrying in wounded.

On 22nd August 1918 near ALBERT, Captain A.J.WHITMARSH was in command of the right assaulting Company. When his Company began to advance towards its objective, it was immediately met by intense machine gun fire from a flank and the left platoon destroyed. Though not supported by artillery Captain WHITMARSH rallied his men and rushed forward, although his left flank was in the air. By skilful tactics he methodically advanced his men in spite of the machine gun fire, and gained BLACK WOOD, an advance of 500 yards. He maintained himself in this position till dark.

On the 26th August he pushed forward as an isolated unit and captured the Village of MONTAUBAN with about 50 prisoners besides inflicting heavy loss on the retreating enemy. This success enabled the troops on the flanks to advance. He continually exposed himself so as to direct the operations personally. The fine offensive spirit shown by the young inexperienced soldiers under his command was largely due to his personality.

During the operation of 23rd October 1918, East of LE CATEAU the company to which Sgt.F.N.BACON belonged, was unable to advance owing to machine gun fire from several directions. This N.C.O. dashed forward towards a post and although under fire from supporting machine guns succeeded in capturing the gun and crew. This had the effect of causing the other machine gunners to withdraw and the Company was able to push forward to its objective.

---

www.ingramcontent.com/pod-product-compliance
Lightning Source LLC
Chambersburg PA
CBHW080837010526
44114CB00017B/2326